Kurt B. Nielsen

# Liberating Organizations

## – Building the Case for Freedom –

ENTRUST SOURCE

Liberating Organizations

© Kurt B. Nielsen 2025

www.liberatingorg.com

DK-6040 Egtved, Denmark


With permission of Author

Entrust Source Publishers

**ISBN: 978-1-942308-60-7**

Entrustsource.com

Co-authors and editors: Paul D. Norton, Christian Myrstad, Robert Fujdiar, Anne Due Broberg, Jacob Honoré Broberg, Arne Christensen, Vibeke Kristensen, Anette Broberg Knudsen, Susanne Nielsen.

Cover and chapter illustrations: Sofia Vasylevska
Layout: Kurt B. Nielsen and
Christian Larsen, ProRex forlag
Print: toptrykgrafisk, DK-6300 Gråsten, Denmark

*In honor of the Swiss Constitution, the preamble:*

*In the name of Almighty God!*

*The Swiss People and the Cantons,*
*mindful of their responsibility towards creation,*
*resolved to renew their alliance so as to strengthen liberty,*
*democracy, independence and peace*
*in a spirit of solidarity and openness towards the world,*

*determined to live together with mutual consideration and respect*
*for their diversity,*
*conscious of their common achievements and their responsibility*
*towards future generations.*

*and in the knowledge that only those who use their freedom*
*remain free, and that the strength*
*of a people is measured by the well-being of its weakest members;*

*adopt the following Constitution*

# Acknowledgments

This book would never have happened without the support of and encouragement from a number of people, who have helped write, build, test and refine the message. I want in particular to express my thanks and appreciation for all their work and time to the following people – my collaborators and *compadres*:

- Paul D. Norton – who has tirelessly struggled to transform my ramblings into proper English and also contributed to important parts of the content. He is known as *the bulldog with a pen*.
- Christian Myrstad – who from the early days co-developed concepts, frameworks, and content.
- Robert Fujdiar – who brought important perspectives from a Czech context to the table and provided an excellent critique.
- Anne Due Broberg – who has contributed to the presentation and formulation of many things, checking for consistency in meaning, etc.
- Jacob Honoré Broberg – who has been a long-time discussion partner and helped shape the message and relate it to other situations.
- Arne Christensen – who has applied his hawk eye to the concepts and structure of the book and found many an inconsistency and suggested numerous improvements.
- Vibeke Kristensen – who tested many of the approaches, tools, and templates in real-life co-training and never shied away from showing me the right way.
- Anette Broberg Knudsen – who has acted as the editor of content and consistency.
- Susanne Nielsen – who has been proofreading this endeavor from the very start.

A special thanks also to all the 90+ people who volunteered to participate in our interview round, providing challenging new perspectives. Read more about them and the results in *Appendix A – Summary of Interviews*.

A host of other people have been inspirations in my and our journey and should all be mentioned, but let us just mention a few:

Anja Wahrich, Arne Åhlander, Bård Kuvaas, Bjarte Bogsnæs, Boris Gloger, Doug Kirkpatrick, Geir Amsjø, John Petersen, Leise Passer Jensen, Lyubomyr Matsekh, René Figgé, Tom Gilb, Tom Mellor, Vlada Fursa and Wynford (Wyn) Jones.

# Table of Contents

7

# Preface

The drive to write this book derives from observing the sad state of engagement in organizations and the consequential sub-optimal value generation. This was combined with a growing awareness of the basic human need for freedom to choose, grow, and contribute and the apparent disconnect with organizational practices. The case for freedom has not been forgotten, but it seems to be sitting on a shelf, gathering dust amid the current public discussion about leadership and organizations. It is a puzzle that most people support democratic government at the national level, but accept autocratic rule in organizations without batting an eyelid, and even hail the imperial CEO. Yet the promises of organizations that create freedom for their people are the same as those of societies. Creativity, innovation, engagement, trust, and taking responsibility will grow if there is freedom. The potential upside is huge. W. Edwards Deming[1] became a major inspiration:

> *A leader's job is to understand his people, understand their differences; optimize their interactions, their educations, their experiences.*
> *– W. Edwards Deming at Western Connecticut State University, 1990*

So what is the reason for this sad state? Is it bad management? Are people just slacking off? Is it a chicken-and-egg situation, where we cannot tell what came first? Or is it just too hard to introduce and live in freedom?

It started to look a bit like a criminal case. The case appears to have gone cold despite the glaring evidence of wholesale organizational dysfunction due to power abuse, rampant bureaucracy, and quiet quitting. It may not yet be a lost cause, but it seems we are living in a post-freedom culture, claiming to be free but succumbing to an elite authority of the heroic or bureaucratic kind.

---

1    W. Edwards Deming: https://en.wikipedia.org/wiki/W._Edwards_Deming

Alternatively, some hold counter-elite authoritarian values with an absolute focus on victims in the so-called cancel culture, which is somewhat irrationally coupled with a claim to absolute individual freedom to be what they want, when they want it – an expressive individualism.

Together these trends limit civil co-existence and foster greater polarization and less engagement with others. This book offers a perspective to change that.

The book is mostly for people working in organizations with complex challenges. It is mostly applicable to organizations with more than a few people and a significant amount of complex knowledge work. We do not address pure production environments or other predictable domains, there is already an abundance of Lean frameworks and practices for these.

The material for this book has been amassed over many years, starting in 2005 when, while working as a system designer and coach, I stumbled upon Scrum. I got excited about this new approach to getting work done using self-governing teams, as opposed to the classic top-down command and control model. I became a Certified Scrum Trainer in 2008 and have worked in this capacity ever since, training and certifying several thousand people inside numerous and diverse organizational firewalls.

The original idea was to publish about Scrum and other agile methodologies in my native Danish language. The conclusion was reached that there was little need and I ended up writing an extended whitepaper *Scrum - a Bird's Eye View* that has served a lot of people.

Time passed and unfolding circumstances called for new directions. Early on, we dealt mostly with software or product development teams focused on getting a good job done. Development teams are well accustomed to teamwork and communication so we touched mainly on the professional aspects of *What* to do, *How* to do it, and *When* to do it. In short, it was all about the tactical aspects – very factual.

We started talking more to Product Owners and leaders, addressing the more strategic aspects of the *Who* and the *Why* of the jobs at hand. We were moving into the value systems of individuals and organizations. That led to a greater need for written material to cover the whole gamut of initiatives and projects, often referred to as *The four Ws – Why, Who, What, and When*. Sometimes when encountering a need for teams to delegate work to suppliers internal or external, there is a fifth W – the *Where*.

Based on this I – together with a group of Scandinavian, Central European, and American trainers and coaches – started discussing how to apply the agile principles and lean thinking throughout the whole organization. This eventually became the Agile Lean Leadership framework that is presented here.

The group shared a passion for impacting the organizational culture and creating more value from its efforts. By then many things had happened, horizons were broadened, and Scrum was just one of the several ways an organization could become agile or even in the broader perspective, be lean. Together we saw how Scrum and Agile worked well beyond their original home turf of software projects and product development and that all sorts of organizations could benefit. The operative term became *Scaling Agility and Lean Out* in the organization.

Many have dealt with *Scaling Up* agile implementations to handle large projects; frameworks abound for that purpose. We were more concerned with *Scaling Out* the fundamental agile patterns found in Lean and Scrum into every corner of the organization, reaping the benefits that we so clearly had seen in projects and product development at the team level.

At the same time, the exercise of *Scaling Out* also led us to investigate the framework's applicability at a deeper level, to areas that are not pure knowledge work. In the general organization, there are many physical boundaries and constraints, it is not all in your head; there needs to be solutions for those circumstances as well.

There was also this new realization about the connection with complexity, something the original Scrum and agile principles didn't touch on much. It was always there, covered in statements about uncertainty and empirical process control, but not specified otherwise. We became inspired by Dave Snowden[2] and his Cynefin framework.

The fathers of Scrum (Ken Schwaber[3] and Jeff Sutherland[4]) with their military background said: *"Scrum is good! It works! Do it!"*. That is of course a great argument, but then Dave Snowden came along and said: *"Now, let me tell you why it works!"*.

We gradually became aware that for an organization to become the best it can be, its people have to engage voluntarily, by being free to choose. Innovation requires engagement, which in turn requires freedom – only this way can an organization be consistently resilient.

When used in the context of organizations, Freedom means freedom from micro-management, exploitation, and abuse by autocratic superiors. But more importantly, it means the freedom to act, while being responsible to the team and the wider organization. It means having the mandate to be the best you can be, to engage, and to be respected as an independent individual. In our modern world, the concept of freedom is often understood as only the first part, freedom from constraints, which is not enough to build a civil society or a constitutional organization based on honoring mutual commitments.

Gradually Agile Lean Leadership emerged through experimentation and theoretical study as a complete framework for *Scaling Out* Agile principles and Lean into the organization, providing the basis for people's engagement, and handling situations above and beyond pure software or product development. The conclusion was clear: There is a real need for a

---

2    Dave Snowden: https://en.wikipedia.org/wiki/Dave_Snowden  and his Cynefin framework: https://en.wikipedia.org/wiki/Cynefin_framework
3    Ken Schwaber: https://en.wikipedia.org/wiki/Ken_Schwaber
4    Jeff Sutherland: https://en.wikipedia.org/wiki/Jeff_Sutherland

simple framework on which to build an organization, enabling it to deal with complexity in a sustainable and resilient way.

We decided to call the framework Agile Lean Leadership because Agile and Lean were the main tributaries to the stream. However, none of the original concepts present a real vision for the whole organization. Agile frameworks (e.g. Scrum and Kanban) are mostly focused on teams and getting things done, which is good. Lean is focused on value streams and removing waste, which is also good. The Agile Lean Leadership framework aims to expand this further out in the organization. It is about leadership, collaboration, and how value creation, initiative, responsibility, authority, decision-making processes, and exception handling operate in an organization honoring Agile and Lean values.

## The Personal Touch

There is a personal perspective on the book as well. A while back I had an accident while playing soccer with my grandchildren, my knee snapped and I was carried from the battlefield by men in white coats. After several failed operations and lots of internal bleeding, the situation ended quite dramatically with experts wanting to amputate my leg. A surgeon at the local hospital defied the experts, pulled me back from the university hospital, and in the end saved my leg after a 3-4 hour long procedure performed by two surgeons.

This was not the only small miracle. A long stay at the hospital followed and my experience with the orthopedic facility was overwhelmingly positive. The collaboration between doctors and nurses, seniors and trainees, and day and night shifts was impressive, a spirit of psychological safety hovered over the place and the patients benefited from the service. There was no traditional hierarchy lording over the underlings with fear and intimidation, instead a general serving attitude dominated.

I was allowed to conduct Amy Edmondson's[5] survey of psychological safety and as expected the score was extremely high; one statement scored higher than anything else *"It is very easy to get help here"*. The whole situation resulted in positive articles in the press instead of the usual complaints about the healthcare system.

It was a collection of extraordinarily ordinary people, who created extraordinary results because they were free to engage, take responsibility, and do the right thing. It gave me a direct understanding of what can happen when good people are given the mandate to operate as free agents instead of always being told what to do.

I believe this is true in every domain, and getting these practices and their background documented became almost an obsession for me, hence this humble volume.

## Encounters en Route

During my and the group's journey, we have encountered many who share our goal, but there is also strong opposition from those who subscribe to traditional *Neo-Taylorist* management. It is clear that this line of thinking is a true anti-pattern to all things Agile and Lean. The Neo-Taylorist approach separates thinking and doing, echoing F. Winslow Taylor's[6] century-old concept of management based purely on numbers and KPIs; numerical efficiency above all else, and a reverence for the expert and the imperial leader. In reviving the Cold Case for freedom, Neo-Taylorism is the main antagonist.

Unfortunately, I found a perfect reference implementation of Neo-Taylorism in our Danish public sector's *New Public Management*. Neo-Taylorism almost always goes hand in hand with the classic hierarchical power structure inducing people to be primarily motivated by moving up

---

5   Amy Edmondson: https://en.wikipedia.org/wiki/Amy_Edmondson and https://amycedmondson.com/
6   Frederick Winslow Taylor: https://en.wikipedia.org/wiki/Frederick_Winslow_Taylor

the power ladder because that is where the freedom, power, money, and perks are.

One book that has made a huge impact completely outside the Agile and Lean domain is, *The Puritan Gift* by the Hopper brothers. It outlines the history of American management from the late nineteenth century to the beginning of the twenty-first. The main thrust of the book is how the rather enlightened management style from the beginning of the twentieth century got distorted after WWII and replaced around 1970 with Neo-Taylorist concepts of imperial leaders, and financial or legal wizards. The pendulum is now apparently swinging back in some companies and organizations, but most of the world is still drifting in a top-down plan-driven direction, whether of the socialist or the capitalist observance.

But there were also really encouraging discoveries, like the research into the importance of teams in complex learning organizations, psychological safety, and intrinsic motivation. From our perspective, W. Edwards Deming is a central figure. His work was key to the American war production of WWII and to the rebirth of Japanese industry from about 1950 to 1970. In his later years from around 1980 to 1993, he tried tirelessly to persuade American business leaders to adopt a better way of leadership. A lot of what we do is founded on Deming's work.

Another important contributor is *Beyond Budgeting,* whose values and goals of Agile Lean Leadership. In many cases, a combination of Beyond Budgeting and Agile Lean Leadership could be the best organizational improvement strategy – creating a pincer movement. Several others will be mentioned in the following chapters.

Then there is a host of other people, who have observed and described the same need for all these positive traits of engagement, respect, self-management, etc. all summed up in the concept of freedom for people. There are also many examples of organizations that have created such an environment, some examples are 100 years old[7]. It is not new as shall be seen.

Finally, recent developments on the geo-political scene have highlighted some fundamental observations of root causes. Freedom or autonomy of the individual in an organization is probably the deepest of all determinants of performance, well-being, resilience, and sustainability to be found. However, not many of those with views on leadership seem to talk or write much about freedom as such. A couple of notable exceptions are professors Bård Kuvaas[8] and Anders Dysvik[9] from Oslo BI and Traci Fenton[10] from Worldblue. Many people want the effect, and the engagement, and walk carefully around the subject, but few tackle it head-on and implement practices that support it.

The war in Ukraine which started in 2022 is about freedom and those who want to take it away from the Ukrainians. In his 2024 book *On Freedom*, Professor Timothy Snyder[11] from Yale highlights the situation. It is a remarkable book that, although speaking about national and global issues, is also relevant to organizations. His analysis of why individual freedom is instrumental to all positive community development resonates with our findings in organizations. Freedom is not just freedom from constraints and outright oppression, it is also freedom to choose, contribute, and become the best possible version of yourself.

Although we have amassed quite a lot of experience during the last 20+ years, there is only so much perspective that can be gained in a lifetime. I therefore embarked on a series of interviews to collect other people's per-

---

7   One of the marquee companies in this space is W. L. Gore (https://en.wikipedia.org/wiki/W._L._Gore_%26_Associates), their idea of the organization came from Bill Gore's experience in the DuPont taskforces originating in the 1920s

8   Bård Kuvaas: https://www.bi.no/om-bi/ansatte/institutt-for-ledelse-og-organisasjon/bard-kuvaas/

9   Anders Dysvik: https://www.bi.edu/about-bi/employees/department-of-leadership-and-organizational-behaviour/anders-dysvik/

10   Traci Fenton: https://www.worldblu.com/about

11   Timothy Snyder: https://timothysnyder.org/

spectives. This was very enlightening and sometimes totally surprising. People from all sorts of backgrounds were interviewed, which influenced the flow of the book quite a lot, the findings are documented in Appendix *A - Summary of Interviews*.

Returning to the case for freedom, yes, it is still there on the shelf, but it is mostly gathering dust, and no active investigation on how to solve the conundrum is happening. This provided the final push to give the book its present shape and form plus its title: *Liberating Organizations – Building the Case for Freedom*.

## Why and Who

This book is written to give readers sufficient facts, arguments, strategies, and tools so that they can investigate for themselves. If they find the facts substantial and plausible, they can then embark on a journey of organizational improvement and reverse the tide of Neo-Taylorism – especially the present-day focus on hierarchy and power. We want to help people and organizations to:

- Create more value out of their efforts for all parties involved, customers, employees, stakeholders, and society at large.
- Develop resilience and sustainability also in relationships.
- Reintroduce respect for people, so that they can choose to engage, thrive, and have pride of workmanship.

At the center is the concept of freedom. None of these objectives will be accomplished if people are not free to volunteer and choose to engage. It is not sustainable if people don't want it, we cannot just program it. Like societies, organizations can only be resilient and innovative if there is freedom for the people to speak up, choose, and act, it cannot be coerced from the top.

> *Freedom without the restraints of responsibility is chaotic and destroys co-operation and teamwork. We all want to achieve the best combination of freedom and responsibility.* — *Bill Gore, Co-Founder W. L. Gore*

The goal may seem overly ambitious and perhaps even too idealistic and romantic. However, all that can be done in complex situations is to look at the evolutionary potential in the present and try to create initiatives that pull in the desired direction and away from the undesirable state. Small steps will have to be taken, with frequent feedback, nobody knows what exactly will happen.

> *The only way to know how a complex system will behave – after you modify it – is to modify it and see how it behaves.* — *George E. P. Box*

This will bring us into the territory of what ought to be, not just what is; this is the territory of ethics. Some may be uncomfortable with that, but it is my take that we need to agree on a certain common value system that allows us to evaluate initiatives and practices; do they help us go in the right direction or not? This question cannot be dodged.

When dealing with complex challenges, we must replace the concept of big up-front plans and power-based hierarchy, or forever be stuck with substandard solutions and slow reaction times because of our low levels of engagement and resilience.

This book just had to be written. The challenges of complexity and rapid change are growing daily. Freedom is under attack both from elites and counter-elites. There is not much prospect of smooth sailing and calm waters in front of us, instead, there is an abundance of whitewater to be seen. It is too early to panic, but it would be overly naive not to sound the bell and wake up the citizens.

> *Well, there's some things a man just can't run away from.*
>
> *– John Wayne in Stagecoach*

18

# Introduction and Reading Guide

If you are engaged in the organization you work for and want to make a difference to help get the most out of its efforts, then you just may have come to the right place.

Furthermore, if you respect and care about your colleagues, employees, and stakeholders; and if you want to see them contribute, take responsibility, and grow to their maximum potential, then there is an even better chance that you have come to the right place.

Finally, do you have a gnawing suspicion that some things are sub-optimal in our organizations, and that effort is squandered without results? That customers and staff suffer under an overly bureaucratic, top-down approach, and that there is little freedom and scope for individuals to engage, grow, and influence direction? If so, you are just the kind of reader we want to find!

*Liberating Organizations* aims to help organizations become more resilient and sustainable and fulfill their mission of creating more value for those they serve – customers, employees, stakeholders, and the community. The purpose is:

*To investigate why freedom in organizations is scarce, and what brought us here.*

*To establish a blueprint for a different environment – a constitutional organization, where there is freedom under the rule of law and not the law of the ruler.*

*To help organizations build a place where freedom exists for people to contribute, create value, engage, and flourish. A place where together, people can be sustainable and resilient, where leadership is a service and not a privilege, and where there is stewardship and not just power.*

This is done by infusing organizations with the motivation and insight to handle the challenges of the modern complex world through the adoption of an Agile and Lean framework, based on the free choices of individuals throughout the organization.

## The Content[1]

The book starts with some broad explanations of the core concepts, followed by a fact-based foundation for assessing the situation at hand: Where are we? How did we get here? Where would we like to have been? And where would we have hated to be? Based on that, what can we do to start moving in the right direction? What is the evolutionary potential in the present?

The book provides practical help for understanding organizational and behavioral patterns, provides a good starting point, and guides your organization towards constant improvement and honest engagement of staff and stakeholders.

The book includes a wide selection of practical methods and templates which we hope will inspire you to research for yourself and start addressing your specific situation. We have included a lot of footnotes and references for further investigation and an appendix with guides to more information on frameworks, principles, and methods.

So the book – although short – will give enough background and sufficient reason to embark on the journey of radical improvement and freedom of choice for people; it also provides the necessary tools for the first steps. It is a tight compilation and an aggregation of good thinking and principles from the last 100 years or so, primarily around the subject of leadership. The authors do not claim to have invented all of this, far from

---

1   Occasionally we have used Artificial Intelligence (AI) tools. We have used text tools to research and discover the context or the origin of certain quotes, we have always checked other sources for these answers, as AI tools often assert something strongly and wrongly (i.e. lie). Many of our black-and-white icon illustrations are originally generated with AI and then hand-improved.

it, it is a compilation of the best thinking and practices to be found with some elements added to the mix for a coherent framework.

The overarching framework is called *Agile Lean Leadership* (often referred to as ALL), as it draws its primary inspiration from agile principles and lean thinking, but there are many smaller tributaries of great thinking and good practices.

**Reading Guide**

The book is framed as an investigation of the cold case for freedom in organizations, a topic that not many seem to be bothered about. You – our readers – are the judge and jury. Is it possible to uncover and present the facts in a sufficiently compelling way so that you accept the analysis and conclusions? Is it possible to present a vision of how the situation could be better? And is it possible to draw a sufficiently detailed map of the road less traveled toward freedom? Will the evidence be plausible enough for you to pass a positive judgment and be willing to take the first steps?

The story unfolds like the *"peeling of an onion"*, with example narratives followed by detailed descriptions in subsequent sections. This leads to a little repetition with the option to read short sequences and still get useful meaning out of the text. There is much more to be said, a workbook sequel is planned and there is a website[2] with references to extra material, full-scale illustrations, and downloadable templates for those who want to dig deeper.

Illustrations are included to give a generalized image by which to remember a concept. There are also examples of concrete templates and artifacts. The illustrations in this book are rather small, they can be downloaded[3] in a better resolution, suitable for print.

There is a lot of references in the course of the investigation, many will just be links to Wikipedia or other media sources to facilitate a more in-

---

2   The book website: https://liberatingorg.com/
3   Book illustrations: https://liberatingorg.com/res/liborg1.0_ill.pdf

depth investigation. Direct quotes will be referenced fully where possible, but many quotes are just from internet sites, that seem trustworthy but do not necessarily provide chapter and verse of the source. When referencing books the site *Goodreads* is used most of the time. There is a comprehensive list of literature at the end.

The book is called *Liberating Organizations,* because the authors want to highlight the critical importance of freedom in the organization. When building such an organization using the Agile Lean Leadership framework, we call it an *Agile Lean Organization.* Occasionally the term *Constitutional Organization* is used to emphasize the idea of the rule of law (commitment to mutual agreements) and representative decision-making. The term *Liberating Organizations* from the book title is used to highlight the contrast to traditional power-based management. Some abbreviations are frequently used to make the presentation more tight:

- ALL – Agile Lean Leadership, the overall framework we present and promote throughout the book.
- PDSA – Plan–Do–Study–Act, also known as the Deming Cycle.
- OODA – Observe–Orient–Decide–Act, created by Colonel John Boyd.
- KPI – Key Performance Indicators.

Occasionally the expression *"Upstairs and Downstairs[4]"* is used, it means the separation of thinking and doing into two different, distinct compartments of management and workers. Another expression is *Value Stream* which originates from Lean and refers to a series of activities that gradually add value to a product or service for the customer or user.

There are several quotes throughout the book mostly from great people who have worked in the area, but sometimes they are just there to brighten your day. They are shown like this:

---

4   Upstairs and downstairs, a tongue-in-cheek reference to the British tv-series Downton Abbey, where the lord of the manor and his family sits upstairs and discuss the placement of the plates, glasses and the silverware, but has no clue as to how food ends up to the plates, as that of course happens downstairs.

> *Well, sister, the time has come for me to ride hard and fast!*
> — *John Wayne in* True Grit

When quotes are provided inline in the text, they are marked by quotation marks, and the quote is italicized, like *"A famous quote"*; specific terms, book titles, and the like are emphasized using italicized text, like *Out of the Crisis*. Terms that are used with a specific definition are capitalized, definition can be found in the *Glossary* in the back matter of the book. There you will also find the *Index* and a *Bibliography*.

In the following when the terms *we* and *us* are used, it means the authors and collaborators of this volume unless the context specifies another group, whereas the *I* and *me* is Kurt B. Nielsen. The book is a consolidated effort of all the authors, on my initiative. Sometimes the authors, *we*, have not been able to refrain from either subjective comments or little personal anecdotes, that were mini-epiphanies for us, they are shown like this:

*It is our firm conviction that the average Team can more than double its performance by adopting Agile and Lean practices.*

We will also present conclusions and propositions this way.

Finally, the book offers evidence along with the interpretation that led us to propose the Agile Lean Leadership framework as a plausible and coherent way of starting the journey toward a Liberating Organization. Please remember that it is a proposed framework, not a recipe or a religion to follow verbatim. Context is everything, every organization is different and must navigate the rapids of change itself, but this could prove to be a useful map to help avoid some of the rocks.

Join us in this investigation of the organizational terrain and follow as we discover the road less traveled to organizational freedom. It may not be easy, but the goal is rewarding, and the journey will be a great experience.

# The Case for Freedom

Let us start the investigation from a bird's eye perspective by trying to make sense of the present state of life in organizations, and perhaps society at large. Let us fly high and try to capture the big contours of the landscape, and then we will dive into the details in later chapters.

The coolness of the mountains
and the deepness of the sea
The blueness of the sky,
The Eagles fly - They do not flee.
The long amber grasses
floating in the breeze,
The smell of sweet flowers
are just thoughts inside of me.
Where men would never venture,
That's where the Eagles fly
On top of purple mountains
You can hear their shrieking cry.

In the mountains are their nests
Hidden from the prey

They won't be fools or be victims
or fall along the way.
They fight for life,
these large strong birds,
They won't let it pass them by.
Examples in our life should be.
To fly where Eagles fly.

— Helen E. Payne Spencer,
Cherokee, Where Eagles Fly

We are setting out to build a case for the freedom of people in organizations. Our impression is that it has been gathering dust on the shelf for 10+ years. Observing organizations we see an apparent lack of freedom for the people in organizations. Our hunch is that many of the challenges and problems with performance are rooted in the limits that are put on people's freedom and ability to fully interact and engage their skills. And whereas there is an abundance of activity around methods and training aimed at helping leaders to empower people, there is precious little focus on the importance of actual freedom from the workforce's perspective. Bård Kuvås from Oslo BI is very clear: "*The positive spiral of improvement starts with the autonomy of people.*"

To get started, we will collect observations and evidence and interview eyewitnesses. We will follow the outline of the workshop method *The Future Backwards*[1]:

- Where are we now?
- How did we get here?
- Where would we have liked to be?
- Where would we hate to have ended up?
- And finally, can we come up with plausible events that could have led to either of the two latter states?

# A Close Look at Where We Are Now

We could spend a whole volume describing the current situation in organizations. We will, however, limit the investigation to a few handfuls of narratives and eyewitness accounts evidence from the field. After several rounds of digging and evaluating, we believe the following few points accurately characterize our present state and how we got there:

---

1 The Future Backwards, by Dave Snowden: https://cynefin.io/wiki/Future_backwards

# Extreme Turbulence and Rapid Change

Information and news (fake or otherwise) are almost instant and available globally. Potentially, anything can be known immediately and without a filter. Companies experience sudden changes in the competitive landscape because of rapid technology development or the appearance of a new and unexpected competitor.

Over the last three to four years we have experienced unprecedented disruption due to pandemics, wars, terror, and natural disasters.

A product that was modern yesterday can be outdated today and personal knowledge and experience can quickly become a ticket to a train that has left. The supply chain we relied on has suddenly withered due to a crisis or war in some remote place on the planet.

All this creates pressure on organizations to assess and react quickly to unfolding circumstances – and change direction if needed. This is called *Agility* by the way.

The result of rapid change and uncertainty is turbulence which can cause confusion or even conflict. Many people will not discover that change is coming until they are in the eye of the storm. They become anxious and lose their sense of: "*I know what is expected of me here*[2]."

# A Crisis in Coherence in Organizations

According to Gallup's[3] research, 77% of the global workforce is *Disengaged*, and 18% is *Actively Disengaged*, which means that they actually are working against the interests of their organization. Western Europe is at an all-time low, below sub-Saharan Africa. In a British study some time ago, it was concluded that 30%+ of British workers were convinced that their job did not contribute to value in society in any shape or form. These

---

2    The first of the questions in Gallup's Q[12] questionnaire: https://www.gallup.com/q12/

3    Gallup: State of the Global Workplace 2022

are staggering numbers and the effects are just now dawning on investors, leaders, and governments.

In the last few years, these trends have taken the shape of so-called *Quiet Quitting*, where people just do a bare minimum to stay out of trouble at work and try to find fulfillment in something else. Lack of engagement seriously limits the ability of organizations to tackle complex problems. People increasingly take back-seat positions in organizations.

In the post-Covid world, there are visible tensions due to different expectations between people in an organization; some expect to work from home when they want, and some young people expect instant gratification and fulfillment of desires at work.

## Desire and Need to Engage People

There is a general realization that for institutions to succeed, people need to be engaged and to *"take ownership"*, to coin a misused phrase. Today, many organizations deal with highly complex knowledge work, where people's cognitive capacities are challenged and stretched, requiring cooperation and communication at a higher level than ever before.

When it is possible to penetrate people's protective, cynical layer, acquired from years of working under hierarchies and bureaucracies, most people want to be involved and contribute. In areas such as IT and product development, Agile frameworks like Scrum and Kanban have been adopted widely, with significant improvement in engagement and increased levels of job satisfaction; other domains have reported similar positive traits.

## Declining Trust in Authorities and Institutions

Many people have lost confidence in institutions and authorities, especially in government and large organizations. They are either too far away from everyday life or seem lost in their own internal procedures with little connection to reality. Consequently, people feel constrained by absurd rules and regulations, irrelevant KPIs and incomprehensible communication. It is like a Kafkaesque[4] nightmare. People in organizations often distrust what they are being told, expecting conveyed information to come with a hidden agenda that may be contrary to their interests.

Trust is a necessary component when trying to solve complex problems. Without it, we don't share information or rely on the work of others. All transaction and monitoring costs rise when trust is low and the time to execute transactions also grows.

Without confidence in the world around us, cynicism and fear creep in, transparency disappears and people start gaming the system out of self-protection.

> *When there is fear in an organization, the numbers are cooked!*
> — W. Edwards Deming

## The Pressure of the Hierarchy

People in teams delivering products and services often voice their frustrations with their organizations, this is one of the key takeaways from our interview sessions. One such frustration is that they frequently feel over-ridden. They are on a meaningful path of work when sudden changes of direction come from above, sometimes from sources without a direct link to them. Hierarchies often devolve into impersonal bureaucracies, alienating people completely.

In Scandinavia, the system of hierarchy is normally not very domineering or abusive, but according to the statistics, 10 to 20% of the people in hierarchies have psychopathic tendencies. Apparently, the very existence of the power structure attracts such people. Nobody likes to be subordinate to such people.

Decisions within a hierarchy are mostly driven by what subordinates believe their superior wants instead of what is best for all in the big picture,

---

4    Franz Kafka: https://en.wikipedia.org/wiki/Franz_Kafka

since this superior may control the individual's future. People want to avoid having their decisions reversed, being told off, or ending up in bad standing with their superiors.

> *In the hierarchy, the boss becomes your customer. Who takes care of the real customer then?* — *W. Edwards Deming*

Finally, the hierarchy is driven by the lure of the ever-higher compensation and status moving up the ladder. It becomes a formidable extrinsic motivator, overriding intrinsic motivation. It is very hard to resist the inherent competition for higher positions in the hierarchy. Read more about the consequences of the hierarchy in *Appendix C – Neo-Taylorism and the Fatal Attraction to Hierarchy*.

## Loss of Confidence in Large-scale Projects

There have been some catastrophic large-scale projects in both the private and public sectors; several IT projects and the building of hospitals in Denmark come to mind. These failures have demonstrated that large institutions are often incapable of managing such initiatives because they are firmly entrenched in a Tayloristic mindset, summarized as the deliberate separation of *"thinking and doing."* This has revealed the deficiencies of expert-controlled, big-up-front planning and a greater appreciation of the need for all team members to engage and contribute when projects are complex.

## A Young Generation with Different Demands

Young people entering the job scene have very different expectations of their workplace compared to previous generations. They want purpose in what they do, to be involved, to have influence, and to have a certain autonomy. They want good, collegial relationships at work, and opportunities to grow and develop their skills.

These positive characteristics have been shown to increase intrinsic motivation leading to engagement. However, organizations may be challenged to meet these requirements, and many interpret them as a pronounced focus on people's own needs, disregarding others and the organization; those stuck in the traditional hierarchical mindset might see it as outright insubordination.

This may not always be unjustified, especially if expectations do not align with the realm of the possible. In our interviews, we uncovered a lot of challenges in this area.

# How did We get Here?

## Centralization, Planning, Command, and Control

The prevailing modus operandi of most managers and certainly the vast majority of business consultants is more planning, stricter processes, and more heavy-handed control. Most managers are deeply entrenched in the *"five-year plan"* way of thinking, which they learned in business school. This trend developed over the last 50-60 years, starting in the US after WWII, it is often referred to as Neo-Taylorism.

It led to deep hierarchical organizations with reduced transparency and speed of response. This unfailingly increased the bureaucracy which stifled any innovation badly needed for solving complex problems.

The concentration of power increases the probability that a single person will assume overall charge and be lavishly compensated for doing so. In many organizations and encouraged by the media, there is a growing infatuation with, if not worship of the strong imperial leader. The pursuit of such power and status then often becomes the ambition of those lower in the hierarchy.

The constant measurement and ranking of people typically found in large organizations induces or amplifies fear which awakens the most basic instinct of all, survival. Many managers use fear almost subconsciously as an instrument to control their subordinates. Today Scandinavian organizations that pride themselves on flat hierarchies and low power distance, adopt subtle forms of psychological warfare instead of old-fashioned brute force intimidation. In any case, people will use extreme measures to survive in fear-driven environments, twisting systems, data, or both to stay out of harm's way.

## Managerial Doublespeak

Marketing has also crept into management over the last 50-60 years, often advocated by consultants who sell their ability to craft sweet-sounding messages and produce motivational posters that are supposed to make people feel good about the organization and its management. Often these messages are not in sync with reality and become a kind of Orwellian doublespeak[5]. People quickly discover this and lose confidence; disengagement is sure to follow. This was also a frequent observation during our interviews with people in the field, from those in the lower ranks of the organization, of course.

## The Good Life and Affluence

In the West, there has never been a period with greater material wealth, better health, or better opportunities for education. Since the 1950s each generation could expect a materially better life than their parents. People can afford interesting holiday destinations, challenging interests, and personal luxuries unthinkable to most a couple of generations ago, and certainly to most people today on planet Earth.

However, after a couple of generations of relative affluence, it seems that nothing is really important, or even interesting, anymore. People are bored but feel entitled to everything, a nice home, instant entertainment, perfect social institutions, personal fulfillment, good looks, fantastic relations, a great sex life, and more! It seems that especially in Western Europe this correlates to the very low engagement at work reported by Gallup.

---

5    Doublespeak: https://en.wikipedia.org/wiki/Doublespeak

There is a dark side to this. Never have there been so many broken relationships and so many depressed people, unable to cope with their everyday life. Some of this is due to the fear mentioned above, but perhaps even more to a loss of meaning and purpose. It is also the case that the latest generations are not automatically on a materially upward spiral, creating further disillusionment.

Finally, there seems to be a worrying loss of sensitivity towards the less fortunate. Lip service may be paid to the needs of others, but people are more likely to close ranks and look inward to preserve their own interests. In some respect, this leads to the next point.

## Expressive Individualism

Expressive individualism is the belief that identity comes through self-expression; through discovering one's most authentic desires and being free to be one's authentic self.[6] The West has gone overboard with individualism to the extent that many crave instant gratification and fulfillment of their particular preferences; they want more and they want it now. This is a real problem in organizations; how to even keep a bunch of expressive individualists in the same room?

Teamwork is especially challenged if expressive individualism is dominant. It becomes difficult to make people invest personally in communal activities such as finding solutions together and attending to other people's needs. There is a tendency to presume that the "system" will take care of that – which it won't.

On the other hand, we are convinced that expressive individualism is brittle and breaks if confronted with real life, real people, and real contributions. It is in fact best suited for couch-philosophers and producers of soap operas. Given the opportunity to contribute for real, experience

---

6    Tim Keller, 2015: https://timothykeller.com/blog/2015/1/9/the-city-the-church-and-the-future

growth, and work with real people, we observe and believe that most people will engage; they just need to be shown the option.

*Nobody changes by being told, they need to be shown!* — *Tim Keller*

# A rough Timeline of how We got Here

Here is a list of important events leading up to the present state, moving backward in time, starting with the most recent important events:

1. 2023. The Hamas attack on Israel further fueled the wider worldwide crisis, calling for more control, and resulting in deeper polarization.

2. 2022. The Russian attack on Ukraine and the ongoing atrocities ignited a widespread fear of the future – certainly in Europe.

3. 2020-2021. The two years of the Covid pandemic left everybody shaken out of their comfort zone and many lost livelihoods and had their lives permanently changed.

4. 2010+. Large-scale failure of institutions both public and private leading to loss of confidence. Pressure from global and mobile markets appeared as well.

5. 2007-2008. The financial crisis revealed the absurdity of just focusing on speculative gains and greed in the financial sector. It made a lot of people lose trust in financial institutions, but also in government. It also brought about heavy-handed control from governments stifling a lot of innovation.

6. 2007. Dave Snowden contributed positively with his Cynefin framework for solving problems in different domains, most notably the Complex domain.

7. 2005+. For many years IT systems intended to rationalize and automate work have been deployed. The problem is that they often did not address the target problem which led to the tightening of rules and regulations, the side effect of which was to stifle innovation and sometimes make the original issue worse.

8. 2001 marked the arrival of important Agile landmarks, such as the *Agile Manifesto* and the seminal book *Agile Software Development with Scrum*.

9. 1990+. New Public Management became the rage spreading the effects of Neo-Taylorism further. The public sector in many places is still suffering.

10. 1990+. In the nineties it became clear that a new perception of management had emerged: It was seen as a separate profession, detached from ordinary work and skills. This is the institutionalized separation of thinking and doing, which illuminates a position high up in the hierarchy as the goal; it is called Neo-Taylorism. The trend started much earlier (around 1970) in the US.

11. 1990+. *Lean* is the Western word for key elements of the Toyota Production System, it became known in the West, and over the years many Lean practices have been adopted, if often not fully understood.

12. 1950-1970. W. Edwards Deming worked in Japan to teach them how to produce quality and build a culture of constant improvement.

13. 1945+. Business schools proliferated after the war, a new managerial class was created based on the ideas of F. Winslow Taylor.

14. 1920+. The large corporations were often institutionalized through tight financial control, a prime example of this is General Motors with its divisional budget control created by Alfred Sloan[7] and James McKinsey[8].

15. 1900+. F. Winslow Taylor formulated his ideas of *Scientific Management*[9] and for some rather obscure reason, it produced a pervasive

---

7   Alfred P. Sloan: https://en.wikipedia.org/wiki/Alfred_P._Sloan
8   James McKinsey: https://en.wikipedia.org/wiki/James_O._McKinsey
9   F. Winslow Taylor, 1911, The Principles of Scientific Management: https://en.wikipedi-a.org/wiki/The_Principles_of_Scientific_Management

wave of change. In Europe, Max Weber[10] and Henri Fayol[11] made their contributions in defining management and bureaucracy.

16. 1850-1890. The American Industry grew enormously and hierarchical management developed further with the separation of line and staff functions, especially in the railroad sector.

17. 1841. Several people quote the year 1841 as the time when the idea of a hierarchy explicitly entered the business. The trigger was the world's first large train accident that occurred on 1841-10-05 in Western Massachusetts. Major Whistler[12] was put in charge of a commission to investigate. He concluded that every organization should be organized hierarchically with precise definitions of responsibility at every node. Those in charge at each node would plan, delegate to subordinates, monitor them, and control their performance. The model was found in the army, specifically the Prussian army.

Before all this, there was the feudal system, the monarchies, the local warlords of the Middle Ages, and before that the Roman Empire, from which we inherited the inspiration for hierarchy and bureaucracy.

## Postlude

The selected narratives may seem overly critical or negative. On the one hand, it is true that the input collected from years of educating and supporting organizations is mostly of the frustrated if not depressive kind.

On the other hand, there is a silver lining in the majority of the observations because most people have good intentions and a genuine desire to change things for the better. All the leaders we have spoken with, appear genuinely to want to develop a value and people-oriented organization. Young people, not yet molded by cynicism or apathy, seem to have a

---

10  Max Weber: https://en.wikipedia.org/wiki/Max_Weber
11  Henri Fayol: https://en.wikipedia.org/wiki/Henri_Fayol
12  George Washington Whistler: https://en.wikipedia.org/wiki/George_Washington_Whistler

growing desire to find a vocation and honestly contribute to a better future.

In many ways, the present can be characterized as the *Post-Postmodern* period, where severe disappointment with and cynicism toward everything – even with the postmodern[13] worldview itself – is prevalent. Left to their own devices, our Institutions only have utter despair in front of them. Nobody has any substantiated hope outside the fluffy-bunny crowd of utopians.

It is fair to say we have tension and a crisis; it is too early to panic, but certainly, it would be naive not to face reality. However, this situation offers a good precondition to initiate change or reformation.

# Where would We like to Have Been?

We have conducted the *Future Backwards* exercise during numerous training and coaching sessions in many organizations and countries, and it has been surprising to find widespread consensus on what would and would not have been desirable outcomes.

The *Heavenly State* (ideal situation), where people would have preferred we were now, features the following characteristics:

If people have the basic material and security needs covered, they want to spend their time and capacity on something that gives them an inner sense of value. This is often referred to as *Intrinsic Motivation*[14] in contrast to *Extrinsic Motivation* (money perks, etc.)

---

13 A broad movement from the middle to the late 20th century characterized by loss of faith in anything absolute, skepticism, irony, and acknowledgment of only the self as judge of everything. https://en.wikipedia.org/wiki/Postmodernism
14 Discussed academically and in popular terms by
- Bård Kuvås: https://no.wikipedia.org/wiki/B%C3%A5rd_Kuvaas,
- Anders Dysvik: https://5c.careers/5c-country-team-members/dysvik-anders/ and
- Daniel Pink: https://en.wikipedia.org/wiki/Daniel_H._Pink

Synthesizing input from the most prominent sources, Intrinsic Motivation has four components:

- **Autonomy** – I have the mandate to decide on a considerable portion of my time, i.e. the freedom to choose and act.
- **Purpose** – I can see a higher purpose in what I do than just lining my pocket.
- **Relationships** – I have positive relationships with the people I work with and am exposed to in daily life.
- **Mastery** – I have the opportunity to grow and become good at what I do.

Of these, the first – autonomy or freedom – is the prerequisite for everything; without that people rarely become the best possible version of themselves and rarely experience fulfillment in their work.

People want the freedom to have their observations and opinions taken seriously without fear of reprisal and they want to be able to ask for help without creating the impression of weakness or incompetence. This is labeled *Psychological Safety*[15] and consists of three elements:

- Nobody should be penalized for admitting a mistake.
- Nobody should be penalized for asking for help.
- Nobody should be penalized for suggesting a better way of doing things.

Again, the foundation of this is freedom. Psychological Safety is not the same as staying in the comfort zone. People may like a bit of smooth sailing, but most get bored quickly and want to take up a challenge and be able to learn, grow, and be proud of their work.

Given the freedom to speak up and a mandate to act, most are willing to take ownership and responsibility, particularly in the context of the com-

---

15  Psychological Safety: https://en.wikipedia.org/wiki/Psychological_safety, especially discussed by Amy Edmondson: https://en.wikipedia.org/wiki/Amy_Edmondson

mon good, where they believe others take their commitments seriously. It boils down to having respect for and trust in others.

Ideally, people want a life-work balance that offers them flexibility, but sadly many of our highly regulated organizations and systems of social benefits and taxes, do not align with those values.

People want transparency; to see the full picture and understand how and why things are done. They want to know that the world is ordered and makes sense to some extent.

Finally, people want to be able to respond quickly to new opportunities or challenges.

Of course, everybody wants to be treated and compensated fairly. The younger generations focus heavily on fair treatment, inclusivity, and justice, whereas the older ones focus more on compensation. We all want more money, holidays, and perks if we can get them, but above a certain level, it is not the driver of our behavior, the desire for intrinsic motivation is.

There are outliers of course, people who are driven by the prospect of great personal rewards or influence, or people who simply want a way to sustain other more interesting areas of their lives outside work. These people exist, and we have to deal with them; but in this present world, organizations cannot expect to navigate the unfolding complex landscape with people who are in the game just for themselves.

## A Plausible Road to the Heavenly State

How could organizations have ended up in this more desirable place instead of the present state? In each organization, there may have been several minor events and many contributing decisions

Globally, the evidence points to one big thing that could have changed the course of events. If somewhere in the 1990s the West had truly learned from what happened in post-war Japan and had not let the damaging

Neo-Taylorist, techno-bureaucratic philosophy take over, organizations could have been closer to the heavenly state. For example, they would have learned earlier from Lean and W. Edwards Deming about respect for people and their freedom. They would have understood the concept of complexity and the necessity of constant feedback loops to adjust the course, and not just rely on central big upfront planning. They would also have trusted the value of people's intrinsic motivation.

Another probable cause dates to the beginning of the 1970s when management started to detach from the ordinary line of the business and become a discipline in its own right, separate from domain knowledge. If this fascination with management had been resisted, we might have avoided the extreme separation of thinking and doing, the creation of the organizational class system, and the excesses of outlandish CEO compensation that have developed over the last 50 years.

The victory of Neo-Taylorism did not happen in a flash. It was a long series of little lost battles, like an invasive weed taking over the garden in the course of a decade or three.

# Where would We hate to Have Ended Up?

Most people also agree on what would be absolute hell for them, and what conditions would make them seriously study job postings.

They do not want to live under incompetent, brutal, or arbitrary leaders in a hierarchy, spending much time on politics or power games. Nor do they want to work under an imperial ruler and just take orders; the young especially do not accept this, they want to have a say in things.

The exception is when a charismatic leader can generate an almost cult-like following, independent of his or her personal qualities. In such cases, a sense of belonging outweighs the lack of personal identity some have. We consider this an undesirable situation, rife with examples of negative consequences.

People also hate to live under a bureaucratic system with incomprehensible rules and regulations and where work is reduced to simple algorithmically compliant tasks. Such workplaces alienate and induce fear which creates its own set of unintended consequences.

People do not in general want to spend their time competing for space in a hierarchy, maneuvering for status and promotion. When the hierarchy is very visible and people are conscious of their rank it becomes a powerful *Extrinsic Motivator* that overrides the *Intrinsic Motivation.* People then enter a game of *Upstairs and Downstairs* or resign and detach – quitting quietly.

## A Plausible Road to Absolute Hell

How then could organizations have ended up here? We have often heard from people – especially in large organizations or the public sector – that just doing nothing, letting things develop as they already do, will end in absolute hell for the people working there. But, in many real-life organizations things did not go all that bad, common sense seems to survive even very counterproductive systems, mostly by people bending incomprehensible rules or flying under the radar.

If organizations had gone fully into Neo-Taylorism, absolute compliance to plans with no idea of how complexity affects decision-making, they could have ended in hell; some have, and some still will.

Finally, if people upstairs in the hierarchy habitually override the initiatives of people on the ground, doing the work, reversing their decisions, changing their circumstances willy-nilly, or in other ways demonstrate their superiority and lack of respect for the downstairs. Then guess what? People check out, take the back seat, and disengage – or leave.

# Then What?

The insight produced by the Future Backwards exercise is usually illustrated in a drawing like the one below:

The
Future
Backwards

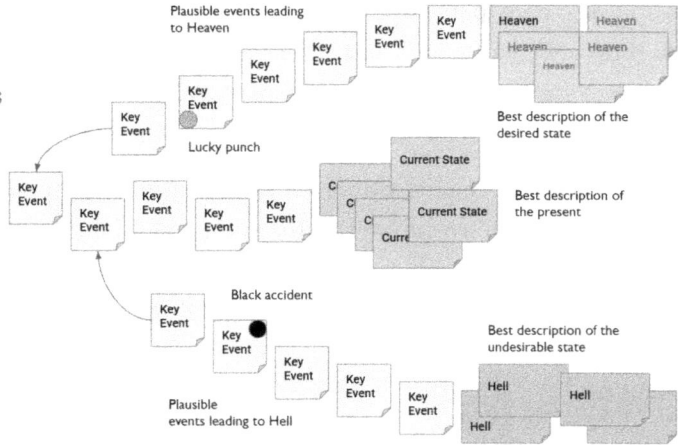

Plausible events leading to Heaven

Key Event / Key Event / Key Event / Heaven / Heaven / Heaven / Heaven / Heaven

Key Event

Key Event

Lucky punch

Best description of the desired state

Key Event / Key Event / Key Event / Key Event / Key Event

Current State / Current State / Curr

Best description of the present

Black accident

Key Event / Key Event / Key Event / Key Event / Key Event / Hell / Hell / Hell

Plausible events leading to Hell

Best description of the undesirable state

What can this be used for? First, if a group does this exercise they will develop a common understanding of their situation, discovering perspectives not previously known. Then with this illustration in hand, the value system becomes clear; what people value and what they don't. That makes it possible to think about changing things for the better and setting objectives to achieve.

Nobody can expect to reach the heavenly state; this is a place that only exists in another *Space-Time Continuum*[16]. Even as organizations change, the world also changes as may our understanding of the heavenly state. Failproof plans are impossible but moves in the right direction can be obtained through smaller interventions and experiments that evolve in the context of existing internal and external conditions.

> We are looking for the evolutionary potential in the present
> — Dave Snowden

# Any Way Forward?

Are there alternatives to the status quo? From our experience and many case studies, we believe there are alternatives. But we would like to com-

---

16  Space-Time Continuum, term from the movie series *Back to the Future*.

bine all those streams of good thinking into an easy-to-understand proposition.

Therefore, the purpose of this book and the whole Agile Lean Leadership initiative is to come up with a blueprint for a better way of organizing. A set of strong arguments, teaching, visualizations, procedures, patterns, and techniques, to give organizations a catalog of insight and a repertoire of concrete interventions so that they can start moving in the right direction.

The details will unfold over the following pages, but for now, let us state that we are aiming for an organization based on other values than power and just efficiency. We call this a *Constitutional Organization* where there is freedom to engage under the rule of law and not just the law of the ruler.

Here is the list of assumptions for our blueprint, our first hypothesis for solving this cold case:

- Having a primary focus on the customers or clients being served, describing them as well as we can, creating a taxonomy, and forming an internal Value Stream to serve them.
- Forming small, cross-functional, and self-governing teams that enable the engagement of the people actually working there, reaching for high internal coherence and low external coupling.
- Introducing cross-team, representative decision-making.
- Establishing forums for handling cross-cutting concerns across the value stream, such as specific competence areas (QA, Design, etc.).
- Having a system for quickly reacting when an unexpected opportunity or challenge appears.
- Enabling radical transparency through open artifacts and events.
- Having solid working agreements between teams working together.
- Using the premises of self-governing structure: No one can use force against others, everyone honors their commitment.

The agreements seen in total comprise the *Constitution*, based on mutual consent, describing everyone's commitments. This is what governs an organization instead of a power-based hierarchy.

# The Inspiration for Opening the Case

The inspiration for opening the case for freedom and this volume comes from various sources. We discovered plausible explanations and alternatives to traditional power-based management in many different places. Here are the ones we consider the most important

## Vanilla Scrum and Agile

During the many years the authors have worked with Scrum in training, coaching, and implementation this has been by far the biggest inspiration. Vanilla Scrum is the most popular and the archetypical Agile framework at the team or project level. Originally Scrum was popularized by Jeff Sutherland and Ken Schwaber[17], based on earlier work by several people. Scrum provides all the building blocks and the mindset so that Agile and Lean can be scaled out into the whole organization. Vanilla Scrum is like the basic two-by-four Lego brick that is a key component in most Lego designs. Scrum is one of several Agile approaches, Kanban also stood out as important from the beginning.

## Lean Thinking

Scrum, as part of Agile, is again a part of Lean Thinking. Lean is a term coined primarily by James Womack[18] in his 1990 book *The Machine That Changed the World*[19], in which he documented the Toyota Production System (TPS). In many ways all this originated in the US before and around the Second World War. The purpose of Lean Thinking is to create more

---

17  See the official "Scrum Guide" http://www.scrumguides.org/
18  James P. Womack: https://en.wikipedia.org/wiki/James_P._Womack
19  Read more about Lean here: https://en.wikipedia.org/wiki/The_Machine_That_Changed_the_World_(book)

value for the customer with fewer resources, but very importantly: through respect for people.

## Cynefin

We were familiar with Dave Snowden's complexity model, Cynefin, and its five domains: **Obvious** (Clear), **Complicated**, **Complex**, and **Chaos** plus the unfortunate **Confusion.** As Snowden says: *"That's where you are when you don't know where you are"*. This model explains that many organizational problems originate from a misunderstanding of which domain you are in. For example, the approach to Obvious work should not be applied to Complex work where there is only fragmented and limited knowledge available; in which case it is necessary to seek knowledge by experimenting in a controlled fashion and watching out for emerging solutions. This line of attack is not what we typically see.

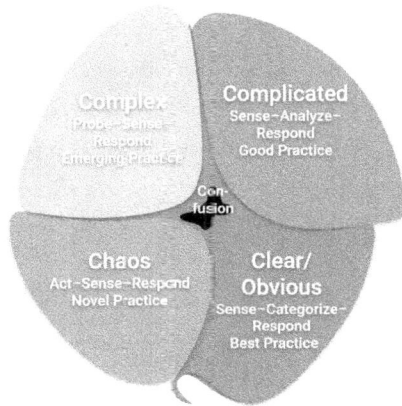

*Knowledge can only be volunteered, it cannot be conscripted!*
— *Dave Snowden*

## Human Nature and Behavior

From the very outset, we knew that there were some tough questions, in particular, the views held about the nature of human beings. Organizations are social systems, collections of human beings, with some structures and processes chosen to try to get everybody to produce value together. A lot of these choices hinge on the view of human beings, and there are plenty of observations and world views to choose from.

# Theory X and Y

Douglas McGregor[20] introduced his *Theory X and Theory Y*[21] in his book *The Human Side of Enterprise* (1960). Oversimplified, he claims that theory X subscribers believe that human beings are only driven by self-interest, and that only through power, rewards, and punishment can they be made to produce something for the common good. On the other hand, theory Y people view human beings as basically good and capable of being self-directing and producing something of value if you just leave them alone. We weren't sure if this model was useful or not.

## Intrinsic and Extrinsic Motivation

There was overwhelming documentation that intrinsic motivation is akin to engagement and where it exists, it produces results.

Many have studied this. Anders Dysvik[22] and Bård Kuvaas[23] from BI Norwegian Business School, Oslo, Norway, are some of the most prominent. They published an article in 2012 about this: *Intrinsic and extrinsic motivation as predictors of work effort*[24], and the conclusions are clear: intrinsic motivation beats extrinsic motivation in producing results and fulfillment for all work in which the worker has the slightest interest. However, extrinsic motivation such as bonuses overrides intrinsic motivation, and people will go for it when there is money on the table.

Intrinsic motivation rests on a combination of Purpose, Autonomy, Relations, and Mastery. So that certainly was a key area to investigate further, and the key concept of autonomy – freedom – stood out.

---

20  Douglas McGregor: https://en.wikipedia.org/wiki/Douglas_McGregor
21  Read more here: https://en.wikipedia.org/wiki/Theory_X_and_Theory_Y
22  Anders Dysvik: https://www.bi.edu/about-bi/employees/department-of-leadership-and-organizational-behaviour/anders-dysvik/
23  Bård Kuvaas: https://www.bi.edu/about-bi/employees/department-of-leadership-and-organizational-behaviour/bard-kuvaas/
24  2012 article: https://biopen.bi.no/bi-xmlui/bitstream/handle/11250/2395261/Dysvik_Kuvaas_2013_%20BJSP.pdf?sequence=1&isAllowed=y

## Psychological Safety

Psychological safety was – and is – very visible in the public debate. Amy Edmondson, the most prominent contributor to the debate, worked on developing an understanding of psychological safety over the last 25 years. It was clear from the outset that psychological safety has to be present if an organization wants to embark on the road to the desired state of freedom.

Psychological safety is a prerequisite for useful feedback, learning, adapting to other people, and generally experiencing that *it is OK to be me here*, this is also a variant of freedom.

# Conclusion

As we have seen in the above arguments, there is a large concentration of complex challenges in modern organizations. We are deeply convinced that yesterday's solutions will not suffice for the problems today. Continuing on the same road will not create the solutions we need. If we keep heading in the direction that most Western societies and many organizations currently are going, then crises will keep following crises.

*We can't solve problems by using the same kind of thinking we used when we created them.* — *Albert Einstein*

The demand for more control will keep increasing to prevent non-conformance, misuse of freedom, and trespassing rules and regulations. Soon the deep frustrations will create calls for the strong man, the Imperial Leader, to come and relieve us of the chaos (and consequently freedom) that we apparently cannot handle, and save the day.

We had some intuitive assumptions about the mechanisms, but the cause-and-effect relationships were not all that clear, we only had fragmented knowledge, but had to do something anyway. We started to look for more evidence, interviewing people in the field, hoping that with more pieces of the puzzle on the table, we would be able to come up with a coherent hypothesis with some explanatory power that was plausible enough to produce some proposals for action. Let us move on to follow the story of management back in time in the next chapter.

*We found that the current status in organizations is characterized by:*
*– Turbulence, uncertainty, and complexity.*
*– Lack of engagement, quiet quitting, and loss of confidence in authorities.*
*– Difficulties in matching the new generations with the jobs in organizations.*

*We identified the main cause of the status to be Neo-Taylorism with its:*
*– Upfront and central planning.*
*– Bureaucratic and power-based hierarchies.*
*– Separation of thinking and doing, managing and working.*

*Another contribution to the status quo is the expressive individualism of the culture.*

*A hypothesis was built for a way forward to a better situation:*
*– Built on agile and lean principles.*
*– An understanding of complexity.*
*– Psychological Safety and intrinsic motivation.*
*– Striving for freedom but with checks and balances – a constitutional organization*

# Investigating the Road
# We Traveled

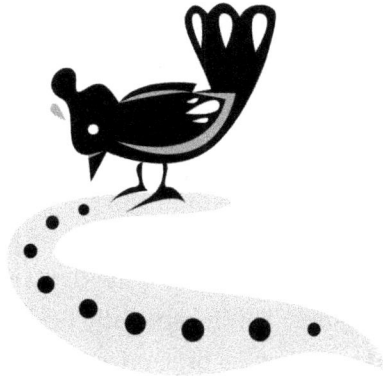

*In the previous chapter, we hovered high above ground to get a perspective of the status quo and determine where we would like to be. Now it is time to retrace the road we traveled to uncover more facts about how we got here. While looking for clues we have often found ourselves at the crossroads of "This Way or That Way". Which would provide the most useful insights and data?*

*In 1915 Robert Frost published the poem "The Road Not Taken[1]". It starts by stating: "Two roads diverged in a yellow wood" and often we felt that same challenge of choosing.*

*It ends with the words"Two roads diverged in a wood, and I—I took the one less traveled by, And that has made all the difference."*

*Our investigation also felt like a road less traveled*

---

1   Read more here: https://en.wikipedia.org/wiki/The_Road_Not_Taken and the full text here: https://www.poetryfoundation.org/poems/44272/the-road-not-taken

This is an investigative journey to discover who has dealt with these subjects before. The first road taken was arbitrarily chosen; provoked initially by a participant in one of our training courses, who pointed me to the two books mentioned below. I have to admit that it was the provocative titles that led me to dive in. This influenced the trajectory of our work and convinced us that there was something here, not just something existing in our heads. Others had seen the same signs.

# How the West Was Lost – The Analysis

One of the biggest puzzles working with organizations is how many managers believe everything can be simplified, planned upfront, and reduced to a neat set of figures. This is especially perplexing when those developing and delivering products or services know that reality is much more complex and that long-term plans can seldom be trusted in detail.

This phenomenon is called *Neo-Taylorism*, which is discussed in more detail in *Appendix C – Neo-Taylorism in Detail*.

## A few Books that Mattered to Us

A few books were recommended to us which became foundational for this book, if not the whole Agile Lean Leadership framework, including the ideas around the Constitutional Organization. The first is *The Puritan Gift*[2] by the brothers Hopper. The second one is *Voltaire's Bastards* by Canadian author John Ralston Saul[3]. Additionally, *The Road to Unfreedom*, *On Tyranny,* and *On Freedom* by Timothy Snyder[4] are very enlightening.

### The Puritan Gift

The book explains in detail how the US became the dominant industrial power from the end of the 19th century and through the 1950s or 1960s,

---

2   Kenneth Hopper and William Hopper 2007, http://www.puritangift.com
3   John Ralston Saul: https://en.wikipedia.org/wiki/John_Ralston_Saul
4   Timothy Snyder: https://en.wikipedia.org/wiki/Timothy_Snyder and https://en.wikipedia.org/wiki/Timothy_Snyder

highlighting the personal qualities of those driving American business at the time. US greatness stemmed from the virtues inherent in the Union, implanted by the founding fathers in the Massachusetts Bay colony in the 17th century. The most important were a strong sense of purpose, personal freedom, and responsibility for the community.

The book explains in acid-dripping language how those qualities were lost after WWII with the rise of business schools and a new managerial class that became an entity separate from the delivery of products and services. By 1970 the *"cult-of-the-so-called-expert"* (as the authors call it) had taken over, and Neo-Taylorism was created.

There is a very good review of the book by Diane Coyle[5] from which a paragraph is included here:

> ... *the Hoppers' first villain is Frederick W. Taylor. He started the process of turning efficient organizational structures into social hierarchies, with top managers increasingly less likely to be engineers or technicians working their way up from the shop floor. Business schools continued this evisceration of the actual process of business, creating a professional cadre of managers, superior in status in pay, and with purely financial and abstract knowledge in place of the tacit skills and experience previously displayed by management cohorts. The downfall was completed by the steadily increasing celebration of greed, sucking the moral heart out of American capitalism.*
> *– Diane Coyle.*

The main evidence harvested from this book is probably that in the last 50-60 years the Western world managed to revert to an almost feudal system, separating thinking and doing and creating a class system, dividing managers from workers. This is attested to by the outlandish rise in compensation for top managers. A new aristocracy is back.

---

5    Diane Coyle, Professor of economics at the University of Manchester: http://www.en-lightenmenteconomics.com/blog/index.php/2010/12/the-puritan-gift/

**Voltaire's Bastards**

The author, Raulston Saul uses even stronger language than the Hoppers, as one might surmise from the title. His angle is that Voltaire's legacy and that of other rational thinkers, has been subverted and that rationality independent of an ethical framework courts disaster.

The Western ruling elites of technocrats and experts are administrators of a system they claim to operate in the name of reason, but very often reason is a smokescreen for short-sighted and self-serving rational calculation. The link between reason and what ought to be has been forgotten with the result that we have organizations and societies obsessed with rational solutions, management, expertise, and clearly defined disciplines.

Saul is a controversial figure. His book evokes either strong admiration or the exact opposite. We certainly do not claim that the book should be taken as pure gospel. The takeaway from *Voltaire's Bastards* is its pinpointing the failures of scientific management in the 20$^{th}$ century. Saul meticulously explains that the technocratic mindset subscribes to the hopeless idea that human organizations and societies can be managed by rational means alone, without constraint or higher goals and responsibilities, or the goodwill of people.

**The Road to Unfreedom & On Freedom**

A history professor at Yale, Timothy Snyder's 2018 book *The Road to Unfreedom* and his 2024 *On Freedom* highlight the gradual and easy loss of our freedom in society. One main theme is the drastic decline of the free investigative press due to the dominance of partisan internet news sources – fake or otherwise. It is an account of the many dark forces on the left and right of the political spectrum that want to lead us in the direction of elitist rule – an oligarchy. Often these forces are linked with criminal or at least borderline criminal activities to weasel their way into power.

In 2017 Snyder published *On Tyranny* in which he proposes ways that individuals can resist the drift toward loss of freedom and practical things that can be done to support those who expose abuse and those who protect the right of others to be heard.

Snyder and his books are considered controversial and somewhat alarmist by a good deal of commentators, but his evidence and arguments are very strong. If we do not resist and constantly pour energy into conserving our decentral freedom we will slide towards a rule of an elite (oligarchy) or pure tyranny.

Our main takeaway is that the mechanisms and developments leading to the loss of freedom in societies also apply to organizations. The ways to resist can inspire organizations, especially in creating and protecting transparency and freedom of choice.

## Neo-Taylorism Conclusions

The dominating theme in the narrative about the road that led us to the present situation is Neo-Taylorism. There are more details of this later on in *Appendix C – Neo-Taylorism and the Fatal Attraction to Hierarchy*, but for now, here are the conclusions we drew for this discussion.

Neo-Taylorism, the cult of the (so-called) expert, has been much more damaging than Taylor himself, as he died at a fairly young age. What are the attributes of this phenomenon? The following section is mostly inspired by *The Puritan Gift* with some editorial liberty, but there is also a strong influence from W. Edward Deming's thinking.

- The first and most important thing is that *measuring* is everything. Managers are those who have been "scientifically" taught how to set goals and measure (Plan–Delegate–Monitor–Control). Everything that has to be managed has to be quantified and measured. The obsession with dodgy statistics and prognosis disguises the absence of domain knowledge.
- Secondly came an obsessive preoccupation with credentials and certification, as the only means of telling an expert from a non-expert is his

credentials. We have never had so many certifications before, often based on bogus assessment procedures.

- Thirdly, management automatically became top-down. What could the non-experts (the lower existences) possibly give the expert other than raw data? The expert who was assumed to have the ability to think, plan, and give answers, would then process and let his answer be known, rippling down the often long chain of command.

- Fourthly, responsibility was inevitably spread among many experts (financial, sales, marketing, human resources, and a host of consultants) and thus no one was really responsible for anything concrete. This transformed the original military-like hierarchy into a sort of mesh, an expert-based bureaucracy, that had to be involved in everything, confusing everybody and slowing things down. Many challenges were then either not addressed, or in the end decided upon by someone sufficiently high up to be above the experts.

- Finally, it came to be believed that you could solve major problems by declaring a certain expert responsible for them. They came to be known as "Czars" of certain things, totally decoupled from the line operation of the organization. People are declared responsible for this, that, and the other; in practice, nobody knows what that means and confusion proliferates.

This has led to several things:

- Experts (including the new imperial CEO, who is the top dog of the experts) tend to be compensated based on some measurable personal contribution to the organization. This leads to a preoccupation with these numbers, which often can be tweaked or faked. When such a compensation scheme is in place, it will be the top priority for the person in question. Someone said: *"You will get what you measure[6]"* – that also applies here.

---

6    Often attributed to quality expert H. James Harrington, but no exact reference can be retrieved.

- Neo-Taylorism has also led to the rise of the Teflon-man (him to whom nothing sticks), whose first concern is to make sure that he cannot be blamed for anything. When there is a crisis and someone smiles, that means he – the Teflon-man – has already figured out who to blame.
- The focus on numbers in general, gradually led to the belief that financial numbers were all that mattered, especially those relating to profit. The business schools pushed the wave further by forcing the concept of shareholder value as the highest goal in businesses. Rampant greed became not only acceptable but even admirable, *"Greed is good!"*[7].
- The rise of accounting and legal staff to the ruling positions, led to the financial wizard manager, whose main contribution is to play financial and/or legal stunts that game the owners, the stock market (and often his own compensation) instead of servicing the clients and taking care of employees.
- A proliferation of individual targets and KPIs that were supposed to foster healthy competition, but instead ended up preventing teamwork and collaboration and leading people to tweak or fake numbers.
- Advocating and even cultivating an atmosphere of fear, driving people who work for the real customers to anxiety or apathy.[8]
- The almost total separation of management and ordinary work has led to bizarre situations. I have had people whom I was mentoring and coaching, literally crying in desperation because of a new boss who boldly claimed that she did not need to know anything about education to run a college; she was a manager and laid plans and made budgets that were to be followed.
- Middle managers with no responsibility apart from monitoring budgets and KPIs. They shift information up and down the organizational ladder, with the predictable loss of real content of around 5-30% for each handover[9]. If we have good handover discipline with only a loss of 10% per handover, then a top leader 7 steps above in the hierarchy

---

7   Gordon Gekko in the movie *Wall Street*, 1987
8   Watch Amy Edmondson here: https://www.youtube.com/watch?v=LhoLuui9gX8

will only have about 50% correct information. Basing top-level strategic decisions on this sort of distorted view of reality qualifies for a diagnosis.

- Top managers move up into a special layer in the atmosphere that suitably could be called the *Managosphere,* much like nobility hundreds of years ago. After a while, they can only exist there with their peers. They cannot breathe the air in the lower layers of the organization and consequently never go there or interact with them.

The characterization of Neo-Taylorism may seem harsh; after all managers in this paradigm are mostly not evil or unintelligent, so shouldn't we be nicer? But in the words of the fictional character Granny Weatherwax[10]: *"We do right, we don't do nice"*. We want to give leaders an alternative to the present state of affairs so they need to understand that Neo-Taylorism and all Agile Lean thinking rest on two different bedrocks. Sooner or later people embarking on the transformation will have to renounce Neo-Taylorism and all its principles and practices.

## Complexity

It became clear that the Neo-Taylorist approach to management is insufficient when applied to significantly Complex work. Examples include its rather exclusive focus on organizational efficiency and the dominant, but harmful idea of driving people by extrinsic motivation as we saw above.

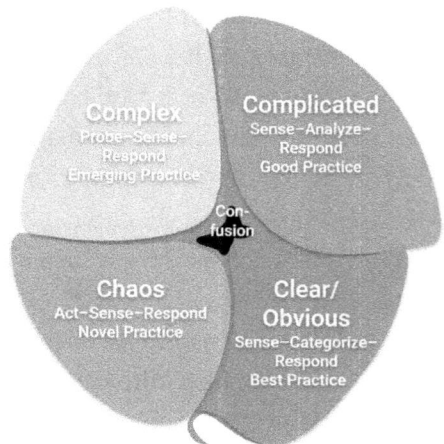

Complex
Probe–Sense–
Respond
Emerging Practice

Complicated
Sense–Analyze–
Respond
Good Practice

Con-
fusion

Chaos
Act–Sense–Respond
Novel Practice

Clear/
Obvious
Sense–Categorize–
Respond
Best Practice

---

9   According to ChatGPT the loss can be as low as 5% in ideal situations, but drop to a frightening 30% when the matter at hand is complex

10   Granny Weatherwax: https://en.wikipedia.org/wiki/Granny_Weatherwax

We delved further into Dave Snowden's Cynefin framework for under-standing the different cognitive domains we may find ourselves in. For a bit deeper discussion, please consult *Appendix B6 – Complexity in 60 Sec-onds*. For now, it is sufficient to mention the five main domains:

- **Clear/Obvious** – Where almost anybody can see what needs to be done and we can have best practices.
- **Complicated** – Where we know knowledge exists, but it requires anal-ysis or research to get at it, we can have good practice.
- **Complex** – Where we only have fragmented knowledge but we have to do something anyway. Therefore we need multiple actors' perspec-tives and experiments to make sense of things, we can have emerging practices.
- **Chaos** – Where we have close to no tangible knowledge, we have to act on intuitive skill, stabilize the situation, and perhaps discover novel practices.
- **Disorder** – The unfortunate zone where you are when you don't know where you are, i.e. you have not carefully assessed your domain. This can lead to all sorts of wrong decisions.

Snowden has elaborated on this fundamental model with descriptions of the so-called *Liminal Zones* between the domains. For now, it suffices to know about the *Zone of Complacency* between Obvious and Chaos. The claim is that by over-structuring things and forcing rules and regulations upon things that should be handled as complex, catastrophic failure can occur in times of rapid change. You fall head-first down into chaos. This is exactly what happens if complex endeavors are handled the Neo-Tay-lorist way, a plunge into Chaos is possible and recovery is very, very ex-pensive.

In most organizations today, there is a high proportion of Complex work to be done. An organization in this situation cannot keep its act together using rules and regulations. They become so comprehensive and brittle that they break apart, often evoking wildly different interpretations of the root cause. This approach may have worked in the industrial age when most work was between Complicated and Obvious, but to cope with complexity we need to understand the value of people's freedom to engage as the basis of gaining knowledge, performance, and fulfillment.

Because Complex work requires hypotheses and experimentation, the only chance of getting serious work done and value created is to bind individuals together with common values, vision, and goals and a personal compass with the freedom to navigate.

Thankfully, most people have a core of decency, self-respect, and common sense and can accomplish things despite organizational disarray. They want to take pride in what they do.

It follows that positive, consistent, and repeatable results are possible when the values and vision guiding people's decisions are supported by the organization. When everyone pulls in approximately the same direction, the force is stronger and value is created at a faster pace. This can only be accomplished if people volunteer their knowledge and skills freely:

> *Knowledge can only be volunteered, it cannot be conscripted!*
> — *Dave Snowden*

We define much of today's work as *complex* because it requires knowledge to be built up through freely offered collective insight and experimentation. Snowden makes a distinction between complex work and that of the other domains to stress the point that effective value creation starts with understanding the domain you are in and acknowledging that a different approach is required.

## Rediscovering Purpose

Another trail followed is that of *Purpose*, inspired by W. Edwards Deming's 14 points for leadership which led us to the work of some interesting people.

Most agree that every organization must have a valid purpose, but it is rare to find a CEO who will confess that greed is alone at the top of the agenda.

However, many of the finely crafted vision statements and purpose declarations have little practical meaning for employees or customers. Nobody trusts them anymore; they are just new compilations of spin and buzzwords, intended to induce warm and fuzzy feelings in people to make them work harder or buy more. Lofty goals are for celebrations, events, and press releases; everyday business is looking out for number one and shareholder value.

Cynicism can be amusing to watch, but a work environment soaked with it is hardly inspiring. The prevailing postmodern attitude combining skepticism and cynicism makes it hard to promote a strong sense of purpose; people just don't believe in any big stories anymore. On the other hand, if a leader succeeds in conveying an authentic vision of a powerful purpose it can generate tremendous power, particularly for those that have never experienced it before. It has to be true though, with a modern word: it has to be authentic.

> *If a leader doesn't convey passion and intensity then there will be no passion and intensity within the organization and they'll start to fall down and get depressed.*                                                        *– Colin Powell*[11]

Back in the sixties, Francis Schaeffer[12] said that the West had slid down the slope and accepted that the only values were *"Personal peace and affluence"*. We are arguing that there are more inspiring and higher purposes. Perhaps it seems foreign to modern readers to fall back on ethical arguments. The modernistic, rational-only worldview said that everything was down to the rational calculation of self-interest. The postmodern worldview, albeit oversimplified, says that everyone constructs their own value system autonomously. The first one is clearly a gross oversimplification, and the

---

11   Colin Powell: https://en.wikipedia.org/wiki/Colin_Powell
12   Francis Schaeffer: https://en.wikipedia.org/wiki/Francis_Schaeffer

second one is useless for anything but cynical couch philosophers' sarcastic outbursts; one cannot build organizations or societies on such an insular view of life.

As we have seen above, most people value being of service and contributing. We need to experience that we exist for more than just ourselves. It is well-documented[13] that people are more content and satisfied with their lives if they serve and do things that benefit others.

Many inferences about good and bad are based on religion or culture, but without entering that discussion, it is fair to say that globally, most people will agree that they value:

- Honesty, openness, and transparency.
- Helping others, especially those who have challenges taking care of themselves.
- Treating others as you would like to be treated (The Golden Rule).
- Respecting others' rights and receiving reciprocal respect.
- Taking care of the environment and not exploiting that or fellow human beings.

Organizations that consistently communicate and demonstrate a powerful purpose have an advantage that can fill an ethical void. We do not argue that an organization should become people's *Raison D'etre*; instead, we simply claim that it is an effective way to create a sense of alignment with a larger goal.

Consistent purpose in an organization implies a long-term commitment to sustainability in its relationships and use of resources and it provides a powerful point of alignment. This contributes to psychological safety and trust which is a prerequisite for constant learning, as we shall see.

---

13  See for example: Borgonovi, F. (2008). Doing well by doing good. The relationship between formal volunteering and self-reported health and happiness. Social Science & Medicine, 66, 2321-2334.

There is also a practical application of clear purpose as it serves as a guiding beacon when the organization is in uncharted waters. Having a strong light on the horizon gives leaders, which in an Agile Lean Organization is practically everybody, something to aim for when they must make decisions about previously unanticipated issues.

There is solid evidence that a clear, common purpose among those people working on a particular challenge is absolutely mandatory. Only in the most simple situations is it realistic to rely on just giving instructions, every other situation requires diverse input and consensus-based decision-making.

## Rediscovering Vocation

Another tributary to our main flow of investigations was rediscovering the importance of vocation. Again mostly inspired by Dr. Deming.

One of the consequences of the Neo-Taylorist view of experts and the imperial leader is a somewhat demeaning attitude towards ordinary work[14]; the work of those who actually deliver something. Autocratic societies have almost always held ordinary work in contempt. The idea is normally that if you truly are *somebody*, you will have people at your disposal to do any real work for you.

With the separation of thinking and doing this trait is evident in many places: in some Middle Eastern societies, in the English aristocracy, and unfortunately in much modern Neo-Taylorist management. There is often an awkward Neo-colonial tension between the creative or highly educated people sitting behind desks and those who are out there getting their hands dirty.

---

14  We use the terms *ordinary work* or *real work* as meaning delivering some tangible result as opposed to telling somebody else to do it, as simple as that.

By contrast, although not perfect, in societies characterized by an assembly of free men such as the old Hebrew, Celtic, and Germanic societies, there was a lot of respect for all kinds of work.

In our work coaching and mentoring organizations, a frequent obstacle to reform is the reluctance of those in higher positions where they have subordinates, to give up or change their role. If they were to start executing real deliverables again, they fear a loss of privilege, respect, or self-esteem.

The Reformation of 500 years ago brought back respect for all kinds of work to the Western world. Martin Luther[15] said the work of the common milk-maid or the baker was God's way of procuring the daily bread for everybody.

In his 2012 book *Every Good Endeavor,* Timothy Keller says that those devoted to work that they are really good at deserve respect for practicing *"The ministry of competence"*, delivering quality to the benefit of all stakeholders and society at large.

Os Guinness[16] in his 2003 book *The Call: Finding and Fulfilling the Central Purpose of Your Life*, concentrates on the personal strength that manifests itself when a person believes that their talents and qualities serve a higher purpose; that they are a unique and necessary piece of the puzzle.

> *Somehow we human beings are never happier than when we are expressing*
> *the deepest gifts that are truly us.* — Os Guinness

There are definitely religious overtones or roots in this line of argument, but not exclusively. We are convinced that the observable facts of human nature and behavior, as documented by psychologists and sociologists, are strong enough to carry the weight of the recommendation. Let us create organizations where individuals are respected for aligning a common purpose with their talents and experience.

---

15  Martin Luther: https://en.wikipedia.org/wiki/Martin_Luther
16  Os Guinness: https://en.wikipedia.org/wiki/Os_Guinness

Good leaders realize the importance of fostering respect for and an appreciation of all quality work in the organization. The most obvious way of kick-starting the process is to lead by example; the leader must deliver excellent quality, and show appreciation for the quality contributions of others. This runs counter to the common narrative where the leader takes credit for success but apportions blame for failure. Organizations are full of opportunities to show appreciation for quality contributions; the magnitude of the positive effect of doing so is often surprising.

This means that leaders are talent scouts, looking to attract people with strong talents that support the grand purpose of the organization. They are also talent developers[17]. This is not just a role or an assignment, it is a serious responsibility that demands a solid combination of domain knowledge, empathy, and interpersonal skills, among other competencies.

All this is not a romantic, fluffy-bunny attitude, but an acknowledgment that to build organizations that fulfill their purpose and create balanced value for all stakeholders, leaders must build up the people in the organization. In an organization operating largely in the Complex domain, its people are assets and investments, not liabilities and costs.

W. Edwards Deming talked about this on several occasions. He mostly used the term *"Allow people pride of workmanship"*, or as in the following quote:

*All anyone asks for is a chance to work with pride.* – W. Edwards Deming

If people are convinced they are in the right place doing the right thing and are respected for it, there is a much better chance that they will participate positively in the much-needed constant hunt for new knowledge and innovation in the Complex domain. This is really just another affir-

---

17  The term *Talent development* is mostly used in connection with planning for people to take over positions in more traditional hierarchies. We use it more broadly here.

mation of the need for intrinsic motivation. This evidence is worth keeping in mind.

## From Reductionism to a Systems View

Finally, we discovered another troubling aspect of the current management paradigm coming from a very different angle. The prevailing Neo-Taylorist style of management has led organizations to focus on the finely granular optimization of details instead of looking at the total. It is a sort of managerial reductionism.[18]

Perhaps unconsciously, the classic hierarchical structure has led to the belief that its branches are independent and can be analyzed and understood completely (assuming everything is Obvious or at worst, Complicated) by the proper expert. This line of thinking typically extends to the individual, who also can be understood completely and controlled like a machine.

According to this line of thought, the output of the organization is the sum of all these entities. It, therefore, makes sense to make simple numerical *Key Performance Indicators* (KPIs) the goal or target for each group or department, sometimes called *Management by Objectives*. Not many managers would subscribe to this view when presented with it, but in real life, this is often exactly what is practiced.

This reductionist assumption is not only wrong, it is mind-boggling, heart-wrenching, and naive. There are scores of real-life stories that portray the calamities of sub-optimization caused by compartmentalized numeric targets without concern for the whole system:

- The purchasing department has as a goal to reduce the cost of production, so they switch suppliers of a component and wreak havoc further

---

18  In a reductionist framework, the phenomena that can be explained completely in terms of relations between other more fundamental phenomena, are termed epiphenomena. https://en.wikipedia.org/wiki/Reductionism

downstream causing other departments' budgets and plans to explode.

* The government decides to compensate public educational institutions for the percentage of passed students. Surprise. surprise! The institution now does not accept students with special needs indicating a risk of lower grades, or grades are gradually inflated.

* The chief of police gets a bonus at the end of the year based on the number of cases solved or won. In December every officer is on the street passing out parking tickets, some bogus, because parking tickets, due to some technicality, count as *Cases*.

* The HR department decides to compensate software developers for fixing old bugs (because the company is plagued by long-standing defects in its products). Hey presto, now all bugs end up being old, as the developers quickly figured out that this would give them more money and they gamed the system – this is a true story.

We could compile a whole volume equivalent of a *Guinness Book of Records* for every domain of numerical targets that were set with the best intentions and nevertheless backfired pitifully. The managers instigating these schemes are of course not stupid, but they keep performing these sub-optimizations contrary to all evidence. A collective blindness to real facts can develop in management circles; a self-inflicted severe cognitive bias. In our opinion, the main explanation is simply that by separating thinking and doing the Neo-Taylorist way, the manager is too far away from the real place of action to see the results of actions and interventions.

The good news is that the evidence is pretty obvious: Look at all the interactions and dependencies in the whole organization, look at it as a system. The bad news is that it is hard, persistent work to make sense of a whole system.

# The Grand Figure W. Edwards Deming

We have included a small section here about the larger-than-life figure: W. Edwards Deming. He talked and wrote a lot about how the corporate world in the West was lost to unhelpful managerial practices, and how the Japanese especially understood how to involve those doing the work in setting the course and finding solutions to challenges.

Deming talked constantly about how leaders should have an *"Appreciation for a system"*. The term *System* can be used in different ways, but here's how Deming defined it in *The New Economics*:

> *What is a system? A system is a network of interdependent components working together to accomplish the aim of the system. The system must have an aim. Without an aim, there is no system.*    *– W. Edwards Deming*

In this context, the word *System* is used to illustrate how all things in an organization are connected and how suboptimization in one area may indeed lead to overall losses in the system. When decisions are made, it is therefore necessary that all those relationships and dependencies are understood and taken into account.

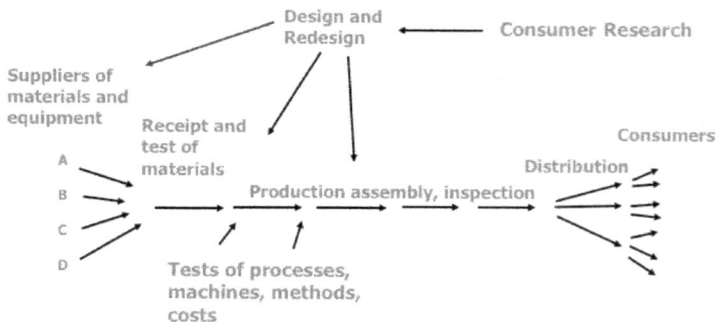

**Out of Crisis, page 4**

As early as 1950 in Japan, Deming used the following flow diagram to explain the whole system to leadership; the idea of seeing the specific purpose of the whole, connected organization, typically exemplified by the customers it serves.

Deming said on several occasions that *"The customer is the most important part of the product development"*. The central part of his teaching was to include the customer in the feedback loop of constant improvement. This was quite a modern concept in 1950.

The idea is that this interconnected system extends to include the customer, the supplier, and potentially society as well.

A system like this cannot normally be reduced to a sequence of numbers and fixed interactions. Therefore, a perfect upfront plan with any relevance to reality cannot be made. What can be done is to try and make sense of the relationships and interactions, and then with that fragmented knowledge create hypotheses and conduct experiments to verify or disprove them. This is exactly what Dave Snowden recommends in the Complex domain.

A deeper study of W Edwards Deming provided an enormous amount of insight and evidence for our investigation. His relentless effort to revitalize the American corporate world until shortly before his death in 1993 (93 years old) is awe-inspiring. The most important highlight is his stress on the PDSA cycle:

- **Plan**. Make the best plan you can. Carefully define the interpretation of results.
- **Do**. Execute the best you can, using all your skills.
- **Study**. Carefully try to understand and make sense of results.
- **Act**. Then decide what to do next, improvements or experiments.

This is the basis of the Japanese concept of Kaizen (改善) – constant improvement.

Keeping the big picture of the system in mind all the time is very demanding. It is understandable and human and much easier to find comfort in some manageable detail and then focus on that. Our brain is lazy and wants simple answers, but succumbing to the desire for simplicity has wreaked havoc on the best of our efforts time and time again.

Helping everybody to stay awake and alert is one of the most important results of an organization with proper checks and balances. The structures and agreed activities and procedures should help everybody keep listening for weak signals of change in the system and keep the feedback channels clean and polished so that quick and informed action can be taken.

Reminding us of always keeping the system view intact, is one of W. Edwards Deming's greatest contributions.

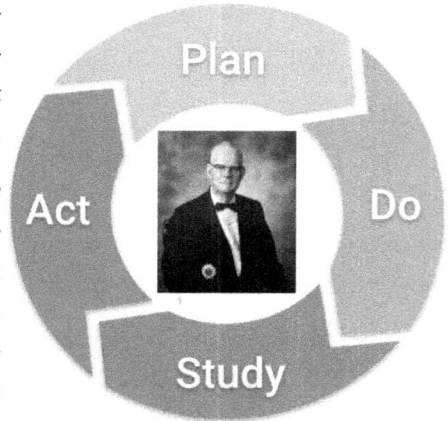

# Looking for Ways Forward

After uncovering the evidence for how the *West was Lost* — managerially speaking, we ventured in different directions to find inspiration from others who traveled the territory before.

## Vanilla Scrum

We mentioned Scrum previously and were somewhat preconditioned having worked for several years as Scrum trainers and coaches, but we were convinced that we needed to dig deeper. We knew perfectly well the power a framework like Scrum would bring to a team setting, a project, or an initiative. This is especially powerful if the project is launched with a sense of urgency and willingness to let the team concentrate on solving the specific challenge. If the surrounding organization understands the urgency, then it is more likely to let the team get on with its job, albeit sometimes using unconventional approaches. But when the organization's demand for compliance and predictability kicks in, it can severely cripple the Scrum teams.

Our quest was to find a way of organizing so the fluid dynamics of the Scrum team could be preserved even when it was scaled out in the whole organization, focusing on the long haul, not just a transient project.

Scrum remains the first and greatest inspiration by far of the Agile Lean Leadership framework. We often refer to it in its most basic form as *Vanilla Scrum*, like vanilla ice cream the core substance before adding condiments. It is the most popular and archetypical Agile Lean pattern at the team or project level and the main framework for working on the borderline between the Complex and the Complicated territory. It is defined by a series of constraints:

- Work is done in fixed Iterations (2-4 weeks long) called *Sprints*. Each Sprint results in a true increment of whatever is being produced.
- There are predefined roles: a Whole Scrum Team consisting of

  - A *Product Owner* who holds the vision and is responsible for prioritization to generate maximum return on investment. He owns the Product Backlog.
  - A *Scrum Master* who is responsible for the process and constant improvement. He supports and coaches the Product Owner, the Team, and the rest of the organization. He owns the Improvement Backlog.
  - A *Team* of 5 to 9 people. They are self-organizing and cross-functional with all the skills required to decide how to execute the work and deliver results.

- There is a defined process or a set of events:

  - Before each Sprint, there is *Sprint Planning*.

- Each day in the Sprint, there is a *Daily Scrum* of a maximum of 15 minutes where the Team and the Scrum Master coordinate and plan for the next day.
- In the Sprint, the Team meets with the Product Owner to refine the upcoming Product Backlog Items in preparation for the next Sprint. This is called *Backlog Refinement*.
- At the end of the Sprint, there is a *Sprint Review* where stakeholders are presented with the results of the Sprint and provide review and feedback.
- Also at the end of the Sprint, The Whole Scrum Team meets to evaluate the recent Sprint, try to learn from it, and suggest improvements, this is called *Retrospective*.

- There are some artifacts visible to all. The common ones are:

  - A *Product Backlog* containing all the deliverables, features, and qualities that should be delivered. These are called Product Backlog Items (PBI). The Product Backlog is an ordered list with the most important Items at the top.
  - A *Sprint Backlog* containing all the Product Backlog Items agreed to be delivered in the current Sprint (the Sprint Goal). These are normally decomposed into individual Tasks by the Team and their progress is shown on the Sprint Backlog.
  - We recommend having an *Improvement Backlog* where the Scrum Master keeps track of impediments and improvements being worked on.
  - Potentially a *Product Burndown* chart showing the progress across several Sprints to enable forecasting of an estimated time of arrival or the amount of Product Backlog Items delivered in a certain timeframe.
  - Potentially a *Sprint Burndown* chart showing the daily progress in a Sprint giving constant feedback to everybody about the likelihood of meeting the Sprint Goal.

Read more about Scrum in *Appendix B3 – Scrum in 6:) Seconds*. Scrum is an indispensable part in the evolution of Agile Lean Leadership because it makes things visible.

*Scrum is like your mother-in-law, it points out ALL your faults.*
*– Ken Schwaber*

## Agile Principles in General

Despite Scrum's prominence, there are several good Agile methods. Here are some takeaways from the *Agile Manifesto*[19], writt:n by a group of software engineers as a statement of what they meant by Agile. It is very software-specific but has general applicability.

* The most important thing is to cater to people ard the way they interact, processes are secondary.
* It is the final product that matters, and the *Custcmer* is the final judge of its quality; paperwork is secondary.
* Finding the right solution is best done iteratively in collaboration with those needing the solution. Sticking to rules is secondary.
* Being able to deliver continuously with quality is primary, efficiency is secondary.
* Agreements between customers and suppliers should optimize collaboration and shared benefits. Winning in court is secondary.
* As we learn about reality or reality changes, the most important thing is to react appropriately, following a plan is secondary.

*...what does it mean to be agile? I mean, my definitior is that you accept input from reality, and you respond to it.* *– Kent Beck*

This certainly added some understanding to our investigation.

## Kanban

---

19  Read more about the Agile Manifesto here: http://agilemar ifesto.org/

While Scrum is the most widespread of the Agile Frameworks, Kanban[20] is the runner-up. It takes its prime inspiration from Lean in production and has a few key characteristics:

- The normal workflow is described as a series of stages (a Value Stream), and visualized including the dynamic flow of work.
- Each stage has a described *Done Criteria*.
- Each stage has a *WIP Limit* (Work in progress) to prevent long queues of work from building up.
- A person prioritizes the work in the input queue.
- The purpose is to achieve optimal flow. A person monitors the flow and adjusts the parameters accordingly
- The metrics are *Response Time*, *Lead Time*, and *Cycle Time*.

Kanban is less prescriptive than Scrum and considered by some to be more useful because it allows constant prioritization. The other side of the coin is that you don't get as much assistance when using it.

Some teams work in environments where Scrum is not helpful, mostly because they cannot foresee what is needed two weeks ahead. For some teams, only part of their work is suited for Scrum in which case a combination of Scrum and Kanban may be called for.

The dynamics of working the Kanban way, the importance of queuing theory, and the metrics from there were important discoveries that helped us synthesize a coherent framework later on.

## More on Lean Thinking

Lean is a Western term generally used to describe the *Toyota Production System* (TPS), which was developed mostly by Taiichi Ohno[21] between 1948 and 1975 and is part of the larger management philosophy: *The Toyota Way*[22]. The concepts originated in the US before and around the WWII.

---

20  Kanban: https://en.wikipedia.org/wiki/Kanban_(development)
21  Read more here: https://en.wikipedia.org/wiki/Taiichi_Ohno
22  Read more here: https://en.wikipedia.org/wiki/The_Toyota_Way

The most prominent advocate was W. Edwards Deming[23]. Read more in *Appendix B2 – Lean in 60 seconds*, but for now, it will suffice to remember the three basic tenets of the original Lean ideas:

- Always focus on customer value-creating activities.
- Always focus on removing and reducing waste.
- Always respect people, and allow them pride of workmanship.

*A happy customer who comes back for more is worth more than 10 prospects*
*– W. Edwards Deming*

The most important practical aspect of what Deming taught us, as mentioned before, is the PDSA[24] cycle. It reminds us to always get active feedback from those we work with, to develop a common understanding, which doesn't come without effort in the Complex domain.

## Beyond Budgeting

For more than 25 years there has been a parallel stream of clear water to the stream of Agile and Lean, called *Beyond Budgeting*[25] (BB); one of its main proponents is Bjarte Bogsnæs[26], who has served many years in the corporate headquarters of large companies. The framework may start with addressing the problem of the central yearly budget, but it does present a comprehensive strategy to reform a company.

We have tried to align our understanding with BB, and we find that there is a 95%+ overlap of our analyses and values, however, we come to the arena of solutions from different angles. BB starts with changing the organization's processes and other global constraints while we typically start downstairs, working with the teams and the value streams.

The main discovery in our investigation of BB has probably been that for an effective change in an organization, there has to be a pincer movement

---

23  W. Edwards Deming official site: https://deming.org/deming-the-man/
24  PDSA Cycle: https://deming.org/explore/pdsa/
25  Beyond Budgeting: https://bbrt.org/
26  Bjarte Bogsnes: https://bogsnesadvisory.com/

starting both upstairs and downstairs. It certainly has to have motivated actors in both places. Read a bit more about BB in *Appendix B5 – Beyond Budgeting in 60 seconds*.

## Democratic Organization

Russell Ackoff[27] wrote a very important book called *Democratic Organization* in 1994. He was a key figure in a few areas that we hardly recognize today, such as Operations Research and System Thinking. He served as a professor of systems sciences and management science at the Wharton School which is part of the University of Pennsylvania. We were familiar with him, but mostly through his fairly well-known quirky *F/laws of Management*, small nuggets of wisdom such as

> *The level of conformity in an organization is in inverse proportion to its creative ability.*

or

> *Good teachers produce skeptics who ask their own questions and find their own answers; management gurus produce only unquestioning disciples.*

It was only much later that we discovered his other lengthy and dense writings on Idealized Design and the theory of organization, the latter best reflected in the book *Democratic Organization*. Ackoff used a different vocabulary than we do today, but it is remarkable how he reached similar conclusions about the necessity of self-determination (freedom) and how to engage people as our own observations indicated other sources confirm – and this was written 30 years ago. The book is largely based on his system thinking and a very modern understanding of the different needs of educated individuals compared to the unskilled labor that most management practices assume. Ackoff reflects and comments on the fact that most people support democratic government in states but gladly accept autocratic top-down leadership in organizations. From 1979 and about 15 years on Ackoff worked with many American enterprises, sometimes

---

27  Russell Ackoff: https://en.wikipedia.org/wiki/Russell_L._Ackoff

alongside W. Edwards Deming, and impressive results were achieved. Here are some very clear statements from the book:

- *"Quality of life is largely a matter of aesthetics; it involves satisfaction to be derived from anything we do; no matter how trivial. These are satisfactions derived from intrinsic values, the satisfaction immediately experienced, and form extrinsic values that arise out of a sense of progress toward an ideal."*
- *"To the extent that the enterprise contributes to the development of its employees, it improves their quality of work life."*
- *"Where quality of work life is poor, no effort to improve quality of outputs will yield lasting results."*
- *"Participation, which is a form of self-determination, is itself a major source of satisfaction and therefore of improved quality of life."*
- *"How can we enable others to improve their own quality of (work) life?"*
- *"How can an organization be designed to provide the participative decision-making required for a high quality of work life while simultaneously enabling its management to deal effectively with the interactions of the parts ... and of the whole...?"*

It is an ongoing theme in the book that people need to experience participation in decision-making. Ackoff's line of argument is very powerful, and he has good suggestions for how to organize to accomplish the objectives. He introduced a so-called Circular Organization with boards of decision-makers enabling participative decision-making, the concept of an Internal Marketplace in an organization, and the idea of a multidimensional organization. More details will emerge later when we match Ackoff's ideas with our proposals.

Some of his observations and proposals are of course context-specific, speaking in a clearly American context and to large corporations. But his writings are very insightful and recommended for further reading.

# Other Tributaries

The case for the freedom of individuals in organizations has been pursued for years by many others. If we had started from a different place, we might have taken a different road. Here are a few more examples of concepts, frameworks, and people that have inspired us.

### Organizational Democracy

The company WorldBlu[28], a global leadership education company headed by the charismatic CEO Traci Fenton, has since 1997 developed and promoted an approach to freedom at work and organizational democracy.

WorldBlu aligns and overlaps with our vision, values, and principles. Again another organization and group traveling on a parallel path towards the same goal. They speak very clearly of freedom - as we do - and argue that when freedom in organizations wins over fear, people are enabled to perform and flourish. Fenton uses the word democracy a lot, where we reserve the word for structures in nations. But it is all about giving people the freedom and the choice to be heard and participate. Read more about the company and the approach in *Appendix D2. Organizational Democracy's 10 Principles*. We are inspired by the strong focus on *Integrity*.

### Strategic Doing

Strategic Doing is the brainchild of Ed Morrison[29] and has been evolving for more than 20 years, providing collaboration and strategy in open, loosely connected networks and ecosystems. The idea is that parties come together to create solutions to complex problems and generate new value based on what they already have collectively. In that respect, it precedes Agile Lean Leadership when a loosely connected group coalesces before it becomes a formal organization. Again, this is an example of a group of

---

28  WorldBlu: https://www.worldblu.com/
29  Edward Morrison: https://agilestrategylab.org/members/ed-morrison/

people working through the same complex territory as us, identifying roughly the same objectives, but taking different, yet parallel paths.

Strategic Doing's approach is fairly comprehensive, and there is a lot to learn from it. It is fundamentally iterative and another variation on feedback loops. It defines a circular flow of questions to keep evaluating: What could we do? What should we do? What will we do? What's our "30/30"? (A term used for determining when an evaluation and realignment will happen). Strategic Doing also defines ten basic skills as a guide to getting something strategic done. We particularly noticed the focus on creating a safe space for people to contribute and develop trust, and the iterative nature of constant evaluating and navigating.

## Inspiration from Unlikely Sources

We came across some people who were challenged by complex environments and came up with non-traditional answers. It happened that a couple of them had military backgrounds.

### David Marquet

Captain David Marquet[30], wrote the book *Turn the Ship Around* in 2013. His epiphany came a few weeks after his emergency assignment as captain of the Santa Fe, a new class of submarine and a ship, for which he had not been trained.

During a routine deep dive exercise, turning the reactor off and running on batteries, he gave the command to go *"ahead two-thirds"* to test the crew's ability to get going again. The commanding officer in the control room repeated the order but nothing happened. Marquet asked *"What is going on?"* and the operator said, *"This submarine does not have a two-thirds setting!"*

Marquet realized that he had a crew trained in obedience and compliance and a captain who was trained for the wrong submarine. His conclusion

---

30  David Marquet: https://en.wikipedia.org/wiki/David_Marquet

was: *"We are all going to die!"*, unless he changed his leadership style. He said:

> *Don't move information to authority, move authority to the information.*

Marquet and his crew escaped the traditional paradigm of management by fear and went from one thinker and 134 doers to 135 active thinkers and leaders. He concludes that *fear* is the single greatest inhibitor of active participation and initiative, leaving people locked in a corner of *What do you want me to do?*

Marquet's main idea is called *Intent-based Leadership,* which includes examples of small actions taken by the crew, which led to a new way of pursuing excellence through collaborative thinking and doing.

### Stanley McChrystal

General Stanley McChrystal[31], led the Joint Special Operations Task Force in Iraq starting in 2003. In 2015, he wrote a book called *Team of Teams* about what he learned in Iraq and later in Afghanistan. It is mostly about how his lifelong training as a commander in the US Army had to be seriously questioned when confronted with the complex environment in Iraq. He came up with several innovations starting with *Radical Transparency* and the concept of a *Network of Teams,* two ideas that fused soldiers to one another via trust and purpose in contradiction of the traditional approach of knowledge on a *need-to-know* basis and strict hierarchy. Here is a quote from the book:

> *Although we intuitively know the world has changed, most leaders reflect a model and leader development process that is sorely out of date. We often demand unrealistic levels of knowledge in leaders and force them into ineffective attempts to micromanage.*
>
> *The temptation to lead as a chess master, controlling each move of the organization, must give way to an approach as a gardener, enabling rather than directing.*
>
> *A gardening approach to leadership is anything but passive. The leader acts*

---

31  Stanley McChrystal: https://en.wikipedia.org/wiki/Stanley_A._McChrystal

*as an "Eyes-On, Hands-Off" enabler who creates and maintains an ecosystem in which the organization operates.*

This is not a fluffy-bunny, romantic view of the world and our challenges in it. McChrystal's implementation came to fruition through strong leadership, relentless training, building trust, and a disciplined approach to knowledge-sharing and learning. We have to push responsibility as far out in the organizations as we can find someone to carry it.

In the absence of brute force command-and-control, such an approach requires an organization to be united in pursuit of a common goal and values. Otherwise, there is nothing to direct efforts in the desired direction. How can this be accomplished in a world that more and more celebrates individuals and their right to do whatever they please? Individuals are important and should be free to set their own course, but this freedom is not absolute, it has to be balanced with a sensitivity to the greater good, otherwise, we revert to the law of the jungle.

McChrystal gave us some very important facts and directions for the final legs of our investigation, and the general idea of a *Network of Teams*.

### Daniel Kahneman

Another bright student in one of our classes introduced us to Daniel Kahneman[32] and especially his 2011 book *Thinking, Fast and Slow*[33]. It is a fascinating read, and it is worth noting that Kahneman got the Nobel Prize in 2002 for proving that the economic theories most people base policies and management on are completely up-the-wall. We regard him as an unlikely source, being a psychologist with a Nobel Prize in economics, he was also awarded the Presidential Medal of Freedom in 2013.

It strengthened the evidence for the unsuitability of Neo-Taylorism in this day and age, as many of the assumptions of Neo-Taylorism are precisely those that Kahnemann proves to be irrational.

---

32  Daniel Kahnemann: https://en.wikipedia.org/wiki/Daniel_Kahneman
33  Thinking, Fast and Slow: https://en.wikipedia.org/wiki/Thinking,_Fast_and_Slow

Kahneman introduced the concept of *System 1* and *System 2*, the first being our intuitive capability of reacting almost immediately, but subconsciously, and the second representing our rational capability of logic and calculation. System 2 is slow and expensive to invoke, so we default to System 1 reactions most of the time. The problem is that System 1 sometimes is wrong – as in really wrong; the good news is that System 1 can be trained.

This then opened the door for the study of Cognitive Biases and noise, which Kahneman elaborates on in the book and the subsequent volume *Noise: A Flaw in Human Judgment*. We will refer to many of these in the following discussions, as they explain so many different aspects of why things go wrong in complexity and what the possible remedies could be. More details can be found in *Appendix B9 – Cognitive Bias and Noise in 60 Seconds*.

### John Boyd and the OODA Loop

John Boyd was an American fighter pilot, a maverick – to use a mild word – and a student of strategy. He came up with the concept of the OODA loop (*Observe, Orient, Decide, and Act*), where he described how we should think and operate when fighting our way through unfolding circumstances. His early cues came from conflict – especially air combat – and later developed his theories into the now generally accepted strategy of maneuver warfare.

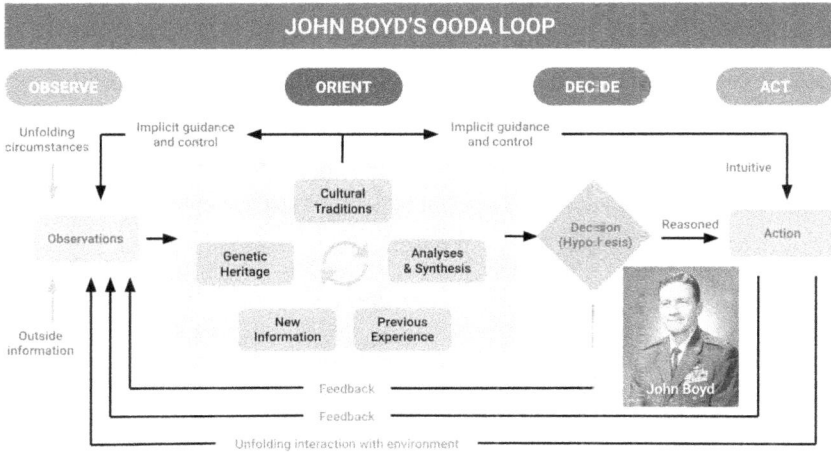

An immediate reaction might be that this is just a more complex version of the PDSA cycle we already have seen. But there are some important new concepts here, especially the orient phase, where according to Boyd, we assess the input, and the observations and sometimes draw subconscious, almost immediate conclusions. This is equivalent to Kahnemann's talk about System 1.

In conflict, those who can outpace, upset, and confuse their opponent's OODA loop can win, because the opponent succumbs to his own biases and noise in the information. In collaboration, it is exactly the opposite. If we in organizations can strengthen and amplify the OODA loops of our Team members and other Teams, we can reduce confusion, bias, and noise and consequently improve decision-making and progress.

This is the basis of our recommendations for how teams should: work in different territories, choose the right approaches, train. and think differently. Read more about this in *Appendix B11 – The OCDA loop in 60 seconds*.

## The old Germanic þing and More

We have worked a lot in Norway, where agile ideas have taken a stronger foothold than most places. Many interesting discussions have occurred and in one of these, the millennium-old concept of a *þing* (from old Norse and English, today mostly spelled Thing) was brought up. It gave us a whole new angle on our concepts of representative decision-making and resolution of challenges, which we will cover in the next section.

In older Germanic society, before central hierarchical kingdoms, a *þing*[34] was an assembly of free men who would meet periodically to resolve challenges and conflicts and agree on binding laws for their territory. In Norway, there is a historic site called *Gulating*[35], from which there are written accounts of the laws in existence back in the day.

Firstly, *þings* were delegate-based meetings where trusted people had the mandate to represent others. Secondly, the laws of *þings* were expressed as commitments entered into by mutual consent, not a command from a central authority. Finally, there was a person governing the proceedings called the *Law-Speaker* (Old Norse *Lagmann*), who knew the law by heart. During the proceedings, he would advise and occasionally call people to order if they contradicted earlier agreements. These observations are important to how we define the structures and roles in Agile Lean Leadership.

We discovered later that this form of delegate-based meeting has existed in many places, most notably in early Ukrainian and later Cossack societies, perhaps also in the North American Grand Council of the Iroquois, and certainly in the mutual consent of the early Hebrew nation implied in the Sinai covenant. Read more about this in *Appendix B13 – Constitution and þings in 60 Seconds.*

---

34  Þhing: https://en.wikipedia.org/wiki/Thing_(assembly)
35  Gulating: https://en.wikipedia.org/wiki/Gulating

# The Human Side

We were not entirely comfortable with our understanding of Theory X and Theory Y as mentioned previously. So we started investigating the area of human nature and behavior.

Not surprisingly, there are precious few brute facts in this territory of human sciences, but many varying opinions. However, we did find some persuasive explanations and models that may be useful. There is some helpful insight to be had by combining the message of the two gentlemen mentioned below. An important topic in leadership discussions is of course the views held about human nature, desires, quirks, and conflicts. A proper organization needs to be able to handle the unpredictable situations that arise out of dealing with human beings.

## Douglas McGregor and Matthew Stewart

Douglas McGregor is primarily known for his *Theory X and Theory Y* introduced in his book The Human Side of Enterprise (1960). He states:

- Management by Theory X assumes that the average employee has little to no ambition, shies away from work or responsibilities, and only works to get benefits and sustainable income out of self-interest. It is believed that all actions should be closely monitored and tracked and the responsible individual rewarded or penalized according to the result of performance. Extrinsic motivation is believed to be what works.
- Management by Theory Y on the other hand believes that people are internally motivated, enjoy working, and work to better themselves. It is also believed that these people thrive on challenges that they may face. They also tend to take full responsibility for their work and do not require the need for constant direction, supervision, or special rewards in order to create results.

While it is quite common to be told by employees that their organization and superiors are squarely in the Theory X territory, it is rare to find managers that subscribe to such a self-image resembling principles from the Stalin era.

It is one of the great mysteries of present-day Neo-Taylorist management style, that on one side it is absolutely preoccupied with plans, rules, numbers, micromanagement, measurements, and KPIs, while on the other side, it speaks warmly of people's self-realization, fulfillment, and the need for deep motivation.

It is our take that the earlier crude and brute-force control mechanism of original Taylorism has been replaced with a more Orwellian (1984)[36], subtle mind-control, and double-speak. This psychological-terror approach induces shame and guilt in the culprits. This is probably why so many today are suffering from anxiety and stress, especially in our Public Sector with its embrace of New Public Management.

### Adding a Dimension

We then discovered Matthew Stewart[37], a business consultant who turned philosopher. In his 2010 article in Strategy & Business[38] Stewart builds on McGregor's work claiming that a better understanding of human reality is obtained by adding *Theory U and Theory T* describing the origins of conflict, particularly in the area of abuse of freedom.

- **Theory U** (Utopian) states that all conflict and undesirable human behavior fundamentally arise out of unhelpful structures, misunderstandings, and false assumptions. If you eliminate those, then the organization or society will revert to its natural state of peace and cooperation. There is an optimal way to be found, where everything runs smoothly.
- **Theory T** (Tragic) on the other hand states that conflict, diverging self-interests, and downright destructiveness are embedded in the human

---

36 George Orwell 1984: https://en.wikipedia.org/wiki/Nineteen_Eighty-Four
37 Matthew Stewart: https://en.wikipedia.org/wiki/Matthew_Stewart_(philosopher)
38 Read more here: https://www.strategy-business.com/article/00029?gko=5d297

condition and will on occasion rear their ugly heads. There will be people who from time to time try to take advantage of others.

Please see our graphic below for a detailed explanation. We have chosen to view the theories along two different axes relating to freedom of the governed:

- The Ability to self-govern in freedom
- The Risk of abuse of freedom.

If you simplify and split the ideas into the traditional 2 by 2 matrix, you get the following:

- No one really wants to identify with the **Controllers** in the upper left corner , this is the spirit of Thomas Hobbes[39], they are basically Stalinists. However, quite a lot think their boss might be one.
- These days practically everybody professes to be **Freedom Lovers** in the lower right corner, an archetype is Tom Peters[40]. Often those actually responsible, believe this is a fanciful and unrealistic view.
- Stemming from the legacy of F. Winslow Taylor, many in practice are **Programmers** in the lower left corner. They believe they can program their way out of challenges by installing the right structures. This is where Neo-Taylorism and New Public Management reside.
- In the upper right corner are the **Constitutionalists**, with mutual consent, respect for all, honoring commitments, and appropriate checks and balances to prevent rogue power games. This is honoring James Madison[41], one of the founding fathers and the fourth president of the US.

---

39  Thomas Hobbes: https://en.wikipedia.org/wiki/Thomas_Hobbes
40  Tom Peters: https://en.wikipedia.org/wiki/Tom_Peters
41  James Madison: https://en.wikipedia.org/wiki/James_Madison

| **T – Tragic** | **Thomas Hobbes** | **James Madison** |
|---|---|---|
| There will always be people who try to hoard privileges and power for themselves at the expense of others. This creates all sorts of conflicts. This is the unfortunate dark side of humanity. | **Controllers,** Hobbes' promoted the absolute sovereign. Human beings are both self-centered and unintelligent. Left to their own devices they will slack off or steal what they do not destroy. Total control by and obedience to an imperial leader is the only way to get results. | **Constitutionalists,** mutual agreements and honoring of commitments. Human beings thrive in freedom. However under the wrong system, they will actualize themselves by seeking absolute power. The answer is a system of enabling constraints, checks and balances and due process. |
| **U – Utopian** | **F. Winslow Taylor** | **Tom Peters** |
| There is an optimal way of creating an organization and environment where everybody works smoothly, effectively and efficiently in the best interest of the organization and everybody. | **Programmers,** scientific management. Human beings are like machines. They generally don't know what they want or how to coordinate their activities. An elite of experts can through a scientifically established scheme of rewards and punishments, prod people into perfect alignment. | **Freedom Lovers,** summer of love 67. Human beings are inherently good, self-starting and self-organizing. They will achieve miracles if only there are no authorities telling them what to do. Let freedom reign and perfect environments and results will self-emerge. |

*Risk of abuse of freedom* (vertical axis label)

**Ability to self-govern in freedom** →

| **Theory X** | **Theory Y** |
|---|---|
| People work only to get benefits and sustainable income out of self-interest. They are disengaged; fear in the form of rewards and punishments must be used to get things done. | People are internally motivated, take responsibility and enjoy work. They work to improve and govern themselves without supervision, being told what to do or rewarded. |

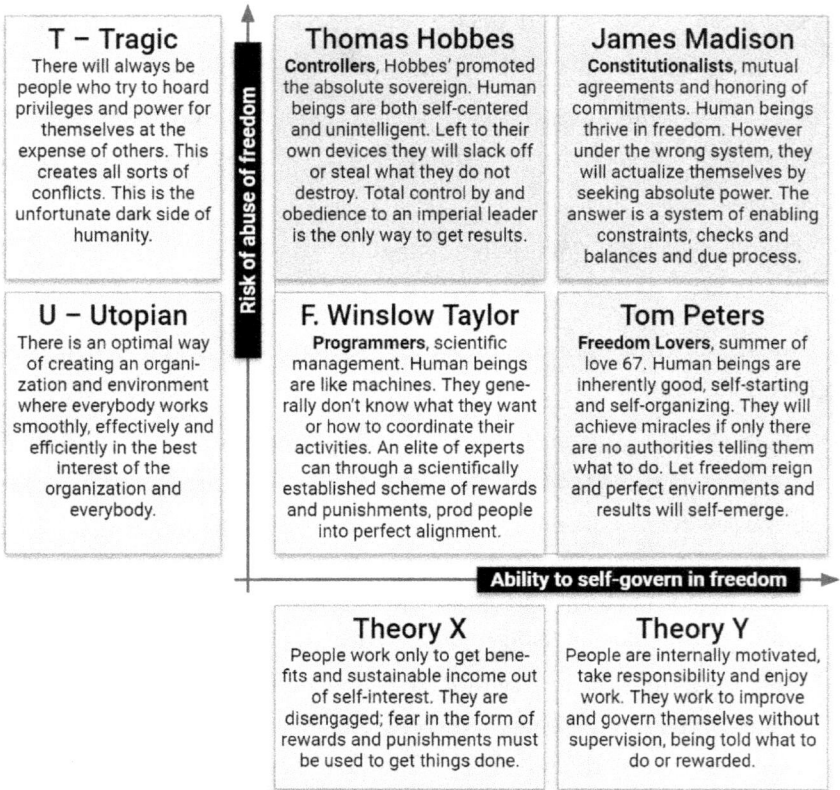

Most of the arguments being hurled at opponents in discussions about leadership are typically from the upper left and the lower right. The Theory Y people seem to expect all Theory X people to be power-hungry dictators. Theory X people on the other hand interpret Theory Y people as having their heads firmly lodged in pink, romantic clouds of delusion.

There is overwhelming documentation that when dealing with knowledge work in the complex domain, Theory Y and Intrinsic Motivation do produce results. We absolutely do need freedom to perform well.

On the other hand, there are people out there to get us, usurp freedom, and exploit others if they can get away with it.

We came to believe that we unconditionally have to focus on the upper right corner of the matrix. Theory Y shows us the way to go, but there is little evidence to substantiate a utopian or romantic claim about human nature. An organization must be able to deal with conflict and occasionally unacceptable behavior. Organizations must have a social contract, a constitution where checks and balances are kept, and unbridled self-interest is balanced by responsibilities to the group and the organization. Checks and balances have to be in place to prevent the organization from being hijacked by power-hungry individuals or dropping into chaos by having no constraints and everybody just doing what they please.

The defining term *Constitutional Organization* was born out of this realization.

## Motivation Revisited

We previously mentioned this line of investigation, but discovered there was much more than we originally realized, especially on the topic of extrinsic and intrinsic motivation which quickly took center stage.

In New Scientist 9th April 2011 pp 40-43, professor Anders Dysvik from Oslo BI said bluntly *"Economists and workplace consultants regard it as almost unquestioned dogma that people are motivated by rewards, so they don't feel the need to test this. It has the status more of religious truth than a scientific hypothesis. The facts are absolutely clear. There is no question that in virtually all circumstances in which people are doing things in order to get rewards, extrinsic tangible rewards undermine intrinsic motivation"*

Later in 2014 he and Bård Kuvaas concluded: *"The more inner motivation the: better job performance, higher organizational commitment, less turnover intention, more additional role behavior, and less job stress and sick leave[42]."*

---

42  Presented at the Annual Meeting of the Academy of Management, Philadelphia PA October 2014 by Kuvaas, B., Buch, R., Dysvik, A.

It is therefore essential to discover structures and methods that prepare the organizational soil for intrinsic motivation to thrive as opposed to the carrot-and-stick approach advocated by neo-Taylorists. We started to look for ways to amplify the fragile intrinsic motivation while dampening harmful extrinsic motivators. The presence of the power-based hierarchy became public enemy number one.

In discussions with Kuvaas, we learned that his years of research, lecturing, and consulting had taught him that autonomy (freedom) is the most important foundation of intrinsic motivation, without which it cannot be sustained. Kuvaas also noted that it is probably the biggest obstacle to true improvement because those in charge are often afraid of losing control, even though it might be an illusion of control.

This evidence helped define the structures of the Agile Lean organization.

## Learning and Psychological Safety

We also realized that our understanding of Psychological Safety and its relationship to learning was superficial, so more work needed to be done.

The term *The Learning Organization* was originally popularized by Peter Senge[43] in his book *The Fifth Discipline[44]*. It is a sad fact that as organizations grow, they typically lose their capacity to learn. It therefore requires a persistent effort to keep the learning capability alive and well.

Today, much of the conversation about the ability to learn takes its cue from the idea of *Psychological Safety* inspired by Amy Edmondson's, (Professor of Leadership at Harvard Business School) lifelong research into how organizations create and sustain a culture of learning. Here is a condensed version of her claims:

* First, create a climate of psychological safety:

---

43  Peter Senge: https://en.wikipedia.org/wiki/Peter_Senge
44  The Fifth Discipline: https://en.wikipedia.org/wiki/The_Fifth_Discipline

- Show respect for others, show appreciation, and admit your own failures.
- Ask honest questions and expect honest answers.

- The following elements must be in place:

  - No one should be punished for seeking help.
  - No one should be punished for admitting a failure.
  - No one should be punished for suggesting a better way.

- Provide process guidelines.
- Enable real-time collaboration. Give people the right tools
- Collect process data. What actually happened?
- Institutionalize disciplined reflection. Conduct retrospectives at all levels, facilitated and focused on action.

*Learning is not a one-time event or a periodic luxury. Great leaders in great companies recognize that the ability to constantly learn, innovate, and improve is vital to their success.* — *Amy Edmondson*

Already in 2008, Edmundson made the connection in an HBR Article[45], where she defined the learning zone as one having high goals but also high Psychological Safety. This is another – perhaps obvious – observation, but quite revealing to us. The graphic below is a slightly edited version from the article.

---

45  The Competitive Imperative of Learning: https://hbr.org/2008/07/the-competitive-imperative-of-learning

## Accountability for Meeting Demanding Goals

| | Low | High |
|---|---|---|
| **Psychological Safety — High** | **Comfort zone**<br>Employees really enjoy working with one another but don't feel particularly challenged. Nor do they work very hard. Some family businesses and small consultancies fall into this quadrant. | **Learning Zone**<br>Here the focus is on collaboration and learning in the service of high performance outcomes. The organizations (hospitals) Edmundson describe in the article fall into this quadrant. |
| **Psychological Safety — Low** | **Apathy zone**<br>Employees tend to be apathetic and spend their time jockeying for position. Typical organizations in this quadrant are large top-heavy bureaucracies, where people fulfill their functions but the ferred modus operandi is to curry favor rather than share ideas. | **Anxiety zone**<br>Such firms are breeding grounds for anxiety. People fear to offer tentative ides, try new things, or ask colleagues for help, even though they know great work requires all three. Some investment banks fall into this quadrant. |

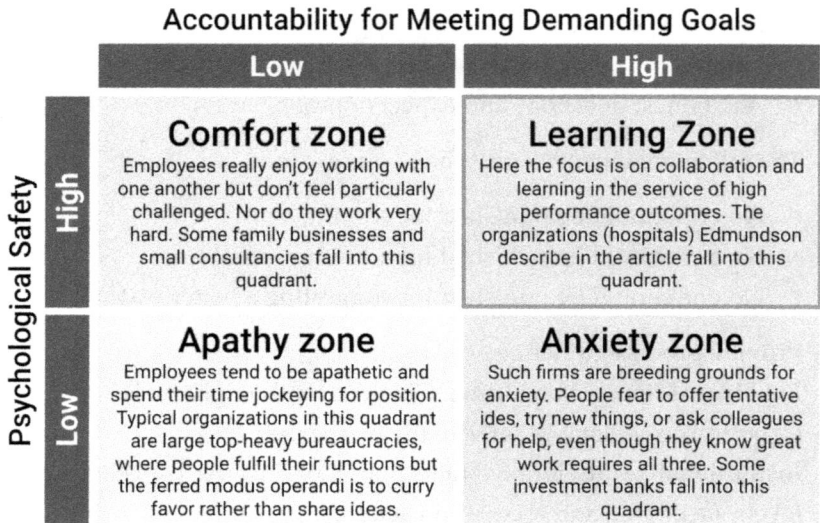

In the same article, Amy Edmondson also defined two opposing views of *Execution-as-Efficiency* and *Execution-as-Learning*. The first is a clear manifestation to F. Winslow Taylor's ideas, and the second completely aligned with our proposal for an Agile Lean Organization:

| Taylorism | | Agile Lean Leadership |
|---|---|---|
| Leaders plan, delegate, monitor and control | ↔ | Leaders set direction and support |
| Employees follow orders and static processes | ↔ | Employees in teams discover solutions and new processes |
| Feedback is normally from the boss and corrective of nature | ↔ | Feedback i two way in the form of advice |
| Fear is often used to push performance | ↔ | Fear is not present as it inhibits innovation |
| No problem solving, leaders have the answers | ↔ | Constant discovery of answers |

In a different setting, Google conducted a massive study of 180 teams trying to discover why some were performing extraordinarily well and others not so.[46]

*They discovered that of the 180 teams they studied, those with a strong sense of psychological safety were much better at creating an environment where people felt safe sharing their ideas and opinions. This led to more productive conversations and fresh, innovative solutions.*

Psychological safety is the dominant factor in extraordinary team performance. It is not the same as coziness or being in your comfort zone all day, there will be friction and sparks flying as different opinions meet and touch. But it leads to learning and discovery. Read more in *Appendix B8 – Psychological Safety in 60 Seconds*.

# Looking Back on the Road Traveled

Our investigations and interviews of people took us in many directions, we have only mentioned the dominant observations that substantially provided both plausible evidence and solutions, but many more sources of input could be mentioned. In the list of literature, the reader can find many avenues to pursue.

With all these facts and observations on the table, we ventured to synthesize all this great thinking into a framework that could provide people and organizations with a practical framework and a way forward, a way to implement.

---

46  Google Study: https://www.inc.com/marcel-schwantes/google-found-most-successful-teams-share-1-trait.html

*We found that the Neo-Taylorist view of organizations is the main antagonist:*

*– It promotes the idea of central planning and the ability to program a perfect state.*

*– It is an exaggerated view of the "expert" as able to discern everything.*

*– It leads to the separation of thinking and doing.*

*Neo-Taylorism is accompanied by the harmful concept of the deep hierarchy, bureaucracy and the imperial CEO.*

*We identified sources of inspiration for doing better than Neo-Taylorism, among others:*

*– Scrum and the wider concept of Agile and Lean.*

*– The importance of W. Edwards Deming.*

*– Old Norse and Germanic þings – assemblies of free men.*

*Any framework for organizations rests on views of human nature.*

*– We investigated McGregor's Theory X and Theory Y*

*– It was enhanced with Mathew Stewart's Theory U and Theory T.*

# Discovering a Liberating Organization

*In the last chapter, our investigation led us to retrace the steps organizations and indeed society at large took to end up in the present state. The investigation furthermore led to the observations and sources that created the foundation of the framework we call Agile Lean Leadership. Now we move on to describe the objectives that we identified and the strategies and solutions that form the blueprint for a liberating, constitutional organization using the framework. Achieving freedom for people to speak up and act is crucial. Let us again begin with a quote from W. Edwards Deming:*

> *The aim of leadership should be to improve the performance of man and machine, to improve quality, to increase output, and simultaneously to bring pride of workmanship to people. Put in a negative way, the aim of leadership is not merely to find and record failures of men, but to remove the causes of failure: to help people to do a better job with less effort*
>
> — *W. Edwards Deming: Out of the Crisis 1982.*

No doubt altering an organization to function in an Agile Lean way represents a major change. For this to happen there has to be a certain discomfort with the present, a vision for a better future, and a willingness plus capability of first steps.

For example, if people are just too comfortable or cozy with the present condition, it is probably not worth trying at all to make them change.

# The Objectives of the Desired Organization

The road we traveled and the evidence collected led to the conclusion that an organization that differs from the traditional power-based hierarchy is required for much of today's complex work. To survive, build products and services that truly serve customers, react swiftly to challenges, and create a workplace that allows people to engage, grow, and thrive, the organization needs some defining characteristics:

- The organization must be fast. Deliver value, learn, and change fast and inexpensively when needed.
- The organization must have a consistency of purpose, be focused on the long term, and be sustainable.
- The organization must be reliable and resilient. It must keep its promises and commitments and have high-quality standards in all aspects. It must be able to react quickly and sensibly to the unexpected.
- The organization must be innovative with free and engaged people who can explore and experiment and therefore be able to handle complex challenges.
- The organization must balance its consideration for all stakeholders and be committed to creating value for all: customers, employees, other stakeholders, and the greater community.
- This is part of the vision for change. Behind all of this lies a fundamental shift towards freedom of the individual, a disassembling of the traditional hierarchy, and a movement from command and control to en-

gagement and trust. The prime objective is to create an organizational soil where these qualities can grow and to convince those at the top of the current structure that there is also great value for them in such an approach. Of course, this is not easily accomplished.

There is a reason that the case for freedom has been cold for so long. It takes hard work in uncharted waters and it seems risky for the current leadership whose greatest fear is *"What if we lose control and wreck the ship?"*. This is a legitimate question to address if we are to have any chance of persuading people to embark on the journey toward an Agile Lean organization. That answer has to be how to avoid running onto the reefs instead of showing them how to salvage wrecks.

Stanley McChrystal – in one of his talks – says that as a leader in a traditional setup, you have to move to the edge of your comfort zone letting people loose – and then go one step further.

But before letting loose, some pre-conditions need to be examined.

## The Human Angle on the Organization

To develop a reliable Constitutional Organization of checks and balances, there needs to be a commitment to freedom but with constraints guarding the common good. It should be:

- An organization that persistently benefits those who contribute positively and keeps people from falling into the trap of either freeloading or exploiting others – exposing those who try.
- An organization that allows freedom of thought, sets the mind free to grow and to contribute but sets limits and heads off the dark side of human nature.
- An organization with radical transparency that pushes authority to where the information is – not the other way around.

Current leadership must desire and underwrite this vision.

We are using language from the territory of ethics, both positive and negative, talking about right or wrong. Readers may wonder why such old-fashioned concepts exist today. Isn't this the postmodern world, where it is accepted that everyone is only accountable to themselves, where there are no grand narratives or absolute truths, and where absolute and expressive individualism reigns?

That may be so, but by now the cracks are showing in this Postmodern worldview. A lack of common values cannot form a basis for personal or corporate life and much less society; holding this worldview, we are like a fish out of water. It will only lead to utter isolation; every man is his own island, perhaps with a single palm tree on it.

If we are to create a thriving organizational environment, we need to get back to a deep sense of value and contribute to a cause that is greater than ourselves. Several psychological studies have been conducted in this area but there is no common agreement on definitions. There seems, however, to be a consensus that human beings need to be fulfilled through:

- Safety: Some security in life, some order, and predictability.
- Autonomy: Significance, I matter, I can choose, I can speak up.
- Challenges: New areas that I can experience and gain proficiency in.
- Belonging: I am fully accepted among my peers and at home.
- Growing: I learn, I understand, and I get stronger.
- Contribution: I give and contribute to others, not just serving myself.

You may remember that these points are almost identical to those of Intrinsic Motivation discussed before.

An organization also has to take a hard look at these points and answer the question: *"Are we prepared for the long haul to achieve these qualities?"*, if the answer is no, then it probably should not start the journey.

# Necessary Endings of Old Habits

Quite often, before anybody can start something new, they have to give up or close down something old that they are unhappy or stuck with. Similarly, organizations have some entrenched views and habits to deal with, mostly related to Neo-Taylorism and its consequences:

- Neo-Taylorism is not a solution for complex work, there must be a willingness to deal with these challenges:

  - No – we do not have enough insight and knowledge to make the perfect upfront plan or budget.
  - No – we cannot honestly measure individuals through KPIs and base reviews and compensation on those KPIs.
  - No – we do not achieve optimal results by sub-optimizing individual areas.
  - No – we cannot separate the contributions of those who think (plan, delegate, monitor, control) from those who work.

- Authority cannot be based on power.

  - Fear and intimidation have to be abandoned as instruments of management.
  - Power tends to corrupt, reduce empathy, and promote hubristic and impulsive behavior, so it has to be limited.

- The traditional hierarchy is not helpful when focusing on engagement.

  - The hierarchy almost inevitably leads to disempowerment and a lack of freedom.
  - Decisions happen a long way from where the information and actions are.
  - A place in the hierarchy becomes the goal, the desire.
  - Position in the hierarchy is often based on seniority or acquired through less-than-honest means, which is resented and unfair.

- Being higher up than others often makes people develop a sense of entitlement.
- Communication channels up and down are too slow and noisy.

- The organization cannot remain curved in on itself.

  - The necessity and beauty of constant feedback from customers, employees, and stakeholders to improve services and products.
  - Rampant growth in bureaucracy has to be curbed.
  - Internal operations and processes cannot be the prime focus.

If an organization wants to journey towards an Agile Lean approach, it must be willing to deal with the previously mentioned dominant impediments.

## Strategies for Achieving the Objectives

After identifying the objectives and examining the constraints and prerequisites, we start looking for strategies that will contribute to the objectives. We have to find some plausible and reasonable first steps. As we know by now, this is all we can hope for because organizations are complex, and we only have fragmented knowledge; although tomorrow we may know better and have to adjust the course. Here is a collection of potential strategies for organizations that strive to work effectively in the complex domain:

- Work in self-managing, cross-functional teams.
- Take measures to develop Psychological Safety. A prerequisite for trust, transparency, growth, and learning.
- Radical transparency, so that all can see the situation as it really is.

  - Goals, progress, impediments, and decisions.
  - This will inspire people, but also reduce the likelihood of destructive behavior.

- Clear roles with mandates and responsibility, e.g. modeled on Scrum.

- Clear working agreements for how one unit takes delivery of services or products from another.
- Enabling feedback loops, PDSA-style:
  - Looking out at customers – and suppliers.
  - Looking in at the organization, processes, and relationships.
- Clear and rapid paths of decision-making, involving people,
  - Direction can be changed transparently and very quickly when needed.
  - Clear escalation agreements when challenges have to be resolved.
- Quick discovery and decisions when encountering threats or opportunities.
- Encourage thoughtful experimentation, giving people an opportunity to find new solutions and grow.
- Clear goals and values, giving people a real sense of belonging and contribution, not just a motivational poster here and there.
- Accountability and a balance of individual and corporate needs through closely connected teams, sharing values and goals.

*We want to be able to turn on a dime, for a dime!* — *Craig Larman*

## The Foundation of Agile Lean Leadership

After all the investigation and collection of evidence, we were convinced we were ready to fire a broadside and define a new framework for scaling Agile and Lean out into a whole organization, building a blueprint for a Constitutional Organization and not an imperial hierarchy. We called it Agile Lean Leadership as it is predominantly a fusion of Agile and Lean thinking.

We described the Agile Lean Leadership (ALL) framework and its foundation in much the same way as other frameworks have done. ALL is a framework to start with and a navigation guide, not a religion or a checklist to follow, the foundation is:

- Four Values.
- 16 Principles.
- A set of structures, practices, and methods.

# The Values – the Bedrock

Any decent system of thought needs some values to which its proponents can subscribe, and write on banners, t-shirts, and coffee mugs. So does Agile Lean Leadership. Our values are not rules and regulations but the glue that along with a clear vision binds people together in the complex domain. For simplicity, we settled on four values to be balanced and kept in mind by everybody. We believe they provide a strong foundation for the ALL framework.

## 1. Purpose, Clear and Worthwhile

An organization must have an aim to work towards. It should be bigger than any individual and be more than just making money. If it helps bind people together over the long term, its stakeholders must find its purpose worthwhile. The purpose will reveal the organization's own values.

## 2. Sustainability in all Things

An organization must have a long-term view, more or less of all things. This implies being able to survive for a long time, removing waste, avoiding draining scarce resources, and building up relationships and human capabilities for the long haul – not wearing them down.

## 3. Resilience in all Things

An organization must expect change and unpredictability. The structures and communication channels must be able to respond quickly to new challenges and opportunities. Everybody must be on the lookout for new knowledge and disciplined reflection must be in place to make sense of things.

## 4. Respect for People

An organization must serve its customers, employees, stakeholders, and community with respect. This includes giving people Psychological Safety and avoiding force and fear, thus allowing them to grow, develop, and have joy and pride in their work.

# The Principles – the Guides

The Principles are guides that organization leaders use as directional road signs. Following the principles implements the values.

## A Clear and Worthwhile Purpose

*1. At every level, be very clear about the purpose, values, and constraints*
Proactive value visibility is a powerful tool. The purpose and value system of the organization is a true north, the compass that indicates the way to make difficult decisions. Constraints also need to be visible; people need to know the options that are and are not available to them.

*2. Balance the value created for customers, employees, society, and stakeholders*
Balanced value for all stakeholders is essential. Focusing on only one aspect will skew the purpose and open the door to all sorts of undesirable side effects. The customer has to be served first and foremost; without him, no money, and no organization. Next, the employees have to see the value, as without them there is no one to serve the client. Then society and finally shareholders.

*3. Hold and display the moral high ground with integrity and strive to build trust*
Values and purpose are powerful if clients and staff trust that they are sincere. The slightest attempt to manipulate people with fake values can backfire catastrophically. Trust is earned over time with consistent behavior and honored commitments. It can be lost in a split second.

**4. Remember, that the final judge of the quality of a product or service is the customer**

Whatever the product or service, in the end, it is only the customer's opinion that matters - does it give him the value he is after? Everyone needs to understand this and be exposed to real customers and their feedback as much as practically possible.

## Transparency and Visibility

**5. Sustain an unrestricted flow of information up, down, and sideways**

Information must be available immediately. The organization must foster a culture where sharing of information is encouraged. No one must be afraid to bring bad news. If there is fear in the organization the leaders will not know about challenges in time. Timely, reliable information is a foundation for resilience and fast changes.

**6. Be in dialog with the customers to fully understand how to benefit and serve them consistently**

Organizations must develop a system of continuous interaction with customers to find better ways of creating products and services while uncovering new or potential needs that can be satisfied. The overall organization-wide learning loop must include the customer.

**7. Shorten the distance of understanding between the customers and the organization**

Organizations must develop forms of communication and activities that maximize understanding between the customer and the organization. Visit the customer and aim to perceive unspoken needs. This makes the organization resilient in periods of changing customer needs.

**8. Create optimal visualization of models, goals, status, progress, and impediments**

Organizations need to show their goals, priorities, progress, and impediments as openly as possible. People (including the customer) cannot react to what they cannot see, so it has to be simple and clear.

## Institutionalized Learning

*9. Strive to see and understand the facts in their full context as a system*
Important facts are seldom simple numbers. Through dialogue, it is important to get the full context and to reach a common understanding between relevant people. It is often the case that decision-makers have to go to "gemba" (the real place) and talk directly to those involved to get proper knowledge.

*10. Build up and sustain a commitment to constant improvement and learning*
There is no final or perfect solution. There are always flaws in any system and circumstances are always changing. The organization has to commit to always learning and navigating toward improved products, services, processes, and relationships.

*11. Strive for collegiate decisions, pushing responsibility as far out as there are people who can carry it*
The best decisions are usually those validated by several people and taken by those closest to the point of impact. In the complex domain, diverse relevant input needs to be taken into account to make sense of things before reaching a decision.

*12. Balance the need for structure and standards with the need for adaptability and innovation*
The organization is a system; there must be a certain order, and to function, it must drive out variability to some extent. However, there is a balance. It must not be over-constrained. If too much variability and slack is removed, the ability to find new ways, to experiment, and to generate ideas is lost.

## Respect and Develop People and Relations

*13. Allow people pride of workmanship and a certain autonomy, building them up to their maximum potential*
The primary assets of an organization are its people from which it needs their engagement, commitment, and full mental capacity. This only occurs if people are intrinsically motivated and proud of what they do. Peo-

103

ple also need to experience growth and progress; the organization must back this up so they can reach their maximum potential.

*14. Be willing to serve colleagues, subordinates, customers, and suppliers; leadership is a service*

The organization needs to engender an attitude of vocation. Every job is a service to someone, externally or internally and everybody receives a service from someone else. Leaders need to display and practice this attitude. Many problems go away if people's fundamental orientation is to serve their customers whether external or internal.

*15. Keep a long perspective on people and relationships; create psychological safety*

Working with people has its ups and downs and relationships occasionally get challenged. People may encounter difficulties that affect their contributions, and customers have their own challenges. The primary objective of the organization is to foster sustainable long-term relationships and to work proactively to adapt and find solutions.

*16. Be transparent and never use fear as a leadership instrument, as fear leads to distortion of data or systems*

Radical transparency is non-negotiable, requiring constant vigilance to keep the instrument of fear out of an organization. Unfortunately, it is a natural human trait to want power over others. Carrot and stick methods inject fear, and fear triggers our deepest self-preservation instincts, often gaming the system to stay out of harm's way.

## Using the Principles in Practice

The principles are practical instruments. When a group of people are considering actions, changes, or interventions, they can use the principles to guide their approach. They can step through the principles one by one and ask themselves the question: "On a scale from 1 to 5, how much does this action amplify or dampen this principle?", (3 is neutral, 5 is optimal amplification, and 1 is maximum dampening). See the example below:

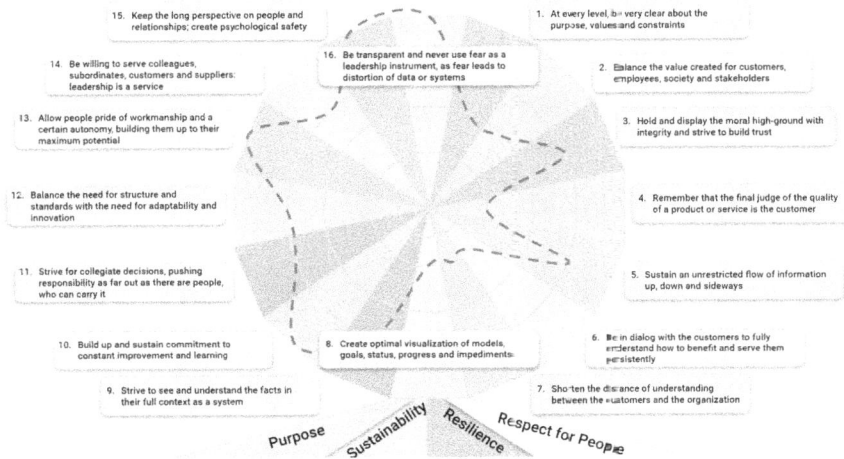

The red dashed line illustrates how different initiatives or actions can be evaluated. The Values are included as reminders: "Do we still base our decisions on the bedrock? The values.".

# The Structures of Agile Lean Leadership

Inspired by our research, we devised a minimalist set of Constitutional Organization structures based on Agile and Lean Thinking. These structures align with the Values and Principles presented above and facilitate our objectives. Except for a few innovations intended to create coherence and linkage, much of what we propose is established practice elsewhere. This is a quick overview, but we will peel more layers of the onion later.

We propose the **Circle Network** illustrated below as an alternative to the traditional Hierarchy. When confronted with a significant amount of Complex work, it is not who takes orders from whom that matters most. Instead, it is critical to see who works with what, who interacts with whom, and in what way. Then we have a better opportunity to make the right decisions – inspect and adapt. This replaces the organization diagram which belongs to the classic hierarchical top-down organizational model.

We call the illustration the **Circle Map**.

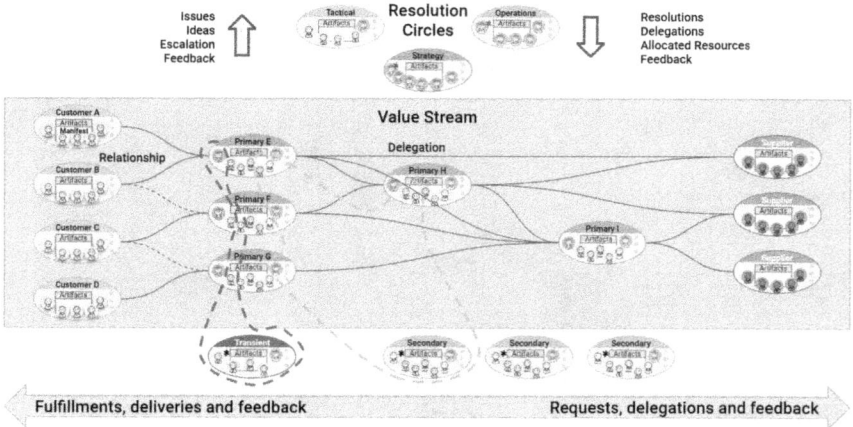

## The Organizational Manifest

First, at the top level of the organization, there is an **Organizational Manifest**, which describes the purpose and the constraints that everybody has consented to. It contains the vision, the mission, the limitations, and strategies. The format is not important, but the organization must take ownership of it, make it highly transparent, and constantly improve it as circumstances unfold. It represents *"the vision and mission"* of the organization and everybody should know and understand it.

## The Centrality of Teams and Circles

In almost all agile practices work is done by Teams. In Lean Production there is also a strong focus on work groups. All the way back to W. Edwards Deming, there is an emphasis on quality in corporate and sometimes communal work. There are many benefits to working in small teams, the most important being that with the proximity of team members, true transparency, trust, and collaboration develop more easily.

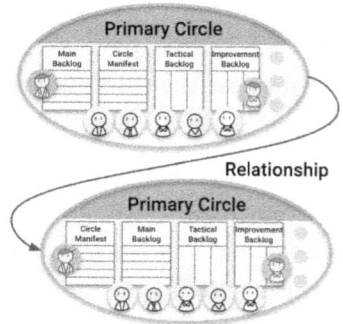

106

*A small self-organizing, cross-functional team is the organizational structure most likely to come up with innovation.* — Steve Denning

In a later chapter, we will deal with the nature of Teams in deeper detail. To maximize independence and maneuverability, teams should be put together to have high internal coherence and low external coupling. In other words, the freedom to get the job done with minimal or no external help.

Inspired by the classic Scrum Team, ALL's basic organizational unit is a Circle. Each Circle has at least one tactical Team, doing real work.

- A circle can have **Relationships** with other Circles between which **Delegations** of work can occur.
- A Circle can be a **Scaled-Up** one with one backlog and multiple Circle Teams[1].
- A Circle can be a **Scaled-Down** one with multiple input streams of delegations to one Team.

## Artifacts in Circles

Circles have artifacts that are similar to those found in classic Scrum:

- **Circle Manifest**: Who we are, what we do, how to interact with us. The Circle takes ownership of this, it is their artifact.
- **Main Backlog**: (Product Backlog in Scrum), an ordered list of Circle deliverables. These are called Main Backlog Items.
- **Tactical Backlog**: (Sprint Backlog) Scrum, Kanban, both, or something better. Main Backlog Items are moved to the tactical backlog and often broken down further into individual Tasks.
- **Improvement Backlog**: An ordered list of potential improvements and impediments.

---

1   Read more about multiple teams in *Chapter 7 Everyday Life – The Practices, Scaled up Circles.*

The organization may use a host of other artifacts, burn-down graphs, lead-time, etc., but the ones mentioned above always make practical sense.

## Roles of Responsibility in Circles

There are a few roles with specific authority and responsibility in a Circle, again largely inspired by Scrum:

- A **Strategy Owner**: (SO, a generalized Product Owner from Scrum), looking *Out* for customers and value, owning the Main Backlog, and prioritizing deliverables to maximize value generation.
- An **Operations Owner**: (OO, a generalized Scrum Master from Scrum), looking *In* for people, improvements, and governing the processes. The OO owns the Improvement Backlog.
- **Circle Team(s)**: Small (5-9), cross-functional, and self-governing. The team(s) have all the primary skills to deliver items from the Main Backlog, they own the Tactical Backlog. If the Circle's dominant work is mostly of the Obvious or Complicated sort, then teams can be bigger.

## How Work is Done in Circles

Circles can operate under very different circumstances embracing the four main cognitive domains (Obvious, Complicated, Complex, and Chaos). For example: standardized production-like work; knowledge-heavy engineering; exploration of new territories; or volatile situations like emergency services. Many Circles work across two neighboring domains. This is workable, but there may be a certain amount of firefighting (Chaos) going on, which can be very stressful and challenging.

Circles will have to choose familiar processes from their main work domain. This can manifest itself in a series of Events (meetings), where planning, execution, and follow-up occur.

If there is enough time to work with iterations (Sprints) of two to four weeks, the Scrum framework provides an excellent starting point for work in the borderline territory of Complex and Complicated. If constant re-planning and rescheduling are needed, Kanban may be more appropriate. This is often the case if the team sits between Complex and Chaos. In the Obvious and Complicated territory, traditional planning can work well, as knowledge and the environment are fairly stable, and many methods well known from Lean can be deployed.

In the case where there is a mix of short-term and long-term work, the best solution may be to combine Scrum and Kanban.

In any case, there should always be feedback loops to learn and navigate, planning cycles, and debriefing, which as with Scrum we call Retrospectives. Never give up on the Retrospective, this is the hub around which learning and constant improvement revolve.

## The Value Stream

The backbone of an Agile Lean organization in true Lean fashion is the **Value Stream**, optimized for effectively delivering value to the clients and beneficiaries of the organization: its Customers. The value stream is usually depicted from left to right, from Customers to Suppliers. Where possible an important goal is that most of the work should be done by small self-managing teams operating as close to the customers as possible. Scaling backward in the organization and delegating work is always a compromise, but sometimes a necessary one.

- **Customer Circles**. Circles representing the categories or classifications of customers the organization services are defined. Manifests describe how we understand the customers and their needs.
- **Primary Circles**. Circles internal to the organization, starting with **Front-line Circles**, serving real customers, followed by **Center Circles** behind the scenes serving internal customers. It is good practice to include one or more **Service Circles** that contain competencies such as finance, HR, facility management, and legal assistance.

- **Supplier Circles,** at the right side of the diagram, external strategic Supplier Circles are documented in much the same way as Customer Circles, but focusing on what these circles can deliver to the organization.
- **Relationships** exist between the relevant Circles, describing the lines along which deliverables can be ordered and exchanged. We call these **Delegations**. Each Relationship has a **Manifest** where the Teams involved have negotiated how to exchange deliverables.

What goes to the right in the Value Stream are requests and delegations, and what goes to the left are fulfillments and deliveries. As always, there is ample feedback – PDSA style – to constantly monitor and react to unfolding circumstances.

## The Resolution Circles

Whenever there is more than one Circle in an organization, there is the potential for conflict. Decision-making in a Constitutional Organization is through consultative and representative **Resolution Circles** which exist for each of the Tactical, Strategic, and Operational disciplines. An Individual from each **Primary Circle** is granted the power to negotiate decisions on behalf of their colleagues in the relevant **Resolution Circle**. This is not a special class of managers.

- **Tactical Resolution.** Appointed representatives from each tactical Primary Circle gather regularly or as needed to resolve backlog challenges to product or service delivery. Primary Circles select their representative, either on a round-robin basis or by selecting the one with the greatest need for a resolution. Not every organization may need a Tactical Resolution Circle.
- **Strategic Resolution.** SOs from the Primary Circles meet to discuss and resolve strategic matters, such as assessing new customer requests or prioritizing internal deliveries. This Circle also manages the allocation of resources as needed.

- **Operational Resolution**. OOs from the Primary Circles meet to discuss and resolve operational matters, such as team composition and internal processes. This Circle also handles internal unfolding opportunities and tensions between team members.

Each of these circles has a person called the **Chair,** with the authority to break any deadlocks. The Chair is normally chosen because of their recognized experience and skills. The three Chairs often function as an **Executive Committee**, able to make fast decisions when time is of the essence.

A Resolution Circle has an associated OO, like a coach facilitating the proceedings and keeping everything on track.

What goes up to the Resolution Circles are issues, ideas, and escalation; what comes back are resolutions, delegations, and allocation of resources. There should always be effective feedback loops to maximize common understanding. Resolution Circles have Main Backlogs of their own; they can delegate items from these to other circles.

The concept of Resolution Circles aligns with the Nordic *Things* introduced in the previous chapter, although Resolution Circles originally came to us by other paths. The main idea is that based upon mutual agreements (laws, a constitution, a covenant) representative delegates meet to make decisions and take action. This may be the natural solution for development in the absence of a central ruling Hierarchy.

## The Secondary Circles

In the traditional hierarchy, people mostly work in functional groups (silos) sharing common interests and skills, which is a good thing and should not be lost. By contrast, ALL teams are cross-functional and multidisciplined, so the concept of **Secondary Circles** provides a platform for information sharing and decision-making between similarly skilled peers and a way to handle cross-team-cutting concerns. Sometimes these are called *Communities of Interest* or *Guilds*. These circles are the backbone of an Organization's management of complex scenarios where it becomes very expensive and sometimes impossible to codify and write down everything. Dialogue between a small group of people with a common understanding of the language and specific disciplines helps preserve and develop their shared knowledge.

Secondary Circles are typically commissioned to deal with specific competencies such as design, QA, architecture, or compliance. Those in Primary Teams with these skills will meet at regular intervals or when the need arises to discuss, decide, and perhaps implement items within their domain. Their home is in the Primary Circle, but they spend some time in Secondary Circles.

Secondary Circles have their own Main Backlog, and participants can delegate items to their own Primary Circle. They can also Escalate to Resolution Circles or receive Delegation from them. Like Resolution Circles, Secondary Circles have a Chair, who will act as a mediator, guide the discussions, serve as an arbitrator if necessary, and an associated OO to facilitate as usual.

## The Transient Circles

If a sudden disruption occurs, one that the Value Stream has not been designed to handle, the best-known practice is to form a **Transient Circle**, often called a task force.

This might be a short-term project that needs to be executed, or an emergency situation, which Dave Snowden calls a *"Sudden drop into chaos"*. We will discuss this in detail later.

Transient Circles comprise those believed to have the best intuitive subject matter competence, who can be trusted to make decisions for the common good. The circle is typically commissioned by the Executive Committee with a charter to stabilize the situation so that normal operation can be resumed. When the situation is under control, the Transient Circle is disbanded.

The purpose of the Transient Circle is to stabilize[2] the situation and get back to near normal. Everybody else tries to keep the Value Stream going as best they can during the emergency.

During its existence, the Transient Circle may have wide-ranging authority. The rest of the organization understands that in an emergency they need to comply. If the ship is in danger of sinking, everybody accepts the captain's orders, there is no time for broad debate.

It is good practice for the Transient Team to have an OO, who is responsible for removing any impediments and getting optimal support from others. The OO should also be alert to anything that can be learned from this extraordinary event. Sometimes this leads to the formation of a new Secondary Circle tasked with developing mitigations for this kind of situation.

As mentioned above Transient Circles can also be deployed to respond to an unexpected opportunity – a positive challenge – or the need to execute a project. However, the principles and practices still apply.

## How does it Work in a Larger Setup?

The overall Circle Network framework works for organizations of up to around 150-250 people, depending on the complexity of their work. We argue that such entities should not exceed "Dunbar's number[3]". This is not an exact number and Dunbar's theories are not generally accepted, but it is a useful range to have in mind.

---

2  "*Chaos is always transient, it will stabilize. If you do not intervene, probably to your disadvantage*" – Dave Snowden.

3  Dunbar's number: https://en.wikipedia.org/wiki/Dunbar%27s_number

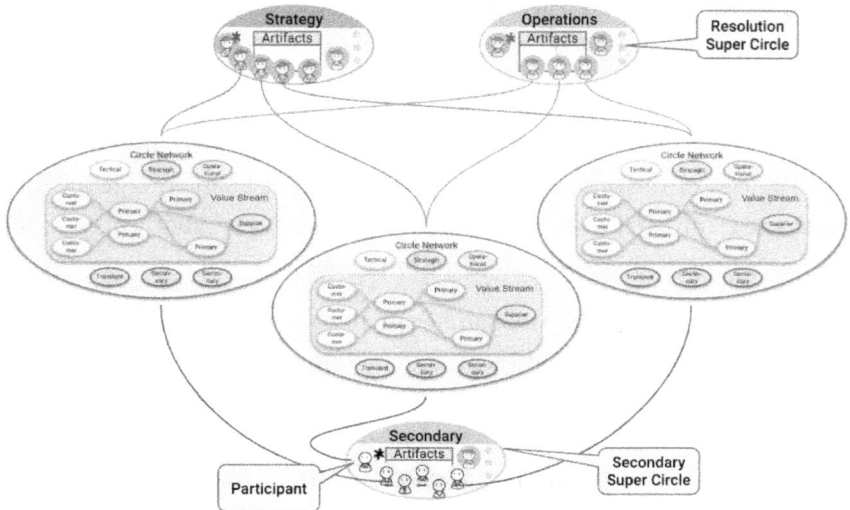

If the organization is larger, it is quite simply more of the same. Such a collection of Circles is called a **Super Circle**, like a division of an organization or a state in a federation.

There will be Resolution Circles and Secondary Circles among the Super Circles, and they will still be operating with consultative and representative decision-making. However, there will not be a central bureaucracy, as inevitably this will seek to spread into every corner of the organization. Super Circles may deliver Items to other Super Circles' Value Streams, but this is more formal than Delegation between Circles as the delivering Super Circle appears as a Supplier Circle to the receiving one. Much more on this later.

## Framework Recap

This kind of organization is created to be Sustainable and Resilient and to reliably serve all the stakeholders (predominantly the Customers). Fundamental to the framework is the overall use of feedback loops, ensuring that learning is accumulated, and leading the organization on the straight path to excellence. This obviously requires the engagement of the people in the organization whose goodwill can be volunteered, but not conscripted. People need the freedom to choose for this to happen.

# The Practices and Methods of Agile Lean Leadership

The practices and methods used in a Constitutional Organization based on Agile Lean Leadership are a work in progress. Here is an overview. Later on, we will take a deep dive into each one.

### 1. Radical Transparency

Radical Transparency is about the broad visibility of information like goals, progress, working agreements, and impediments. Examples include Manifests, Main Backlog, Tactical Backlog (Sprint and/or Kanban), Improvement Backlog, Story Maps, Roadmaps, and competency matrices.

The Constitution of the Organization which everyone is invited to consent to and honor in their decision-making may be regarded as the sum of all the Circle and Relationship Manifests.

### 2. Establishing Routine and Recognizability

Everybody needs some order and predictability. Within Circles and in the interactions between them there has to be some easy-to-understand and simple enabling constraints. This is exemplified by the events in Scrum and Kanban and through the discipline of delegation and escalation.

### 3. The use of Self-governing, Cross-functional Teams

A small group of people with complementary skills, a common goal, and the collaborative spirit to reach it is the best-known structure to give people a voice and foster respect, transparency, and teamwork.

### 4. The split Leadership Concept

A unique dynamic is created by granting leadership responsibility to the Strategy Owner (SO, Product Owner in Scrum, a mini-CEO *Looking out*), the Operations Owner (OO, Scrum Master in Scrum, like a mini-COO *Looking in*), and the Tactical Team (Circle Team, developers in Scrum, responsible for the delivery and the factual competencies). It avoids the dark side of the power hierarchy which often leads to a sense of entitlement. Instead, it creates checks and balances which to some extent immunize the Circle against those wishing to grab power inappropriately.

### 5. Extending the Team Concept to Circles

A Circle may be scaled up (with one SO, one Main Backlog, and several Circle Teams each with their Tactical Backlog), or scaled down (one Circle Team but several request or delegation streams (Backlogs) from several sources). In fact, a Circle doesn't need to follow a specific practice such as Scrum, as long as Relationships and Delegations are understood, agreed upon, and committed to. Of course, the Circle must have internal structures that create a desired effective environment.

### 6. Sustained Learning and Constant Improvement

The most fundamental property of an Agile Lean Organization is to constantly learn and improve. Tools and conditions for achieving this goal include making it *safe* to speak up and to fail in earnest, capturing exceptions, disciplined retrospectives, and daily stand-ups.

### 7. Organizational Mapping

By making relationships between circles explicit, visual, and transparent, members of the Organization can achieve a shared consciousness about what they are, their goals, and how they operate.

A Roadmap is a useful artifact for visualizing important constraints and forecasts. It is good practice to have one at both the organizational and Circle level. Manifests for Circles and Relationships, decision-making processes, and principles of escalation all contribute to a common mental model – a high-level nautical chart to sail by.

### 8. Handling Interrupts, Impediments, Opportunities, and Crises

Even the best of Organizations will eventually run into circumstances for which they were not designed[4]. The Constitution, i.e the Manifests, must contain working agreements dealing with interrupts to protect Teams and performance, how to train crews, and how to re-team in Transient Circles in a crisis.

# Summing it all Up

This first high-level sweep over the Agile Lean Leadership territory has provided an overview of the framework, putting all the important concepts and ideas on the table, so we can start to decompose them and understand their benefits and challenges.

The ALL Framework provides a good starting point, a blueprint, for an organization embarking on a journey toward engagement, leadership, and freedom. As with everything complex, context is crucial. In each situation, people will choose their particular approach but focus on different aspects as they judge what will be best for them. It is a bit like a theater production of a Shakespeare play or an opera by Mozart, there is a stage setting with different arrangements, orchestration, props, and backdrops. Sometimes new stagings introduce new ways of getting into the core content.

Likewise, ALL is not a simple set of checklists or prescriptions to follow, but rather a set of proposed enabling constraints to be contextualized in the actual organization and circumstances. A simple list might work in an organization working mainly in the obvious domain but would be ineffective where high levels of complex work exist.

There may not always be a complete implementation of everything in Agile Lean Leadership – far from it, but it is always beneficial to recognize

---

4    All models are wrong, but some are useful: https://en.wikipedia.org/wiki/All_model-s_are_wrong

the ideal blueprint. Sometimes only a small portion of an organization will embark on this journey, perhaps just one team, but it can still be very helpful. However, such an approach requires that the rest of the organization is willing to accept a Manifest that specifies the collaboration between the parties. This has to be there to protect the freedom in this free territory.

Prepared this way with this arsenal of insight, we are ready to dive deeper into the benefits, challenges, and risks of introducing Agile Lean Leadership.

*We identified plausible objectives for an Agile Lean Organization:*
*– Be fast, deliver value fast, learn fast, and change when needed.*
*– Have consistency of purpose and be sustainable.*
*– Be reliable and resilient, and keep promises and commitments.*
*– Be innovative, and be prepared to explore and experiment.*
*– Have balanced empathy for all stakeholders.*

*We identified the bedrock of values and principles for an Agile Lean organization: Four Values and 16 Principles.*

*We presented a model for an Agile Lean organization.*
*– A value stream of Customer Circles, Primary Circles, and Supplier Circles.*
*– Representative decision-making through Resolution Circles.*
*– Secondary Circles for cross-cutting concerns*
*– Transient Circles for the unexpected.*
*– Manifests for Circles and relations, governing among other things Delegations.*

*Several helpful practices were discussed.*

# Benefits of a
# Liberating Organization

*We now have all the relevant facts from the investigation on the table and have a blueprint for a practical framework for how things could be better, we called it Agile Lean Leadership . Now, let us look at some concrete benefits that building an organization on the Agile Lean Leadership framework can produce. What benefits will accrue from crossing the fence to liberty? Again a quote from W. Edwards Deming can help us get going:*

> *The aim proposed here for any organization is for everybody to gain – stockholders, employees, suppliers, customers, community, and the environment – over the long term.    – W. Edwards Deming: The New Economics, 1993.*

*It was repeated and extended decades later by the Business Roundtable, 2019[1]:*

*...we share a fundamental commitment to all of our stakeholders...*

*Delivering value to our customers...*

*Investing in our employees...*

*Dealing fairly and ethically with our suppliers...*

*Supporting the communities in which we work...*

*Generating long-term value for shareholders...*

*Each of our stakeholders is essential. We commit to deliver value to all of them, for the future success of our companies, our communities and our country.*

---

1    BRT: https://www.businessroundtable.org/business-roundtable-redefines-the-pur-
     pose-of-a-corporation-to-promote-an-economy-that-serves-all-americans

# Benefits for the Organization

## Less is More

The organization can experience a wealth of benefits from the changed conditions in an Agile Lean Organization, we will just mention a few:

- Better common vision and understanding – less confusion.
- Better engagement – less quiet quitting.
- Better psychological safety – less fear.
- Better maneuverability – less waiting for decisions.
- Better handovers and communication – fewer mistakes and delays.
- Better learning and ability to adapt – less top-down plans and control.

These soft values do not stand in isolation, but are intertwined, overlap, and work together. Here are some observations:

Gallup's studies of engagement in the global workforce[2], conclude that the differences between the organizations that come out in the top 25% relating to engagement and those in the bottom 25% were:

- 10% in customer loyalty/engagement.
- 23% in profitability.
- 18%/14% in productivity (sales/production).
- 18%/43% in turnover (high-turnover/low-turnover organizations).
- 64% in safety incidents (accidents).
- 81% in absenteeism.
- 28% in shrinkage (theft).
- 58% in patient safety incidents (mortality and falls).
- 41% in quality (defects).
- 66% in wellbeing (net thriving employees).
- 13% in organizational citizenship (participation).

---

2  Gallup $Q^{12}$® Meta-Analysis of 112,312 business and work units including 2,708,538 employees: https://www.gallup.com/workplace/321725/gallup-q12-meta-analysis-report.aspx

121

These are impressive numbers, by any scale of measure. Amy Edmondson's writings about psychological safety in medical care systems demonstrated similar outcomes concerning patient safety, errors in treatment, etc. Other reports in the media show significant improvements in employee relations when the properties of Agile Lean Organization are present.

The Agile Lean Leadership framework offers a major opportunity to improve customer interaction as well and create sustainable positive relationships. There is little research in the area, but lots of anecdotal evidence. When those on the frontline dealing with customers use ALL principles, they have the freedom to act upon customers' feedback, creating a greatly improved bi-directional relationship between customer and supplier. This includes increased respect, loyalty, and willingness to engage. The organization has a much-improved understanding of its customers' actual needs and more relevant input for further development of products and services.

Let us now look at the potential benefits of ALL organizations from different angles, starting with the people in and around the organization.

# Benefits for the Stakeholders

## Benefits for the Customers

### Better Attention to Needs

Agile Lean Organizations' true north is oriented toward those they serve; they understand that the most important part of product and service development is the customer, who experiences greater attention and more involvement with its partners.

Classic hierarchical organizations sometimes measure customer service by its efficiency, boiling it down to *how quickly you can get rid of the customer wanting attention* – it is anything but *service*. Sales, service, and supply departments may interact with the customer in isolation from each other, failing to respond directly to real customer needs and sending conflicting messages.

## Better Communication

In the same way, Agile Lean Organizations are always looking for better ways to keep the customer in the loop, often including technology allowing customer access to relevant people in the organization. For example: closed chat, video messaging, and case tracking tools.

Good communication helps develop mutual respect leading to better customer relationships and greater sustainability – a win for both parties.

## Better Value for Money

Especially for the development of complex products and services, Agile Lean Organizations are more competitive because their approach is better able to meet customer needs on time and within budget. This is not always apparent at the outset, but because it avoids the false starts and blind alleys of traditional development it is better value for money in the long run.

In a study of traditionally run complex projects, Standish[3] found that only 23% of IT projects were successful, 58% were challenged, and 23% were outright failures. Also, 50% to 70% of effort in large-scale complex projects or organizations is wasted because the effort does not deliver anything of value to the customer.

Stakeholders should expect to see quantifiable results in this area, however new ways of identifying produced value will have to be found to provide tangible evidence. One viable route is to focus more on quantifying objectives and to agree on how to measure this, another quality measure is to keep track of the ability to react in a timely fashion to unfolding circumstances.

---

3   Standish data 2018: https://www.standishgroup.com/sample_research_files/Demo-PRBR.pdf

# Benefits for those Working in the Organization

### People Delivering Products and Services

Those doing the actual work in the Value Stream(s) of the organization should experience tangible results of an Agile Lean Organization, especially in the overlapping areas of engagement, psychological safety, and intrinsic motivation. Whether they are called retrospectives, evaluations, or something else, feedback and learning loops are an important way to engage people, refresh their memories, and keep them current.

Notably, Agile Lean Organizations tend to have less staff turnover contributing to continuity and reducing the costs associated with hiring and training[4] new people. There are also many examples of how much easier it is to attract the right people and talent if the organization follows these principles.

They are also better able to handle unplanned work and interruptions so that people's ability to concentrate and solve complex problems is improved.

Finally, because teams are self-managing and largely self-sufficient, delays caused by external decision-making are greatly reduced, enabling the Team to maintain velocity.

### Middle Management

Current middle managers will spend less time relaying information and decisions up and down the hierarchy and attending status meetings and instead more time doing meaningful, value-generating work, typically making sure everybody has a common understanding and removing obstacles for people working and clearing their road.

If the Agile Lean Leadership framework is implemented fully, they may assume roles as Strategy or Operations Owners in Primary Circles; they may be experts in certain areas and assume Chair positions in Secondary

---

4    Today's buzzword here is *onboarding*.

Circles while being valued Team members in Primary Circles. This can be seen as a positive move, as long as it does not signal a loss of status. One group – the bureaucrats – will not see this as desirable. Sadly, we do not have much to offer them apart from re-training; bureaucracy is not sought after in an Agile Lean Organization.

## Executives

The intended outcomes of Agile Lean Leadership are long-term, which should align with the motives of the executives in traditional organizations, although this is not always the case. However, if seen from the perspective of sustainable customer relationships and resilience in the face of constant change, executives should gladly embrace the benefits. In addition, managers who care about their workforce can take credit for its improved performance and increased dedication and growth.

## Board Members

Board members are the owner's representatives and should see the value of Agile Lean Leadership for the Organization. In particular, the radical transparency provided substantially increases the reliability of forecasts which are based more on fact than fantasy, providing a solid foundation for future decision-making. Forecasts may not become more popular, but they should be closer to reality, especially if the organization adopts the practice of estimating and forecasting in ranges, the best estimate and a worst-case one, when aggregating a useful indication of uncertainty can be calculated. The transparency will also reveal the true capability of the organization much better, enabling improved strategic decision-making.

# Benefits for the Broader Community

## Robust and Sustainable Institutions

Society benefits from having robust and sustainable institutions. That includes public institutions but also businesses and non-profit organizations. It is an enormous cost to society if institutions are started, built up, start to disappoint, and then fail and close and have to be restarted in a new form.

With robust institutions society is more stable. Ordinary people can make plans, invest, buy property, or get an education with reasonably robust expectations for the future. People need to trust their social institutions and each other, because if there is no trust it will be replaced with control with its associated higher costs and sense of alienation. If there is high trust, then transaction and monitoring costs for any deal are at an all-time low[5].

If institutions develop freedom for people, allowing them to take responsibility and make decisions, it has wider ramifications, people will be experienced in acting in civil society with respect for each other.

**Greater Value Generation**

We contend that Agile Lean Organizations produce a better return on investment (ROI) in the long run. Society has less waste, and more resources to provide a better quality of life for its citizens and increased global competitiveness. Better value creation allows society to become sustainable and invest in resilience.

**Greater Resilience in Times of Challenges**

If a society has organizations and institutions built for the engagement of its people, decentralized decision-making, and accountability, it will be more resilient in times of challenge or crisis. Central control means long delays in reaction and a single point of failure which can break catastrophically in times of rapid change.

It is surprising and worrying that this fact doesn't seem to be on the radar of policymakers in these times of multiple overlapping crises.

---

5   One of the most efficient markets known is the diamond market in New York City, run by Orthodox Jews, who trust each other absolutely.

## Benefits for Owners

Owners have invested in the organization, and fundamentally they want a return on their investment. Naturally, they want greater value generation, they should also appreciate increased long-term sustainability and resilience[6]. However, it is quite rare to hear this view in the debate, more often the discussion is skewed towards short-term expediency, as in *"Any low-hanging fruit in the first quarter?"* Many years of preoccupation with short-term results and speculative gains have rendered many incapable of thinking long-term. An organization with higher resilience represents a lower investment risk than others, with less risk of catastrophic failure. Svenska Handelsbanken is a bank that persistently has outperformed others based on similar organizational principles.

For public organizations and non-profits, it is a bit different. They are not in it for the money, but nevertheless have a concept of value, and want value generation – although not monetary – to be sustainable and resilient and with as low overhead as possible.

# Beneficial Side-effects of Freedom

When people have the freedom to decide substantial things in their domain and they get the affirmation of others, they grow and become more robust psychologically. When freedom persists, and decisions are implemented and not reversed, the individual develops a more positive attitude to life's challenges. Conversely, a constant feeling of pressure from above and minute control producing low self-esteem can be crushing and demoralizing.

A beneficial, albeit anecdotal, by-product of freedom is that people become more alert to change in their circumstances, increasing the effective-

---

6     We are in fact now focusing on approaching small to medium sized organizations, where we can get into dialogue with owners or their immediate proxies. In larger organizations – as we found in our interviews – the sight of the real bottom-line is frequently lost in internally defined metrics and KPIs.

ness of the sensor network of those in the organization. Intelligence gathering is of higher quality and faster, which increases resilience. If people have no mandate to say or do anything, they subconsciously lose interest in being alert – what's the point?

As with any relationship, collaboration within an organization is only really valuable when it is entered into freely by mutual consent. New collaborations occur spontaneously, some only in the heat of the moment, and some for longer, and may end up being institutionalized. But they serve a purpose, almost without overhead.

Freedom coupled with voluntary transparency reduces the need for governance and control, especially regarding small things. Governance and monitoring people take time and consume resources. During our interviews of eyewitnesses, we encountered some middle managers who claimed to spend 50% of their time on control-related matters, up and down. If there is freedom to trust, this waste is reduced.

# Case Studies

Organizing for agility is not yet commonplace, but there are many examples of organizations built on values and principles similar to Agile Lean Leadership.

- *Corporate Rebels* has made it its business to assemble evidence of companies that have successfully organized in agile and self-governing ways. They run a comprehensive educational program and 150 key examples can be found on their website: https://www.corporate-rebels.com/bucketlist.
- Beyond Budgeting refers to such organizations as Empowered and Adaptive Organizations, and they have an abundance of examples of companies, read more here: https://bbrt.co.uk/beyond-budgeting/bb-bbo.html . You also find brief statements about Toyota, Svenska Handelsbanken, and Southwest Airlines.

- Leise Passer Jensen and Brian Dahl has a useful list of Danish companies in their. book *DamnGood Leadership*.
- Svenska Handelsbanken used a highly decentralized self-governing model with minimum control before there was anything called Agile or Beyond Budgeting. Their story has been told in numerous places, you can read their own version here: https://www.handelsbanken.com/en/about-the-group/our-story[7].
- Another marque company is the California-based tomato processor Morning Star; probably one of the most radically managed companies. It has practically no hierarchy, relying on self-forming relationships. No one has power over anybody else and you honor your commitments. A description of their management practices can be found in many places, here is one to start with: https://www.corporate-rebels.com/blog/morning-star .

We will just mention a few examples where we have had hands-on experience.

## RiksTV

RiksTV[8] is a Norwegian company delivering TV and streaming services to its customers via the Internet and over the air. Their business model makes sense due to the very special terrain and geographical challenges in Norway. We had the privilege to work with them some years ago implementing a comprehensive *network of teams* model for their organization.

Among the benefits achieved by RiksTV was *radical transparency* achieved through a well-designed system of review presentations and feedback together with retrospectives that aggregated their findings. There was rep-

---

7  Handelsbanken whitepaper: https://scrummaster.dk/lib/AgileLeanLibrary/Topics/BeyondBudgetting/Handelsbanken_Consistency_at_its_Best_2.pdf
8  RiksTV: https://www.rikstv.no/

resentative decision-making and a commitment to psychological safety, enabling people to speak up without fear of reprisals.

One area in which we were involved was a large product development project. It was challenged because some of the external development partners were not accustomed to agile supplier-customer relationships and because an existing contract prevented the desired flexibility.

An important detail with a great impact was the collaborative estimation of project parameters (cost, effort, and value) expressed as ranges; one number for the expected result and one for the worst case. This highlighted and clarified the uncertainties and risks, resulting in a much improved common understanding among leadership and developers.

Despite being more traditionally minded, even the board accepted the idea and could see the benefit of knowing that projects had an expected and worst-case cost and that there were *unknowns* that could only be discovered en route.

## NAV in Norway

NAV[9] is the abbreviation for the Norwegian Labour and Welfare Administration. Having trained several of their people we have a good insight into their operation, and their successes are well-documented in the media. NAV is especially impressive as it is a public institution with the usual political and budgetary constraints. But in Norway, the public sector has to a great extent embraced everything agile and lean. Let us just mention two examples:

In 2020 during the Covid pandemic, Norway shut down like so many other countries. Parliament quickly passed a bill giving extraordinary compensation to organizations that had to send people home. The question then became how to get the money to the recipients. Teams at NAV are highly agile and self-managing, with a mandate to get things going.

---

9    NAV: https://www.nav.no/en/home

They quickly assembled a group of highly skilled people who conceived a way to do it. In three (3!) days they launched an online application for organizations to get their payment – very impressive. In Denmark, similar decisions were made in parliament, but nine months later, there was still no technical solution; I believe they were still debating who could make decisions as this crossed several organizational silos.

NAV has been extremely progressive in another area too. There are NAV offices all over Norway, some of which were part of an experiment allowing them to develop their own processes, abandon traditional budgeting, and decide their own way of spending money. They were no longer forced to use certain central functions such as purchasing. There were constraints; they still had to produce accounts and use some central systems, but the only thing that needed approval was an increase in headcount.

The result was reduced costs (an unverified number mentioned is 30%) and more engaged staff, with all its attendant benefits. Recently, after this first successful experiment, NAV extended the framework to all its offices. In a statement, it commented that *"if you actually trust people to be responsible, the vast majority will reciprocate by being just that, and cost and waste go down."*

## A final example

A production plant of an international company in the medical supply business implemented a set of project and product teams to serve specific customer classes. They largely left the rest of the organization as it had always been, not the least in order to fly under the radar so that they would not upset their American owners. They left the traditional line organization in place, but line managers were now not in charge of people's work in the teams; instead, they were the masters, the teachers of the domain, supporting and teaching team members. We had our share of cultural challenges as we worked to train a sister facility in Mexico, but due especially to a couple of very talented women from the Danish operation, the approach was accepted and an unprecedented level of psychological safety developed as people contributed and spoke up. This was a big step in Mexico, where bosses were normally really bosses.

The change was driven by the resident Danish plant manager together with some very effective staff members. It became very successful, so much so that the plant manager was promoted and successfully implemented similar structures and models in seven or eight other plants around the globe.

Locally the story did not end well. A crisis occurred and the central finance department cracked down on the operation, like a starcruiser in Star Wars, and demanded more control, better plans, and tighter budgets. A new plant manager was employed who was primarily loyal to the central bureaucracy, so sadly all agile activities and practices withered.

# Decoding the Organizational Impact

Introducing freedom to an organization is an experiment or a test of a hypothesis, and as such it needs monitoring, as all experiments do. Are we on the right path? Do we need to change course to achieve our objectives better? Are there any surprises, or things that did not work out the way we had expected?

## Looking through the Constitutional Lens

Whenever there are questions about monitoring development and finding the right metrics, the knee-jerk reaction is to think about money, sales, cost, and reporting hours – aka commercial metrics. They are all good and necessary, but not the only ones that matter, so we often use the term *"applying the Constitutional Lens"*.

Softer values such as engagement, psychological safety, freedom, etc. are inherently difficult to measure, like many things in the complex territory.

Whenever there are people involved, complexity fellows, they say one thing today and another tomorrow.

The Constitutional Lens consists of posing the following questions:

- What do I observe that relates to the freedom of people to act and decide?

  - Are we actively denouncing the use of power or fear against others?
  - Are there any cases of attempts to hoard power?
  - Are any lapses, cases of misuse of power, or fear captured and dealt with?

- What do I observe relating to kept commitments?

  - Are there people who do not seem to subscribe to this principle?
  - Are any lapses in honoring commitments captured and dealt with?

- What do I observe regarding willingness to speak up (psychological safety)?

  - Are people free to admit a mistake without fear?
  - Are people free to suggest better ways of working?
  - Is it easy for people to get help or decisions when they need it?

- What do I observe regarding the distribution of benefits?

  - Is the current benefits system causing unnecessary tension or dissatisfaction?
  - Are any misconducts in the appropriation of privileges captured and dealt with?

- What do I observe around using the Constitution – manifests and working agreements?

  - Is the Constitution still aligned with the circumstances that have unfolded?
  - Do we need amendments to the Constitution?

The Constitutional Lens gives you another set of observation points, improving the ability to make sense of the organization and its environment and act responsibly.

## Metrics Showing the Impact of Agile Lean Leadership

Questionnaires aiming to analyze *softer values* are notoriously unreliable, often failing to account for different cultures, generations, and educational profiles, which can skew the way questions are interpreted. They also fail to detect when people deliberately provide false answers that they think will benefit them, or they might suffer from cognitive biases seeing the facts through distorting glasses.

Finally, people cannot be bothered with questionnaires anymore, they only respond if they have extreme experiences. Furthermore, the bias of the expert who designed the questionnaire tends to contaminate the results, and therefore a lot of customer and employee research produces little real value.

Nevertheless, if a team accepts the questions as relevant and commits to using a questionnaire as a baseline for discussions about improvement it can be useful.

Another approach to gaining insight into people's perceptions and experiences is *Micro Narratives*[10] which in this context is a collection of small stories produced by individuals. Viewed together, the stories create a 'map' of the broader streams of observations and experiences. Micro Narratives also include a process of 'self-signification' or 'tagging' by respondents to help understand the significance of stories.

To get people started with their collection of micro-narratives we say: *"Tell us about an important experience relating to ..."* and add the subject we want to collect stories about – e.g. freedom. Then, based on some prede-

---

10  MicroNarratives: https://allgoodtales.com/micro-storytelling-useful/

termined criteria, we ask them to evaluate what it means to them, adding any significant criteria of their own.

The narrative approach to collecting insight into people's views is especially useful when dealing with customers because you often don't know them as well as you do your colleagues, and it is very hard to find a common understanding through a questionnaire.

## The Freedometer

We have developed the following *Freedometer*. It consists of a questionnaire to assess the freedom experienced by team members and a radar chart for visualizing the answers. With all the limitations of questionnaires, it can still be helpful to create a common understanding of the team status quo and trigger discussion of improvements.

1. I generally have the freedom to decide and act within my domain.
2. People with authority regularly encourage me to take initiative and decide.
3. In my Team people generally make decisions and announce intent.
4. My decisions are rarely unreasonably reversed by an authority.
5. I am often acknowledged for taking the initiative or making a decision.
6. I regularly show appreciation for other people's accomplishments.
7. When I observe something unusual, people normally listen to me.
8. In my Team, we aim to be transparent and seek common understanding.
9. In my Team, we generally have each other's back and strive to help.
10. I appreciate having the freedom to do the right thing and take responsibility.
11. I am willing to grant others the freedom to decide and act, even when I know better.

12. I do not normally fear my Team members' reactions to my acts and decisions.

| | Agile Lean Leadership Freedometer | | | | | |
|---|---|---|---|---|---|---|
| # | Question | 1 | 2 | 3 | 4 | 5 |
| 1 | I generally experience I have the freedom to decide and act within my domain | | | | | |
| 2 | People with authority regularly encourage me to take initiative and decide | | | | | |
| 3 | In my Team people generally make decisions and announce intent | | | | | |
| 4 | I normally do not experience my decisions unreasonably reversed by an authority | | | | | |
| 5 | I often receive acknowledgment for taking an initiative or making a decision | | | | | |
| 6 | I regularly show appreciation for other people's accomplishments | | | | | |
| 7 | When I observe something unusual, people normally listen to me | | | | | |
| 8 | In my Team, we try to create transparency and common understanding for each other | | | | | |
| 9 | In my Team, we generally have each other's back and strive to help | | | | | |
| 10 | I appreciate having the freedom to do the right thing and take responsibility for that | | | | | |
| 11 | I am willing to grant others the freedom to decide and act even when I know better | | | | | |
| 12 | I do not normally fear my Team members' reactions to my acts and decisions | | | | | |

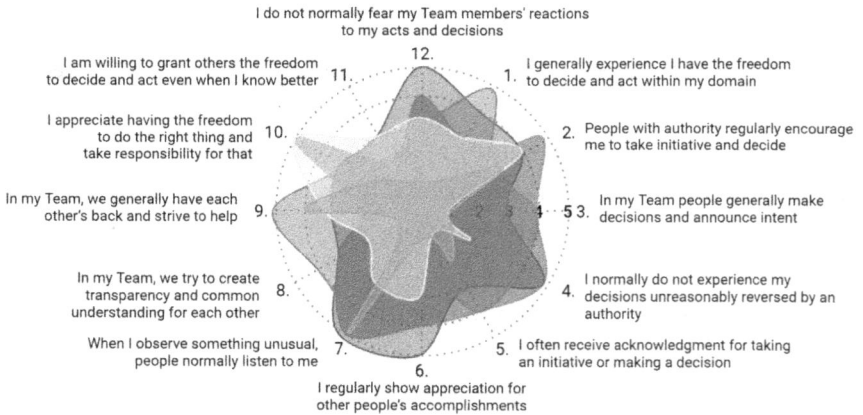

## Freedom Micro Narratives

Freedom and constitutional organization are not topics that people talk about much, so questionnaires may not be the best way to gain insight. Micro narratives may work better. We like to prompt people to tell a few small stories with questions like:

- When dealing with other people in the organization I have had these important experiences relating to my sense of freedom.

- Recently I have had some important encounters that influenced my sense of freedom in the organization.
- I tried to take some initiatives and the responses shaped my sense of freedom in the organization.

Then we ask them to evaluate their narratives in how they affected the following parameters on the following scale: '-2' – Very negatively, '-1'– Somewhat negatively, '0' – Neutral, '1' – Somewhat positively, and '2' – Very positively.

We have found the following parameters useful, but they are by no means the only ones possible.

- It increased my general sense of freedom to take initiative and make decisions.
- I experienced that people around me backed me up and encouraged me.
- I received recognition for my initiative from unexpected sources.
- I received practical help from this encounter.
- I felt that people wanted my opinion and listened.
- I saw that giving people space and freedom produced great results.
- I experienced joy in letting people decide and act outside their comfort zone.

We encourage people to define a couple of their own parameters if they have another important angle on the narrative. This produces a very rich dataset, which should not be interpreted mechanistically because context is important to understanding the answers. On the other hand, similar or regular fact-finding missions in a larger population may reveal trends and developments not necessarily visible to the naked eye.

*We found that there are a number of identifiable benefits for the organization itself:*

*– Better value to customers per unit of effort and cost.*

*– Dealing fairly with customers, staff, and suppliers.*

*– Investment in freedom and engagement of staff pays off.*

*We identified benefits for all stakeholders: Customers, staff, the broader community, and owners.*

*Although not accepted by everybody, there is an abundance of evidence in various case stories documenting the validity of an Agile and Lean Organization.*

*Changing an organization is an experiment, how can this be monitored and perhaps influence course changes?*

*– Using the Constitutional Lens on observations of the organization.*

*– Using the Freedometer.*

*– Using Micro Narratives.*

# Challenges, Risks and Countermeasures

*As seen in the previous sections, there needs to be a vision of how things could be better in organizations. We must understand the benefits that can be harvested if we are to persuade people to strive for an Agile Lean Organization.*

*The journey to agility and freedom is rife with challenges, risks, and distractions that can pull you off course. These need to be addressed and remedies offered.*

*It is a bit like Bunyan's Pilgrim's Progress where many obstacles are encountered on the road. No doubt, there will be mistakes, but we must commit to learning from them and then get on with doing the right thing.*

> *The more efficient you are at doing the wrong thing, the wronger you become. It is much better to do the right thing wronger than the wrong thing righter. If you do the right thing wrong and correct it, you get better.*
> *– Russell L. Ackoff*

# Can a Constitutional Organization be Sustainable?

Very often when a discussion about an alternative non-hierarchical organization starts, someone will immediately dismiss it with statements like: *"That is just not the way things are"*, *"there has to be a single person who can decide and be held accountable"* or *"that will never hold up over time."*

It is understandable, as most people, especially in larger organizations or public institutions, have never experienced the phenomenon of freedom. Until they were discovered in Australia in 1697, the phrase *black swan* stemmed from the belief that such creatures did not exist. Now the expression means an event that comes as a surprise but has a major effect. So for many people, an Agile Lean Organization is a black swan; we don't see many of them around. Indeed, such organizations are still quite rare, but they exist and are doing very well.

There are some valid arguments and difficulties that hamper the development of a Constitutional Organization, leading people to try to keep order by brute force and fear instead of by mutual consent. We will examine this right now for bigger organizations. Small, owner-managed organizations present a different case which we will tackle at the end of this section.

## The Iron Law of Oligarchy

The *Iron Law of Oligarchy* was introduced by German sociologist Robert Michels[1] in his 1911 book *Political Parties*. The *Iron Law* states that rule by an elite, or oligarchy, is inevitable in any democratic organization as part of its *tactical and technical necessities*. Bureaucratization and specialization are the driving processes of the iron law.

Michels was convinced that as an organization grows, no matter how democratic and self-governing it may have been at the start, it will even-

---

1   Robert Michels: https://en.wikipedia.org/wiki/Robert_Michels

tually and inevitably develop oligarchic or elite tendencies. So for Michels, true democracy is impossible, especially in large and complex organizations. The relatively high level of adaptability and maneuverability in a small-scale self-governing organization succumbs to what he calls *"social viscosity"* in a large-scale organization. Michels says that self-governing and representative decision-making is incompatible with large-scale organizations. If this is true, it is bad news for the creation of Liberating Organizations which then may be a lost cause.

Michels documented his findings from studying political parties and trade unions; he found quite a lot of evidence that those original democratic institutions drifted toward the rule of an elite. Slightly paraphrased Michels sums it up like this:

> *Any large organization has to create a bureaucracy to maintain decision-making capability as it becomes larger. Daily decisions that have to be made all the time cannot be made by large numbers of disorganized people. If an organization is to function effectively, centralization must happen and that means that power will end up in the hands of a few. Those few – the oligarchy or the elite – will then use all means necessary to preserve and further increase their power.*

Our first comment to this is that this brief statement rests on at least two presuppositions that we would like to challenge:

* Disorganized people probably cannot make effective decisions. However, lack of central control does not make them disorganized. We contend that small self-governing Circles (teams), organized around Value Streams with forums for decision-making and conflict resolution, is a viable alternative that robustly preserves people's freedom.
* Michels claimed that for leaders *"The desire to dominate … is universal. These are elementary psychological facts."* Once in power, people strive to preserve their power. This may be somewhat true, which is why we need a Constitution with checks and balances to which everybody has committed. We have to curb the human lust for dominance we so eas-

ily develop. It can be done, hard work maybe, but well worth the effort.

It is significant that in his later writings, Michels saw this rule as not only inevitable but also desirable. Michels relocated to Italy and joined the Fascist Party in 1924.

One of Michels' arguments was that central bureaucracies have to evolve and be granted authority to make and execute decisions, as not everybody can be involved in everything in large organizations. Since bureaucracy has the ability and opportunity to control access to information, power can be successfully hoarded and centralized. This often happens without much resistance from those it was supposed to serve, due to apathy and indifference. The elite will inevitably grow to dominate the organization's power structures and control their subordinates. This echoes the fundamental fascist idea that a strong man is needed to control the apathetic masses.

Not everybody agrees with Michels, who has been criticized from many sides. One important voice is that of Adolf Gasser[2], a Swiss sociologist and political scientist, who taught constitutional history at the University of Basel. He believed that although oligarchy was a tendency within organizations, it was not inevitable. Gasser argued that the *Iron Law of Oligarchy* overlooked the role of personal commitment and democratic processes in countering the concentration of power. He emphasized the importance of processes and agreements within organizations that could promote transparency, accountability, and mechanisms for grassroots involvement. He wrote the book *Communal Freedom as Salvation of Europe*[3] which we will return to later.

---

2   Adolf Gasser: https://en.wikipedia.org/wiki/Adolf_Gasser
3   *Gemeindefreiheit als Rettung Europas* published in 1943, a second edition in 1947

# The Issue of Bureaucracy

Michels' conclusions follow Max Weber's[4] theory of bureaucracy. Weber proposes that the most appropriate way to run an organization is to structure it into a rigid hierarchy of individuals governed by strict rules and regulations. Accordingly, such a bureaucracy should be characterized by specialization and division of labor, formal written records, competence as the basis for job appointments, standard operating procedures, and an impersonal bureaucracy.

The Frenchman Henri Fayol[5] (1841–1925) was a mining engineer who ended up being in charge of a large mining company. Over the years, he developed a set of 14 principles that he was convinced were foundational to running a large company. In 1916 he published *Administration Industrielle et Générale*, one of the first works with a clear theory for management and still one of the most elaborate. Although Fayol is not well known, his ideas about administration, line of command, etc. have had a profound influence over the last 100 years. His view of management as those who plan, delegate, monitor, and control work is still with us today in *Prince2*[6] for example.

There is the ever-present influence of F. Winslow Taylor and his *Scientific Management*, but he was never very specific about processes and bureaucracy, he pointed more to the importance of the expert and the ability to create a perfect system of stick and carrot that could compel workers to do what the experts wanted.

Later, the business schools would capitalize on these ideas and create a new breed of managers who are educated to manage everything without domain knowledge, focusing entirely on budgets, top-down plans, KPIs, and reporting.

---

4   Max Weber: https://en.wikipedia.org/wiki/Max_Weber
5   Henri Fayol: https://en.wikipedia.org/wiki/Henri_Fayol
6   Prince2: https://en.wikipedia.org/wiki/PRINCE2

In 1957, C. Northcote Parkinson[7] formulated *Parkinson's Law*[8] (in slightly humorous and sarcastic terms) about bureaucracy, which he claimed would always develop into a body trying to maximize its own size. Furthermore, since those in a bureaucracy are distanced from the real work of the organization, their lack of real understanding makes them tend to believe that everything is simple or obvious, when in fact much of it is complicated or complex.

According to Parkinson, bureaucrats tend to create work for each other, which they think is important but is in fact just waste. In the end, a mature bureaucracy will grow at an almost constant rate driven by people's desire to have subordinates. Parkinson argued that if you have a 6% annual growth rate in the administrative body, then eventually any company will die. The whole workforce will be part of the bureaucracy and none in the actual value stream. Bureaucracy, like an invasive species, requires careful control and pruning to prevent ecological harm.

## The Issue of Hierarchy

In the classic theories of management presented so far, the existence of a hierarchy of power is assumed. Here is how we normally understand hierarchy:

- Someone at the top, several layers of middle managers and workers at the bottom, where real work happens.
- Everyone in the hierarchy takes orders from above and is

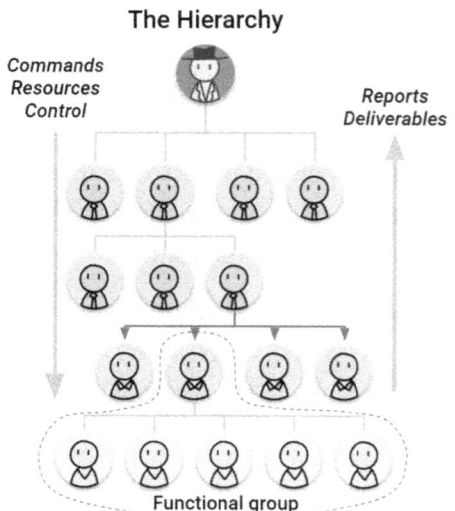

The Hierarchy

Commands
Resources
Control

Reports
Deliverables

Functional group

---

7   C. Northcote Parkinson: https://en.wikipedia.org/wiki/C._Northcote_Parkinson
8   Parkinson's original Law: https://www.economist.com/news/1955/11/19/parkinsons-law

accountable – in this context often seen as being liable for punishment in case of non-compliance.

- Everyone gives orders to those below:

  - Plan – what needs to be done and when.
  - Delegate – Decide who is going to do it.
  - Monitor – Supervise that the right process is followed.
  - Control – Verify and accept deliverables.

- People at the bottom of the hierarchy just do what they are told.
- People are typically assembled in functional groups where they report to a superior.
- Coordination between such groups is vertical. To address one in another group, you have to go up the hierarchy and get permission to go down another branch.

The hierarchy exists for compliance and predictability. The presence of the hierarchy creates a number of problems for freedom:

- W. Edwards Deming said: *"In the hierarchy, the boss is the customer, who takes care of the real customer?"*
- Since the hierarchy is inevitably based on the power of superiors over subordinates it works against self-management and representative decision-making.
- People often are afraid to make decisions for fear of a superior reversing them, they therefore tend to look for solutions that they think will align with the will of their superiors and not necessarily the best solution.
- Furthermore, it may attract the wrong people to the hierarchy, those who want power over other people more than the power to do something.
- It is hard to avoid a certain level of fear of the boss since he has the person's destiny in his hands.

- People's compensation is normally strongly connected to their position in the hierarchy. If going up the ladder is the only way to advance – then people will want to climb.

The classic management style is a kind of brand or ingrained worldview that most executives and managers subscribe to and identify with. Bob Emiliani[9] has written about this in one of his membership-only blog posts. Therefore it takes great effort to even discuss possible better ways. Read a more thorough discussion of the impact of the hierarchy in *Appendix C - Neo-Taylorism and the Fatal Attraction to Hierarchy*.

# General Countermeasures

It is particularly relevant that the theories of efficient management and bureaucracy were developed from the late 19th century until World War I which was a period of immense optimism and confidence in man's ability to understand and control everything. The admiration for science and technology was almost absolute, so Taylor's term *Scientific Management* was clever marketing that resonated well.

However, by the time Michels' theories came to light after World War I, that optimism was completely shattered and he descended into disappointment and cynicism.

This is a recurring pattern. In good times we drift toward naive optimism believing in human goodness, and the ability to develop perfect systems that secure eternal prosperity. But in times of crisis, the pendulum swings to the side of disillusion and cynicism, ending in the call for a strong leader, the Imperial CEO, to take charge and create order.

We tend to alternate between two forms of alienating autocracy: first, the systems and bureaucracies inspired by Weber, Fayol, and Taylor, and second, the heroic, imperial strong leader of Hobbes' and Michels' liking. The evidence seems to indicate that people subscribe to Theory X (as pre-

---

9    Bob Emiliani: https://bobemiliani.com/blog-posts/

sented in Chapter 2), and swing between believing that the expert can create a perfect system or that brute force is the only way forward.

The *Iron Law* and other theories mentioned above should make us acutely aware of the involuntary drift toward oligarchy and bureaucracy if it is not being confronted.

## Protecting the Constitution

Switzerland has a unique democratic constitution[10], its preamble goes like this:

> *In the name of Almighty God! The Swiss People and the Cantons, mindful of their responsibility towards creation, resolved to renew their alliance so as to strengthen liberty, democracy, independence, and peace in a spirit of solidarity and openness toward the world, determined to live together with mutual consideration and respect for their diversity, conscious of their common achievements and their responsibility towards future generations, and in the knowledge that only those who use their freedom remain free, and that the strength of a people is measured by the well-being of its weakest members.*

This is a good start for an organization's Manifest. In his book *Communal Freedom as Salvation of Europe*, Adolf Gasser explained how democratic institutions can survive, using the Swiss model of society as inspiration. He described the requirements – slightly paraphrased:

* They have to be built up from bottom to top by free people who have the power to defend themselves.
* Free people join or form independent local communities which include financial independence, and are free to determine their own rules.
* Local communities combine into a higher unit e.g. a canton or a value stream.
* There is no hierarchical bureaucracy.

---

10  Swiss Constitution: https://www.fedlex.admin.ch/eli/cc/1999/404/en

- There is competition between local communities e.g. for services delivered or compensation.

It is no surprise that Gasser took the Swiss model of society as an inspiration. Our proposal for structures and processes in Agile Lean Leadership is a re-interpretation of Gasser's ideas. So it is time to propose the first countermeasures based on these ideas:

> *#1. Let the self-governing unit have dominion over hiring, firing, and compensation, and let them decide how to spend their money and the processes they follow. All of course within reasonable global constraints.*

From this follows some practical measures to secure the governing principles

> *#2. Follow the way of the Constitutionalists[11], providing people with ample freedom under the rule of law (the Constitution) but with constraints, checks, and balances that prevent the strong from grabbing power and preventing bureaucracy from spreading.*

This Constitution, the set of working agreements in the organization, has to be negotiated and consented to. Commitments have to be made and Operations Owners (OOs) have to facilitate and enforce them – much like the Law-speaker (Lagman) of old Nordic þings did. Checks and balances always have to be upheld. The OO role is special and crucial to Constitutional Organizations – as we will see later – always focusing on upholding freedom and commitment to the Constitution among other things. As we look at some areas in more detail the OO will be the primary agent for countering challenges and risks.

---

11  Constitutionalists with reference to Mathew Stewart and his combination of Theory Y and Theory U, read more in Chapter 2.

## Protecting and Amplifying Freedom

Individual freedom of choice is the foundation for everything we advocate. Small agreements or protocols about how team members and teams interact help keep it in everyone's mind.

Occasionally, there will be those who try to take control and assume power; sometimes by macho-style brute force and sometimes in more subtle, passive-aggressive[12] ways, like disapproval or exclusion. It is in a sense the bullying of the weaker individuals. It is important that everybody is aware of this and steps up and defends the victim, it is especially the responsibility of the OO.

> *#3. Use non-threatening intervention, e.g. "I wonder why you say this, do that, or do not engage in conversation."*

This invites the person to modify or even retract some of what was said or done. Sometimes it even dissolves the matter as the person actually did not mean it, they were just clumsy and insensitive.

> *#4. Broaden the scope or appeal, and say something like: "Apparently, we do not share the same view of this, perhaps we should take it up a notch, and see what is best for us all."*

Agile Lean Leadership has Resolution Circles, where contentious issues can be discussed and resolved; traditional organizations have a line of command and other structures for this.

---

12  Passive Aggressive Behavior: https://en.wikipedia.org/wiki/Passive-aggressive_behavior

> *#5. Insist on transparency. "Let us discuss this in the Team" or "Let us involve our OO, he might have a good idea." Show your team what goes on: "Hey, I just received this email, I thought you should know."*

Those with ulterior motives will often single out people and try to intimidate them or play the game of *divide and conquer*, perhaps even introducing fear into the relationship between colleagues. Teams provide some protection against this, it is not about me, it is about the team. When outsiders know there is transparency in the Team, it dampens the consequences of such attempts. Always be very suspicious if someone tells you that they cannot talk about this or that, there are cases where matters cannot be made public, but they are rare when there is a culture of trust.

Freedom must be promoted. Those who have lived without it may find it hard to change their habits. If we want people to use their freedom to participate in decision-making and to take responsibility, we must show them the attractiveness of freedom, and the potential of a more fulfilled life. And we have to help them grow in three key areas (the three Cs):

1. **Competency**. Help them develop the skills to do the job. *"You do not want incompetent people walking around pushing buttons on a nuclear submarine"* –David Marquet.
2. **Clarity**. Help them develop a clear vision of where they are heading, so they can make the many small, daily decisions that lead in the right direction.
3. **Character**. Help them develop integrity, humility, and willingness to serve so that they can be trusted to make good decisions that influence others or are made on their behalf.

> *#6. Listen to people's need to gain new competencies and challenge them if they don't seem to have an ambition. Also discuss it in the Team setting, "What does the Team need to get better?"*

People normally want to improve, and it increases life quality and energy to experience improvement, the importance of facilitating this is hard to overestimate.

> *#7. Show and discuss objectives and goals in the Team – radical trans-parency, to build a common mental model.*

A cornerstone of Intrinsic Motivation is a clear and commonly accepted goal, amplifying this should be fundamental to everybody involved and it will help them to stay on track.

> *#8. Discuss and agree on common values, and help each other live up to those values. Praise those who exemplify behavior that strengthens those values.*

Highly competent people who have clarity and character are not easily intimidated and can live effectively in freedom. It is worth noting that any system of self-government requires an educated population in all these three areas. So it is not enough just to have the right system or process, this is an unfortunate Tayloristic misunderstanding.

> *#9. At each step ask yourself: "How can I present this information or knowledge in the most easily accessible form for my Team Members?", "How can I respond in the most effective way to my Team members' need for knowledge or feedback?" Furthermore: "How can I extend this to other Circles collaborated with?"*

Another angle on amplifying freedom is to make information as accessible as possible. A special strategy is called *Supporting each others' OODA loop*. In a collaborative environment (as opposed to a competitive or confrontational one) it is not about upsetting each others' OODA loop but rather optimizing it so that others can effectively Observe, Orient, Decide, and Act.

> *#10. When you are about to start or execute something, tell those around you: "I intend to do so-and-so now, what do you think?"*

Another way to amplify freedom is by communicating intent. This is something that David Marquet has talked about a lot. Communicating your intent to others invites them to ask questions, propose a better way, or even correct you, thus building their confidence and engagement in the process. It is an easily agreed, but powerful behavioral pattern that fuses a Team together, maximizing common understanding and strengthening each person's OODA loop.

> *#11. How can I decide matters in a way that preserves the choices for me and my Team as circumstances unfold?*

Finally, when making decisions, look to keep your options open until the last responsible moment. None of us know what tomorrow will bring; options are good.

## Dampening Bureaucracy and Centralism

If we do not constantly pour energy into dampening it, there is a natural mud-slide towards bureaucracy and centralism. It is a battle that takes place almost every day, and everyone is involved in this battle.

Both tendencies exemplify cognitive biases that make us comfortable with rules and rigid constraints that mistakenly push matters into the Obvious/Clear domain. Because the things you don't know much about often appear simple and obvious, many think the work of others can be managed with checklists and best practices.

> *#12. Never let anyone have the authority to introduce unilateral rules and regulations for others, especially not legal, finance, accounting, HR, and purchasing. Such rules and regulations have to be assessed for what is good for everyone and for the whole system.*

If certain areas of work really are in the Obvious and Clear domain, it is ok to define best practices, but frequently it is an oversimplification made by people not familiar with all the details.

> *#13. Whenever the creation of a central authority is proposed, always challenge the assumptions for its need, and ask why Teams cannot decide alone, bilaterally, or collectively for themselves.*

In Agile Lean Leadership we would consider placing such an authority in an appropriate Secondary Circle if it cannot be left to the individual Teams or bilateral agreements.

> *#14. Whenever there is a call for employing people who are not part of the Value Stream, always ask "Why can't this competence be within the Value Stream?"*

To uphold the vision of putting customers first, Agile Lean Leadership aims to include as many as possible in the Value Stream (Primary Circles), but perhaps this new authority and skill is better developed in a Secondary Circle.

> *#15. At regular intervals perform a sanity check of existing rules, regulations, reports, and other existing artifacts. Eliminate those that do not provide value.*

Rules and regulations are much easier to introduce than to remove, and once in place, someone has a job to enforce them and will resist their removal. Weeding out unnecessary administration is key to removing waste in Lean.

## Dampening the Effects of Hierarchy

Agile Lean Leadership uses representative, delegated decision-making in place of a hierarchy. There can be some resistance in existing organizations, so piecemeal, or partial implementations are common. In such cases, it may be necessary to dampen the negative effects of the remaining hierarchy.

> *#16. Existing management must actively decide to grant the necessary freedom and independence to Agile Lean Leadership initiatives, commit to it publicly, and be its sponsor.*

This creates a *Free Zone* where different rules apply, which should be respected and promoted positively by all. A Manifest for the *Free Zone* must be written by the zone's members, negotiated with, and approved by the existing management, which will withdraw and take no part in the daily operation of the zone.

> *#17. Compensation and other privileges must never be linked to a position of power over others as this creates a fatally powerful attractor for the dark side of human nature.*

As long as status, money, and power are tied to a position in the hierarchy this extrinsic motivation will take precedence over any intrinsic motivation of working for the common good and demonstrating a serving attitude.

*#18. To live and work in a 'free' system, people must commit to and accept responsibility. They must constantly support, maintain, and develop the practice of freedom.*

When liberated from autocratic rule, some things change immediately in the euphoria of the moment, but other things take a long time to settle, so patience is a virtue. The process is often easier with new management.

## Dampening Apathy

The threats to freedom do not only come from the outside. Participating in decision-making can be hard work, and it can feel easier to just go with a knee-jerk reaction and let others decide.

*#19. Whenever Team members shy away from taking decisions and responsibility, know that abdicating the freedom to decide reduces the ability to do so next time.*

There has to be psychological safety so that people can speak up or take action, however that does not mean staying in their comfort zone, people should not avoid participating in difficult issues to gain a brief moment of comfort while sacrificing the long-term freedom to engage.

*#20. When team members claim to be victims or to have no authority to decide anything, remind them of what they can do without asking anybody or getting new resources. Choose to act.*

There is always something that can be done now, for example, read about Liberating Structures[13]. Freedom is often reclaimed inch by inch. It is not helpful to retreat into a victim role.

---

13 15% Solutions: https://www.liberatingstructures.com/7-15-solutions/

> *#21. Whenever team members edge away from doing anything and slip into apathy, remind them that they have consented to the fundamental principle of honoring their commitments.*

It takes five positive experiences to balance a negative one, so defaulting on commitments has dire and costly consequences for trust in the organization.

> *#22. Whenever possible, celebrate small victories and acknowledge the freedom to decide and act. Ask what can be learned from those situations that did not yield the desired result.*

When people act and are reinforced by their peers, they gain the confidence to do it again at the next opportunity. Any mistake or unsuccessful experiment should be viewed primarily as a learning opportunity.

## Dampening the Quest for Power

Apart from pathological cases, people's quest for power seems to stem from a lack of identity, rooted in something bigger than themselves. Some build their identity on their accomplishments, people's approval, money, good looks, celebrity status, and similar extrinsic things. A few have an identity rooted in something truly bigger than themselves, often taking the form of a religious conviction.

Unfortunately, identity can also be founded on the ability and opportunity to dominate other people. It is not particularly attractive, but there is evidence that lack of identity and low self-esteem are traits shared by bullies, dominant team members, imperial CEOs, and autocratic leaders of nations. They only feel they matter when people squirm and jump at their command.

> *#23. Try to uncover people's real positive objectives and goals and work toward creating a path for them to accomplish them.*

The best strategy is to try and help such people to find an alternative attractive object or positive accomplishment to build their self-esteem on, this can divert their desires to a more positive trail. Normally unhelpful behavior cannot just be stopped, it has to be replaced by something else, something positive.

> *#24. The Manifest should include the notion that. "Nobody can use force against another person to make them do things."*

Advance agreement by mutual consent has to be reached about what this means and how it is enforced.

> *#25. Whenever domination rears its head, it must be confronted, politely but firmly. Try saying "I wonder why you are trying to force this person to do this or that?"*

Confrontation and enforcement are necessary, it is part of the checks and balances in the organization. The Operations Owner (OO) has a special responsibility in this – politely but firmly.

# The Challenges Relating to Stakeholders

Now, let's take a quick tour of the challenges for an Agile Lean Leadership or Constitutional Organization starting with those relating to the organization's stakeholders.

# Challenges Relating to the Community

### Regulation and central planning

In our part of the world (Scandinavia), regulation is a favorite occupation for politicians. It is a deeply held (naïve Neo-Taylorist) prejudice that everything can be planned upfront, programmed, and regulated. In recent years the European Union has excelled at issuing regulations even farther from reality than we were used to.

Small companies and startups are often deeply frustrated and feel they have to operate in legal gray zones, under the radar. The regulations are so complex that many companies are not sure if they are following them or not. Only large companies can afford the legal staff to ensure compliance.

A recent regulation commands everyone to make a detailed account of their work time, preventing flexible work arrangements, and obliging some small businesses to avoid having employees. How this can work in today's hybrid work environment is hard to see.

Overregulation curtails freedom and suppresses entrepreneurial activity. It moves organizations into the *Zone of Complacency*, with potential catastrophic failure during times of rapid change.

### Unions and the Welfare State

Both of these institutions were created to fulfill a noble purpose, and have largely done so. But, over time, bureaucracy has grown wild, stifling freedom. Unions are very often against the flexible agreements that would benefit their members as their power base is strict rules of employment and compensation. The welfare state with its high taxes also leads people to speculate more in getting public grants and tax evasion than on innovating and serving customers.

### The Educational System

Sometimes educational institutions lead the development of knowledge and innovation, and sometimes they are woefully behind. A familiar example is the backward thinking that business schools impart to their un-suspecting students. Both in management and economic theory, the knowledge that graduates depart with is seriously flawed. Management training is mostly a revamped Neo-Taylorism with additional manipula-tive techniques to make staff believe that they matter. In economics, most of the principles taught are outdated, oversimplified, or just wrong. In the 1990s Daniel Kahneman and Amos Tverski[14] proved that the model of hu-man behavior used in economic theory was often oversimplified and plain wrong; he coined the hypothetical creature an *Econ* as opposed to a *Human*. Kahneman got the Nobel Memorial Prize in Economic Science in 2002 for this contribution. With the notable exception of the progressive Oslo BI, the old false principles are still taught and used by most educa-tional institutions and policymakers.

## Challenges Relating to Customers

Customers who are not familiar with the ideas of nonhierarchical organi-zations can find it hard to understand and act in this environment.

### Expecting Traditional Supplier Relationships

Traditionally, customer interaction has been governed by the protocols of expected behavior, negotiation style, and a certain power game, reflected in the phrases *bargaining power*, and *where there are winners there must be losers*. This results in adversarial customer relationships, with each side trying to get the upper hand or exploit the other. This should not be so with a Constitutional Organization's relationships with its customers or suppliers. Of course, each party has to look after its own interests, but they should balance this respectfully in order to create value for all.

Some customers may even oppose the flatter structure of a Constitutional Organization, they expect to talk to people of equal rank and status and regard it as an insult to be engaged by someone of perceived lower status.

---

14  Amos Tverski: https://en.wikipedia.org/wiki/Amos_Tversky

### Unwillingness to Engage in Collaboration

For anything but the simplest items, delivering products and services to customers requires collaboration, dialog, and a common understanding. The aim of a Constitutional Organization is to understand customers better and discover their needs, but this may seem like getting too close for some. In our experience, it is not that customers don't want a closer relationship, it is just very unusual, so a little finesse, sensitivity, and patience are recommended when explaining the approach.

# Challenges Relating to Owners and Board Members

In smaller owner-led companies the owner's presence is clear, but in larger organizations, a non-executive board of directors represents the real owners. The granting of freedom to those in the organization has to be approved, not opposed by the owners or the board. Executives need to be confident that they will not be overridden or ousted when the first crisis hits and the owners have to trust the people in the organization; if they don't, their only option is to enforce control.

The whole organization must work to create trust with its owners; this seems self-evident, but often the relationship is marked by suspicion of exploitation on both sides. Building trust starts with mutual respect, radical transparency, and honoring your commitments.

Unfortunately, both parties have cognitive biases based on stereotypes. It is easy to think of the owners as exploitative and the owners think of their staff as just out to get an easy paycheck. Not that these views are always unjustified on either side. However, perpetuating a confrontational culture gets organizations nowhere. People in an organization should be aware of the owners' fear of losing control and being taken advantage of and must acknowledge that the owners' detachment from daily operations obscures their view of the details and consequences of their decisions. Therefore perpetual open and honest communication is critical to the development of bi-directional trust.

A special challenge exists when owners are disengaged. Normally there is little that can be done apart from creating radical transparency and inviting them to participate in events such as reviews or collaboration sessions. Otherwise, the best remedy is adhering to a clear, simple Manifest for the organization, an agreement stating how communication with the owners happens.

## Challenges Relating to those Working in the Organization

Now let us take a look at the challenges people inside the organization can present on the road to freedom. Again it is mostly about trust and being willing to serve.

### Executives

Executives are those employed by the owners as stewards of the organization, and remember there is a hierarchy here too. The owners have the right of ownership and have given the executives a revocable mandate, responsibility, and power for achieving and sustaining the organization's vision and reaching its objectives. Executives may be afraid of falling out of favor with the owners, but commitment to long-term cooperation and the experience of solving difficult challenges together builds trust and reduces fear and suspicion on both sides.

Everybody in the organization should be mindful of this dynamic. Executives must have timely and reliable information, and they must be able to rely on the commitment of their staff.

However, another set of challenges for executives revolves around the perception of status. Any change in management principles may seem to harm the executives' status among their peers. An effective countermeasure is to have a value proposition that demonstrates the benefits of the new leadership structure and that it represents a rational and forward-thinking road to take.

## Middle Management

Middle managers are different from executives because their jobs are likely to change the most when moving to a Constitutional Organization. It is no longer about *Plan-Delegate- Monitor-Control,* but about fulfilling new roles as Strategy Owners, Operations Owners, or experts in certain fields. It is also about showing respect and a serving attitude more than displaying power. It is participating in effective teamwork, radical transparency building, and representative decision-making.

Understandably, anxiety or outright fear may exist within this group which can easily feel victimized in such a transformation. Others get what they want, but middle managers seem to lose something. They must be included through invitation and given the freedom and psychological safety to choose how to participate.

Deep inside most of us resides the idea that status comes with rank and position, but in a Constitutional Organization, it is different because status stems from being effective and respected in a new role. Often people cling to their existing titles and are prone to experience a loss in status following any change. Demonstrating appreciation of these new roles is absolutely central to getting traditional middle managers on board on the road to freedom.

The best way to get middle management on board is to have a crystal clear value proposition for the new roles that are acknowledged across the organization. It has to cover compensation, career path, and the basis for status and appreciation.

There will be those who have a hard time making the switch; fear of a loss is a much stronger emotional driver than looking forward to a gain; patience and consistent communication are crucial. Unfortunately, *thoroughbred* bureaucrats have no role in a Constitutional Organization and need to be repurposed if possible.

## Bureaucracies

Every organization needs some structures in place and people to maintain and ensure compliance – some bureaucracy. However, it is an invasive species that can easily spread across the whole organizational garden. People who just administer rules and regulations are inclined to believe that they are the most important in the organization, even when far removed from the real value stream. In Cynefin terms, this constrains the operation within the Obvious/Clear domain, even approaching the Zone of Complacency. Such organizations are very brittle and can break catastrophically in a crisis. Bureaucracies also tend to become more granular over time, stifling initiative and engagement. Here are the areas of the most heavy-handed bureaucracy:

- **Accounting and Budgeting**. There are countless examples of incredibly detailed forms, accounts, and reports that nobody really uses. Budgeting is often the biggest challenge to reasonable behavior, it is a corporate raindance full of rituals and very little practical positive impact, but everybody believes it is important. Detailed budgeting by oversimplified metrics and reliance on past performance inevitably leads to suboptimization.
- **Time Tracking**. This practice is prevalent across the board, but while it may have some value in predictable factory work, its utility in the complex domain is zero or even negative. Asking people to account in detail how they spend time may be impossible in the complex domain, it causes irritation and can compel people to game the system resulting in the collection of useless data. There are of course situations where services are sold to customers by the hour, and accountability is needed there.
- **HR**. The employment of people – especially in larger or public organizations – is often handed over to *expert* recruiters, who, detached from the action in the Circles and often with little domain knowledge, decide who to employ, promote, dismiss, and even how teams should be

composed. This prevents sustainable self-governing and dramatically reduces engagement.

- **Legal**. Sometimes the legal department has to review even the smallest of matters for fear of non-compliance. This introduces enormous delays and often leads people to fly under the radar using non-discoverable and non-transparent ways to get things done. During our interview process, a number of people declined to participate due to fear of non-conformance with the legal department.
- **Purchasing**. In much the same way, the purchasing department is often a significant obstacle to collaboration and progress. Furthermore, being removed from where the work is done, they do not suffer the direct consequences of the adversarial supplier relationships that they often create.

People who are subjected to unreasonable control and reporting demands will be frustrated and disengaged. If you look up the word frustration in the dictionary it says: *"When people are hindered in their meaningful and purposeful activities"*. So be prepared to do a bit of gardening and weeding out of wild shoots of bureaucracy here.

*A bureaucrat is one who has the power to say "no" but none to say "yes."*
*– Russell L. Ackoff*

### People Delivering Products and Services

The people delivering value in the value streams and those supporting them, are normally very positive about changing to a Constitutional Organization. Like most citizens in the world who express a desire to live in free societies, and be able to influence their own lives, so do people in organizations. This requires that they subscribe to the organization's values and goals and are willing to participate and engage openly. Occasionally, some challenges are encountered:

- People don't trust change initiatives. Many have been burned repeatedly or are numbed by frequent forward and backward changes and reorganizations. People often suspect that the initiative is just another way of squeezing more work out of them. However, a serious invitation to participate can persuade them otherwise.

- Over the years skilled experts have developed and ruled little kingdoms that are hard for them to give up. Finding a way to let their passion flourish in the new setup, can produce impressive results.
- The quest for work/life balance is rightly a hot topic, not least because the term positions work and life in opposition. Some are unwilling to commit to work if it affects their ability to prioritize their private lives. But freedom is not just one-sided, it comes with taking responsibility, and there has to be flexibility on both sides.
- To garner support and commitment for change there has to be time to concentrate, but people are often so overloaded with requests and commitments they have no free mental bandwidth or time to focus on getting a new structure to work.
- People may be afraid of participating, speaking up, or taking initiative, due to previous negative experiences. Psychological safety must be in place before anything can be expected to work.
- Cultural and generational differences can make forming teams based on trust and commitment an uphill battle. As much as we stress the benefit of diversity and perspective on complex problems, they can be difficult to overcome. There has to be enough overlap of values and common goals that people can communicate, and develop trust, forming teams with this sufficient overlap by choice – not coercion.

# Common Pitfalls

## Starting without Proper Commitment

In all the excitement over freedom, self-governing, engagement, etc. a common mistake is to start implementing changes only to find out that some authority has halted or sidetracked the effort. It can be tricky to find a balance. On the one hand, you need a sponsor in high places so the initiative doesn't get flattened, but you also want to start doing something beneficial right now.

Our best advice is to identify the boundaries of your mandate and move a little outside of it to establish a slightly more free zone. If you demonstrate success, you will have the opportunity to expand the boundary and attract more sponsorships over time. It is more evolution than revolution, but it helps every one to get started and see results without slipping into apathy or resignation.

# Unclear Career Paths

We have touched on this issue before, but it deserves special treatment because it can be a real obstacle for many. If the hierarchy is replaced by an agile, lean, and constitutional organization, those with titles like *Manager of...*, *Head of...*, *Chief of...*, or *XYZ Expert* face serious changes in the way they are perceived by themselves and by others. We were probably naïve in believing that the benefits of a Constitutional Organization are self-evident and that any reasonable person would immediately accept this value proposition, but this is clearly not the case.

If moving up the hierarchy is no longer an option, people need an alternative growth path with ways to develop their skills, financial opportunities, and sense of their own status and worth. We all want to be respected so it has to be clear that these opportunities exist, albeit slightly different in form. People have to know that they are not falling behind in income or they will naturally resist any change to a constitutional model.

This has to be stated clearly in the manifest and other artifacts, but to develop and maintain trust it also has to be practiced and communicated daily.

### The Roles and Mandates are not Clear

The new roles and mandates in a Constitutional Organization are geared toward responsibility, not power, and are therefore different than in a traditional organization. Starting on the road to freedom without a solid common understanding of what these are can create tension and disappointment.

A common mental model and language are necessary and can be developed over time as people develop their roles and relate them to others through dialogue, illustration, and real action.

### Overspecialization

Neo-Taylorists focus on the expert and specialization almost exclusively, which is not helpful when the work is mostly in the complex domain. Overspecialization often comes at the cost of less communication.

## People's Positions are Dictated

A final challenge is when, without dialogue or invitation, people are simply told: "*Now you have this or that role*". In a Constitutional Organization, assignments emerge from engagement and commitment by mutual consent, not as residuals from the power structure.

When creating new organizational structures, try to have people volunteer, perhaps for a couple of things, negotiate, and see if you can solve the puzzle collaboratively. Volunteers may not get 100% of what they want but will normally compromise to create space for others and to get the job done. This creates a commitment that can be trusted and contrasts with those pushed into roles who may pay lip service to the commitments until they find an exit.

Of course, life is organic, and people and circumstances change, so the exercise of setting teams and choosing roles has to be repeated from time to time to allow people to adapt and realign with the current situation – that is resilience and sustainability in action.

# Sustaining Freedom in Crisis

Some give up the quest for organizational freedom, often due to a crisis of some sort. This is how a crisis often unfolds:

1. A large project looks like failing, or a large customer has been lost.
2. The potential financial consequences become clear.
3. Executives, especially those with financial responsibility, declare a state of emergency.
4. They demand order, more control, more reporting, and tighter budgets.
5. If the crisis is resolved positively, it is interpreted as evidence that more control was what was needed and that people cannot handle freedom responsibly.
6. If the crisis does not end well, usually heads will roll and the interpretation is that enforcement of control was too late, too weak, or the problem was the result of some scapegoat's wrongdoing.
7. In either case confidence in freedom is lost, and people will again be subdued into compliance.

There is no denying that crises – sudden drops into chaos – do happen and may require extraordinary measures which may be hard and prone to mistakes. But the knee-jerk reactions described above are expressions of the cognitive bias that failures can only be the result of someone who did not do what they were told or were slacking off. But crises do not need to have a single root cause, random things happen, circumstances change and there may be other unexpected external factors[15] that could never have been planned for.

Any functioning organization will have business continuity planning and risk management processes in place. This should cover natural disasters, supply chain disruption, unplanned factory closure, loss of key customers, etc. Those contingencies should still be in place and activated, and the issue seen as what it is – a crisis, not a failure of the organizational model.

---

15 The Covid pandemic in 2020 and 2021 and the Russian war on Ukraine starting in 2022 represent such unplannable *Black Swan* events.

So what can we do? Transient Circles as described in Chapter 3 are like a temporary task force brought together in a crisis with the power and skills to stabilize the situation before returning to their previous roles, without creating a new power structure.

During a crisis, it may be absolutely necessary just to do what the smartest people say. But when a near-normal situation is restored, we give them due credit, dissolve the transient mandate, and return to a – perhaps new – normal state.

Transient Circle members must be identified and trained as the *Crew*, just as the first officer can take over from the pilot and fly the plane if needed. The organization must trust these people to have exceptional intuitive skills in order to grant them this extraordinary, but transient mandate.

If this practice is written in the constitution, understood, and accepted, it will prevent sliding into an oligarchy. Such organizational behavior has to be learned and practiced, but it will always be necessary to have contingency plans in case of emergencies. Remember:

- They must have Competency – knowing what to do.
- They must have Clarity – knowing where to go.
- They must have Character – be able to decide for the common good.

We consider this the best practice for crisis management without lapsing into permanent command and control.

When the crisis is due to unacceptable mistakes or agreement violations, a Transient Circle composed of Operations Owners may be formed to deal with the threat. It may result in people getting reassigned, retrained, or even dismissed, depending on circumstances. We will address how to do this later.

# Looking back at the Risks and Countermeasures

We found that many things can challenge the development of freedom in an organization, and many do not believe that is possible at all. We found an abundance of recommendations for countermeasures and got some great input from the people – the witnesses – we interviewed.

It may seem that the challenges and risks are much more abundant than the potential benefits, but that is more the nature of our human observation biases. Negatives are easily spotted in detail, positives seem more fluffy and less measurable. Negative experiences take up more space mentally than positive ones, it takes roughly 5 positive experiences to balance one negative one.

*We found voices that claim freedom in organizations is impossible in the long term.*

*But also voices that describe how it can be sustained.*

*There are clear obstacles in most organizations, most notably:*
*– The current hierarchy.*
*– The current bureaucracy.*

*Threats to freedom in general need to be countered in many ways.*
*– The good news is that there are many avenues to be pursued*

*Challenges related to the different stakeholders were found.*

*A few common mistakes were also seen.*

*Finally, the challenges of crisis handling were explored and a framework solution was presented.*

# Growing a Liberating Organization

*After a deep dive to uncover plausible benefits, challenges, and pit-falls, we now have a practical framework – a blueprint – for a Constitutional Organization that we believe will be liberating for all those involved. The next step is to look in detail at how this blueprint can be implemented. It cannot be forced and like a garden must grow organically. The soil has to be prepared, seeds sown, and nourishment provided. There will be a harvest in the end, but some occasional weeding may be necessary. General Stanley McChrystal is a great inspiration:*

> *... The idea of a chess master no longer works ... I backed into a different model ... of leading like a gardener. The gardener creates the environment, the ecosystem ... that allows the plants to do what they do, and do it very, very well.* — *Stanley McChrystal, video 2015*[1]

---

1 Stanley McChrystal, YouTube 2015. https://youtu.be/yHR1kK1_cE0

*The role of leadership is to prepare, seed, feed, weed, and finally harvest. Captain David Marquet, another military leader, said his job was to make it possible for everybody to be a leader in their respective circumstances.*

> *The leader-leader structure is fundamentally different from the leader-follower structure. At its core is the belief that we can all be leaders and, in fact, it's best when we all are leaders. Leadership is not some mystical quality that some possess and others do not. As humans, we all have what it takes, and we all need to use our leadership.* — L. David Marquet

Developing a garden in rough terrain requires preparation, a vision for the grand future, and the willingness and ability to get started. After the first steps, something will probably be different than originally thought, and after due assessment will require a course correction. Kathie Danemiller[2] popularized the following formula for change:

$$"D \times V \times F > R"$$

Where **D** is Dissatisfaction with the present, the **V** is the Vision for a better future and the **F** (First Steps) is about the *willingness* and *ability* to take First steps. These three factors have to be multiplied and the resulting number has to be greater than **R** – the Resistance in the organization for whatever reason towards this particular change. Although this formula is a crude approximation it is nevertheless helpful as a mental model for starting the journey towards freedom in an organization.

We have presented convincing evidence of dissatisfaction with the present, a vision for a better future, and some potential challenges and pitfalls contributing to resistance to the change. Now we must raise the **F** factor to achieve success.

How can we encourage a willingness to work on promoting freedom? The benefits have been documented, but their perception by the people in the organization must be strong enough to gain critical mass. There has to be an emotional attachment to see it through to fruition.

*In the end, the human heart does what it wants.*    – *Timothy Keller*

This chapter is about the practical action that can be taken. Our goal is to present plausible evidence for strategies and straightforward actions that enable the first steps toward establishing and sustaining freedom.

*Sometimes, if you want people to change their behavior, you have got to give them the tools that allow them to do so!*    – *Dave Snowden*

---

2   Kathie Danemiller: https://en.wikipedia.org/wiki/Formula_for_change

Professor Isac Getz[3] puts it slightly differently, a bit paraphrased from a 2011 article[4]:

> *People will not change based on knowledge alone, they need to undergo two fundamental emotional experiences: exasperation[5] with the present state and admiration of the better alternative. Exasperation isn't criticism. It's a call for action, not for analysis. Similarly, admiration isn't appreciation. A person may appreciate others, yet not be willing to join them. But a person admiring others mostly wants to act to become part of them.*

We start by presenting a radical path – a *High Road* – to freedom in the organization. It describes a leadership style based on the constitutional model that can apply to any organization of a certain size and ideally, the whole value stream should be involved. Often this will not be the case, sometimes with valid arguments that it is too revolutionary and risky. This High Road is another *Road Less Traveled*, so we will also present ways to get started on a smaller scale. Nevertheless, it is important to keep the blueprint for the Constitutional Organization as a backdrop even if taking a more evolutionary approach. We need to remember where we are going and why, even when moving at a slower pace.

# A High Road to a Transformation

Based on constitutional principles, the *High Road* leads directly to the desired Liberating Organization. It changes the foundation of the value stream from a hierarchy to a network of self-governing circles empowered through representative decision-making; it is a radical, but greatly rewarding path. In Lean and Toyota parlance this would be a *Kaikaku* – a radical change.

---

3   Isac Getz: https://en.wikipedia.org/wiki/Isaac_Getz
4   Liberating Leadership: https://www.academia.edu/27744967/Liberating_Leadership_Creating_a_Freedom_and_Responsibility_Based_Organization
5   Exasperation: Being so frustrated with someone or something that you feel like you're at the end of your rope. You are fed up and ready to act!

It may be argued that a lesser-known Japanese term *Kakushin* is more appropriate. It refers to a more innovative or transformative change instead of just a big change. A *Kakushin* approach will often result in a complete departure from the current situation, something that is of another nature altogether. That can certainly be said of going from a hierarchical, feudal type of organization to a Constitutional Organization based on freedom of the individual and representative decision-making.

改革

*Kaikaku*

革新

*Kakushin*

It is a bit like changing the engine of a ship in mid sea, one day it runs on steam, the next on diesel. It sounds daunting, and it can be, but it will certainly be intense and interesting.

A great example is *Toyota's Production System* (TPS), where the top-down assembly line was replaced by a network of production stations with multi-skilled teams. There was a need for adaptability at each station of these places, so the team members were directly involved in designing the system and in problem-solving.

The process of the High Road is illustrated below:

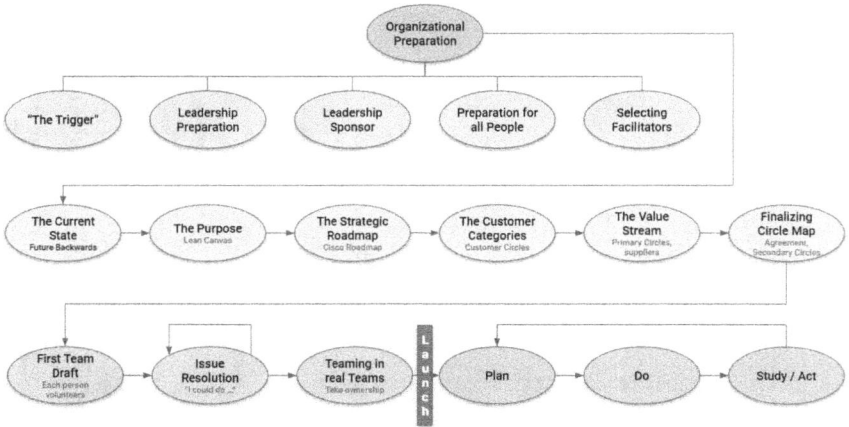

The first principle in this approach is to invite, rather than direct people to participate and contribute. It may be uncomfortable for some, but it is a prerequisite for those currently in authority to demonstrate commitment to the process and provide psychological safety. There must be a respected sponsor who guarantees that the undertaking is genuine, that whatever is found will be taken seriously, and that no one will be punished for uncovering unpleasant facts.

This does not imply a big-bang implementation without experimentation and verification. Instead, it is a carefully designed set of steps that gradually develops a common understanding – a mental model – of the organization's ecosystem and builds trust in the unfolding solutions. Each step is evaluated and consideration is given to the safety of moving forward. It is always possible to back out, but in any complex system, it is never possible to return fully, any intervention changes the system irreversibly. And so it is here.

Borrowing significantly from Russell Ackoff's *Idealized Design*[6], this is a process of discovery where, in pursuit of radical innovation, an organization steps collectively and carefully into the liminal territory between

---

6    Idealized Design: https://eaasos.info/Content/Downloads/AckoffGuidetoIdealize-
     dRedesign.pdf

Complex and Chaos. This approach identifies how the organization should be built from scratch without current constraints. It then works backward, to the present looking for plausible interventions to move us in the right direction. It aligns with the Cynefin approach to Complex territory, where the goal may be unclear, but we can at least move in the right direction. There is also a touch of Strümpfer's[7] designed conversation here.

The process is designed for co-located people; doing it remotely is much more difficult and requires even more careful preparation. Let us step through the process illustrated by the diagram above:

# Organizational Preparation

### The Trigger

In the introduction, we said that to change in an organization there must be a certain dissatisfaction with the present (a *Trigger*), a vision for a better future, and a willingness and ability to take the first steps. This should be thoroughly discussed, documented, visualized, and communicated. It is an honest assessment of the current situation, a comprehensible vision of what can be achieved, and an earnest willingness to change, acknowledging that once underway, the route may diverge from the original roadmap.

### Leadership Preparation

With a thorough understanding of what will happen and the expected results, the current leadership or owners must agree with, and support the new vision. Preparation will typically consist of a few training sessions and workshops. To avoid confusion, leaders must be well prepared, they will be expected to be committed and to answer questions about the process and ultimate aims and objectives.

---

7   Johan P. Strümpfer: https://www.linkedin.com/in/johan-p-strumpfer-3711809/

Often leadership must get acceptance from the owners or the board of the organization, they have the right to be informed transparently so that they can decide. There are many ways of working through such a presentation for approval. Our best advice is to:

- Use for example the *Lean Canvas* to present a quick overview of the initiative, the *Why*, *Who*, and *What*. Remember to collect known or discovered constraints and risks.
- Then expand this into a roadmap of deliverables and activities, the *When*.
- If there is a desire to go the whole nine yards, then build a complete *Impact Map*

  - Show Objectives, Risks (*Why*), and the proposed Strategies (*What*) and the relationship between them, which Strategies contribute to which Objectives or mitigate which Risks – and how much.
  - Show Stakeholders (*Who*) and their relationship to the Objectives, Risks, and Strategies including the priority of Stakeholders, and which ones are the most important.
  - Perhaps in a separate table show the Strategies we already have thought of should certain undesirable consequences unfold. How can we block or mitigate these consequences? Bear in mind that this is Complex, we may have to come up with mitigation schemes en route, we only have fragmented knowledge.
  - Armed with this the initiative can be prioritized and the best choice of Strategies can be chosen, including their implementation sequence, documented on a *Timeline* – the *When*.

**Leadership Sponsor Commitment**

A well-respected person in the current leadership should step forward to be the official *Sponsor* and be integral to the interactive process of determining the form, structure, and composition of the initiative as it unfolds. The Sponsor publicly commits to the initiative and puts their authority and capability behind it. The integrity and character of the Sponsor provide purpose and stability when things may seem confusing in the middle of the process.

### Preparation for all People

Everybody in the organization is given the opportunity to participate in training and discussions about the structure and process of the impending initiative. At this point, it is important to know if there are enough people who recognize the *Trigger* and want to work to effect change. If not, what concerns, fears, or questions are holding them back? To get a clearer sense of where people stand, we often ask them to produce and self-assess micro narratives[8] detailing their most important positive and negative observations or opinions on the matter.

Reforming an organization is highly complex. It cannot be done by coercion and requires people to participate freely. If these conditions cannot be met it will be necessary to seek alternative approaches.

### Selection of Facilitators

The final step in the preparation is to select a number of respected people to be the *Facilitators*, who are needed to help the temporary teams if they get stuck in some way. The *Facilitator Team* will select one of them as the chair with the authority to break deadlocks and convey the team's decisions and progress.

It can be helpful to let people in the organization propose those they trust and support to be Facilitators. As a rule of thumb, we propose a rough ratio of one Facilitator to every 15 people involved in the process.

## Process for Defining Circles

It is now time to explore how the new organization's Circles should be composed. This part of the process is a shallow dive into Chaos for six consecutive half days, or longer if necessary.

---

8    Micro narratives, read more in *Chapter 7 Everyday Life – The Practices* and *Appendix D - More Tools and Practices*.

On day one of Circle formation, the invitees line up according to their primary discipline. Divide the total number of people by seven to find the number of teams. Let us assume 16 teams, then count along the line to 16, starting from one again until the end of the line is reached. Then the people with the same number (1 to 16) will form a temporary team, effectively taking individuals from each discipline in turn, the result being a group of cross-functional Temporary Teams of roughly seven members each.

**Day 1 – Assessing the Current State**
When addressing a complex situation, it is very important to understand current circumstances. We may have only a fragmented understanding, but together we can build a more complete common mental model of the situation.

Each Temporary Team performs the Future-Backwards[9] exercise, resulting in a *State-Event* display supported by the Facilitators. The result is:

* An improved common understanding of the present – where are we right now?
* An improved understanding of defining events that brought us here.
* An improved understanding of where we would really like to be now – Heaven.
* An improved understanding of where we would really hate to be now – Hell.
* Two sets of plausible events that could have brought us to Heaven or Hell, if something different had been chosen or done at some point in the past.

The resulting State-Event displays are presented to two other Teams (e.g. those teams with a number one higher and one lower than the one in question, we call the team number +1 and -1 and so forth in the following) who may ask clarifying questions and critique the assumptions or conclu-

---

9   The Future Backwards, read more in *7 Everyday Life – The Practices* and *Appendix D - More Tools and Practices*.

sions. The originating Teams may introduce changes based on the feed-back, they then declare a release candidate for each Team.

The Facilitators collect the State-Event displays and extract consolidated values and objectives from them. What does each Temporary Team seem to express?

## Day 2 – Aligning the Purpose

The day starts with a review. Facilitators present the consolidated values and objectives and there is a vote to find the most important ones (e.g. using poker chips[10]). After some deliberation, and perhaps a re-vote, the top five are used as signposts for the rest of this process.

Next, each Temporary Team develops a proposal for a Lean Canvas[11], with the Facilitators' support, this documents the rationale for seeking this new organizational structure. The resulting Canvas is subjected to Ritual Dissent[12] by two other Teams (team number +2 and -2) before the Temporary Team declares a release candidate ready. The Facilitators ensure a clear, unique value proposition with a Vision and Mission on the Canvas.

The Facilitators collect the Lean Canvases and consolidate the Vision and Mission statements.

## Day 3 – The Strategic Roadmap

The day starts with a review. The consolidated Vision and Mission statements are presented and voted on. The top three of each are used as signposts for the rest of this process. Later, when the real Circles are in place, the Strategic Resolution Circle will refine this to a single Manifest containing a vision and a mission statement for the organization.

---

10  Poker-Chip Voting, read more in *07 Everyday Life – The Practices* and *Appendix D - More Tools and Practices*.

11  Lean Canvas, read more in *07 Everyday Life – The Practices* and *Appendix D - More Tools and Practices*.

12  Ritual Dissent, read more in *07 Everyday Life – The Practices* and *Appendix D - More Tools and Practices*.

Next, each Temporary Team builds a proposed *Roadmap*[13] for the organization, starting at the top with a lane for customer objectives, and then they perform a Ritual Dissent (this time with teams +3 and -3). The Roadmaps are collected and consolidated by the Facilitators.

### Day 4 – The Customer Categories

Again, the first thing on the agenda is a review. The consolidated Roadmap is presented lane by lane and voted on to establish consensus on the most important things. There should be no more than 10 items per lane. At the end of the process, the timing on the Roadmap may need to be adjusted, but the result is a release candidate for the Roadmap.

Each Temporary Team then tries to reach a common understanding of the categories of customers that the organization serves, defining a so-called Customer Circle for each major category. These "Customer Circles" will in the future organization be serviced by a dedicated Frontline Circle committed to meeting the customers' best interests. Ritual Dissent is performed (now with teams +4 and -4). The result is a set of Customer Circle Manifests describing who these customers are and what they want.

The proposed Customer Circles are consolidated by the Facilitators and the Sponsor.

### Day 5 – The Value Stream

Review again. The consolidated Customer Circles are presented. People have the opportunity to raise concerns about the Circles and Manifests, by adding Post-it notes, which are then reviewed. If the Sponsor and Chair of Facilitators agree that the result is close enough, the process continues (with possible changes), otherwise, the Customer Circle exercise is repeated starting with the current status.

The Temporary Teams develop a proposal for the Primary Circles and Supplier Circles, what should these Circles be able to do (not who is in the

---

13 Roadmapping, read more in *07 Everyday Life – The Practices* and *Appendix D - More Tools and Practices.*

Circles), Relationships, Manifests, and Competences. Ritual Dissent is performed (+5 and -5).

At this stage, it is OK to propose some Secondary Circles, but it is not the main focus, the Value Stream comes first – delivering to customers is always the organization's principal aim.

Starting with one Frontline Circle per Customer Circle and one Service and Admin Circle, the teams Iterate until they find a workable proposal.

Circle proposals, Manifests, and lists of Competences are collected and consolidated by the Facilitators.

### Day 6 – Finalizing the Circle Map

The final day also starts with a Review before the consolidated Value Stream – Primary Circles – are presented. There is an opportunity to raise concerns about Circles and Manifests (with Competency lists), by adding Post-it notes to applicable items. Proposals for Secondary Circles may be posted, but there is no formal process for commissioning Secondary Circles at this stage.

The Circle Map is reviewed and a Confidence Vote[14] is taken. If the Sponsor and Chair of the Facilitators agree, it is accepted, otherwise, the exercise is repeated starting with the current status.

## Process for Setting Teams

To avoid trying to solve too many things at once and getting lost in personal preferences, the process of designing the Circle Map paid little attention to those who would work within the Circles. It is now time to start staffing the Circles.

---

14  Confidence Vote, read more in *Chapter 7 Everyday Life – The Practices* and *Appendix D - More Tools and Practices*.

### Day I – Volunteering and first draft

To ensure a good common understanding of what needs to be done in the individual Circles, the agreed: Values, Vision, Mission, Roadmap, and Primary Circles (Value Stream) are recapitulated and reviewed.

Then people are invited to volunteer for the teams. Each person is asked to prepare a minimum of two proposals for what they think they should do and where they should be. The proposals are handed over to the Facilitators and should contain the following: Their preferred Circle with priority (1 or 2), their ideal role (SO, OO, or Team member), three relevant competencies, three values, and a maximum of three prerequisites (e.g. education, tools, etc.). People are recommended to write a short narrative about why it is important for them to join this Circle. It is also OK for people to suggest participating in certain Secondary Circles if they have specific skills that could help resolve cross-team concerns.

During a break in the action the Facilitators collect the envelopes and try to make sense of the proposals, looking for a plausible way forward. After the break, assuming they have a practical solution the Facilitators present the first iteration of the Primary Circle Structure to everyone and identify the volunteers for each role. Competency Matrices are filled out for each team, obvious challenges are described and highlighted by the Facilitators and everybody reflects overnight on how to meet the challenges.

If the Facilitators do not see a plausible solution, they can suggest redoing the envelope exercise, this time broadening the volunteer's scope to three or four roles.

### Day 2 – Iterative issue resolution

The first iteration of the staffed Primary Circle Structure is reviewed, with the opportunity to post proposals to resolve challenges. The volunteers may have to reconsider their commitments: *"Perhaps I could take this other position"* or *" I do have that competence as well"*. They can also secondarily make suggestions for others "I think so-and-so could take that role". Finally, people can suggest changing something in the Circle structure to resolve the challenge.

Challenges that can be immediately agreed upon are accepted and the artifacts are updated. A Confidence Vote is taken. If the Sponsor and the chair of Facilitators agree that the result is close enough, the Primary Circle Structure is offered as a release candidate.

Otherwise, Transient Teams are formed to discuss the remaining major issues and may repeat the process the following day, to a maximum of three iterations.

### Day 3 – Teaming up in Real Teams

We are almost ready to launch. The Primary Circle structure is reviewed once more and improved if small improvements are apparent.

- Each real Primary Circle conducts an intro session with presentations and clarifications; there are now real OOs for each Circle that facilitate this. Manifests and Competency Matrices are amended and are owned by the Circle.
- Relationships with other Circles are negotiated and Manifests are written for the Relationships.
- The need for Tactical Resolution Circles to discuss the progress of deliveries is identified, but it is simpler if they can be handled bilaterally. Do not worry too much, these can always be commissioned later. Go for the simplest solution.
- Proposals for Secondary Circles can be made by anyone who discovers a need, these are collected by the newly installed OOs.
- Occasionally the need for Transient Circles operating outside the normal Value Stream will be discovered such as special one-off projects.

Unless something alarming occurs, everything is now ready. There may be some practical details like office space to be resolved, but make it as simple as possible, the top priority is getting into the new operating model as quickly as possible while everything is fresh in people's minds. Delays at this stage are always harmful.

## Launch of the new Organization

The big day has arrived. There may still be some internal optimizations, but the Value Stream is ready to get deliverables flowing to customers which takes precedence over internal adjustments.

There will always be little wrinkles to iron out but the OOs will be actively assisting by removing impediments and facilitating communication.

It is important that nobody panics because it is not perfect, it never will be. Just maintain the flow of customer deliveries then iterate: Plan-Do-Study-Act.

## Rapid Adjustment in the Formative Weeks

An organization is a complex organism and no matter how well-planned, the new structure never completely matches reality. It is therefore important to be prepared for rapid adjustments in the first weeks of operation. Here is a list of things that can be expected.

- **Getting the Strategic Resolution Circle in gear**. The SOs must get organized. They should define their Manifest, Artifacts, and decide how they will work together. They should also choose the Chair of the Strategic Resolution Circle. They may not be at liberty to do this themselves, as constraints may be imposed by owners or the legal framework for the organization. This Circle will have a backlog of strategic initiatives that the members work for the common good and occasionally they will delegate objectives and deliverables to their Circles. There will be one OO who will support the Strategic Resolution Circle.
- **Getting the Operational Resolution Circle to work**. This is similar to the Strategic Resolution Circle, but the objectives are different and the focus is looking inward at the organization. This Circle acts like a human sensor network, monitoring the organization and ensuring that proper adjustments are made to optimize collaboration.

- **Discovering needs for Tactical Resolution Circles.** If bilateral collaboration and communication are insufficient, Tactical Resolution Circles can be created with the OOs' help; there should be at least one OO to support such Circles.

- **Discovering needs for Secondary Circles.** Team members in the Primary Circles may discover a need to develop skill-based areas with people from other Circles, such as design, QA, compliance, or system architecture. The OOs will facilitate the creation and operation of such Circles, calculating how much effort to allocate, the frequency of meetings, the artifacts needed, invitees, etc. An OO will also support such a Circle.

- **Discovering needs for Transient Circles.** Sometimes unusual and unexpected challenges or opportunities occur. If the Primary Circle(s) cannot absorb such a sudden drop into Chaos into their normal operation, a Transient Circle may be commissioned according to the overall Manifest for the organization.

- **Fine-tuning Relationships between circles bilaterally.** Bilateral Manifests covering collaboration between Circles are simply amended when better ways are discovered. OOs facilitate this.

- **Defining and documenting principles for Escalation.** Escalation is a special form of delegation – asking for a decision, not a delivery of something – and any change to the principles is handled in much the same way as ordinary Delegations.

- **Team misalignment**. Sometimes teams end up mismatching the needs of the Value Stream, this could be missing or superfluous competencies, personality, or value tensions. Such tensions have to be resolved.

- **Circle Map improvement**. From time to time a better set of Circles can be found, e.g. scaling out and having a Circle behind the Frontline to deliver components to the Frontline Circles.

## Continuously Tending to the Organization

Although at a lower intensity, this is similar to what happened during the formative weeks of the change. It is important to attend to the organization's health and well-being. Never think of an organization as a machine that simply works once wound up and set in motion. It is organic and therefore complex, and everyone, especially the OOs, should accept responsibility for finding improvements and removing waste.

Periodic retrospectives for the whole organization are recommended to ensure that there is a place where ideas can be collected, discussed, and prepared for decisions. The community of OOs has an important role to create and test hypotheses for continuous organizational improvement.

# The Low Road – A Free Territory

The High Road may seem too risky or even dangerous to many, so various incremental introductions of Agile and Lean methodology have been attempted over the years. This is called a *Kaizen* approach – a series of small incremental changes. In classic Lean methodology, there is a time and a place for *Kaizen, Kaikau,* and *Kakushin* approaches.

This has often been done when introducing Scrum, Kanban, or other Agile methods, with a team or a small group of teams being sanctioned to work this way and it can work, at least initially. We call this a *Free Territory*. Sometimes, the intention is to let the approach spread to other areas once experience has been gained, but this is not always the case. For example, many banks have deployed Agile methods in their IT system development, but not in the main part of the organization. It is also worth mentioning that such territories or free zones often don't last very long.

If there is a traditional hierarchy above and beside the Free Territory, it will always be felt like an intrusion, sometimes threatening the authority of the hierarchy. When the first crisis occurs, the hierarchy – typically in the form of the finance department – strikes back with a demand for traditional budget control, more reports, and status meetings. If such a liberated Territory is to be sustainable, there must be a commitment from a highly placed sponsor with authority to back up the structure. The evidence from all sorts of organizations indicates that self-government can only endure if core freedoms are constitutionalized and cannot be retracted on a whim.

## The Necessary Freedoms

Those in the Territory govern themselves in the following areas without the need to ask for permission and without the fear of being micromanaged by a central authority. In all these areas there will be substantial agreed and enabling constraints, allowing people autonomy:

- Use of resources including money, competencies, space, and tools is the minimum. Often, central accounting will need things for the organization's accounts, but they should primarily act as advisors to the Territory, not controllers.
- The Territory has to be self-governing with respect to hiring, firing, and compensation; they know who best fits their teams. Central HR should act only as an advisor.
- The Territory chooses its internal organization, how to organize and work in Teams, and who assumes which roles. The Territory is responsible for its customer and supplier relationships, whether external or internal. In complex situations, strong performance depends on good relationships. For example, to avoid conflict a central purchasing department cannot overpressure suppliers with which the Territory needs good relations. It follows that the Territory will itself negotiate manifests (working agreements) with customers and suppliers. Also, central legal departments should act as advisors and not as a police force.

## Relations with the Rest of the Organization

The traditional parts of the organization (the hierarchy) must accept the self-governing status of the Territory including the expenditure of money, which seems to be the hardest part. It must negotiate a workable manifest for the Territory with a minimum of constraints and once in place, the organization must adhere to the working arrangements expressed in the Manifest. This may include preventing interference from the central powers and assisting the seemingly unorthodox elements in the Territory. Some things need to be stated in the Territory's Manifest, or the charter as it is sometimes called:

- How the Territory delivers to its customers. There may be organization-wide commitments or compliance constraints that set limits for how this happens.
- Visibility and transparency. This is a core commitment of the Territory which should strive to exceed agreed standards of transparency as a means of developing trust. Territories must avoid developing an exclusive mindset that views the rest of the organization as old-fashioned or less sophisticated, and therefore a pretext for being less transparent. Announcing intent is an important and respectful way to give the organization advance notice of what the Territory is about to do, and it may even produce useful input.
- How the Territory can draw upon the services of the rest of the Organization. There should be simple rules enabling the Territory to get optimal internal accounting help from the organization, for example. Countless examples exist of teams soliciting external suppliers because the internal option was too hard or expensive to use.

The OOs must lead from the front, demonstrating transparency and facilitating common understanding. They will spend considerable time and resources explaining the Territory's value proposition to the rest of the organization, frequently answering the question. *"Why are we doing this?"*

The last important thing to mention is the periodic Reviews (Sprint Reviews in Scrum). This is where the rest of the organization can see what has been accomplished and provide feedback and new ideas. When executed correctly such reviews enhance everyone's Psychological Safety and demonstrate the value of transparency, trust, and keeping commitments.

## How to Get Started on the Low Road

Find a suitable organizational unit to start with, a place of extra opportunity, challenge, or motivation. Often this has been internal IT, product development, or perhaps Corporate Budgeting; if in doubt, start with a customer-focused area, then run a compressed version of the process described above:

- Identify Customers/Stakeholders, and create manifests for them.
- Develop a Manifest for the unit/Circle in question.
- Build a Master Backlog of this Circle's Objectives and what deliveries they must execute.
- Based on the Master Backlog, develop a Competency Matrix. Do the competencies match the needs that can be seen in the goals of the Circle? It might be necessary to invite new members or strengthen current competencies.
- Identify other organizational units whose collaboration and services are needed. Create Manifests (working agreements) with them.

Iterate from there, spreading the practices to other collaborating units.

# The Frontline, Facing the Customers

A variant of the Liberated Territory approach is to start at the deep end, where the customers are. Customers are usually the only sources of income, so when adopting an Agile Lean mindset to liberate the organization, always focus on creating value for the customer, while taking an incremental approach to transformation.

First of all this forces the organization to look primarily at its customers instead of being distracted by internal processes, which contribute little to creating customer value. Secondly, many organizations already have realized that they need to improve in the area of customer relations. And finally, it is an area where rapid feedback and results can be expected.

One challenge is to avoid taking a short-term view of customers. There are clearly motivations to look for the *"low hanging fruit"* and a focus on *"making the numbers for the quarter"*, but this should not obscure the fact that long-term customer relationships are what make businesses resilient and sustainable.

It is possible to introduce a Liberating Organization here at the frontline and create a Free Territory as a limited experiment that can be rolled back if it doesn't produce the expected value. The experiment will provide quantifiable results within weeks or a few months and is a *"safe-to-fail experiment"* as Dave Snowden calls it, that does not burn the whole budget but does bring value, insight, and knowledge.

Customers are becoming increasingly diverse, and changes happen fast. Most organizations know they have difficulty collecting customer intelligence and can't keep up with what their customers really want. Customer needs have become very complex and traditional customer survey methods don't work anymore. A radical new approach is needed.

A variation of the Low Road approach is to work backward to understand and describe customer needs, then rethink how best to serve them, forming Frontline Circles to deliver the optimal customer experience.

These Circles constitute a special territory facing the external world but with solid delivery agreements with the traditionally organized internal units. The aim is that over time the value of the liberating approach becomes apparent and spreads to other areas. In Lean terms, it is a Kakushin approach to the customer-facing corner of the organization.

## Rapid Customer and Service Discovery as a Starter

If changing the frontline organization seems too daunting, there is a more limited experiment that can be run which we call *Rapid Customer and Service Discovery* (RCSD). It starts with the organization agreeing to send a small expeditionary team for a short time into customer territory. We call this the Discovery Transient Circle (DTC).

- The goal is for the DTC to return to the Organization with proposals for changes to products or services that would produce more value and aid new customer acquisition.
- First, objectives are identified and agreed with the organization. What is to be discovered? Are they willing to accept and act upon the facts that may surface?
- A timebox is agreed upon; what is the runway for achieving results? As a rule of thumb, it should be between 3 and 6 months, unless it has been tried before, in which case it can be a little shorter.
- Recruit volunteers for the DTC. Agree on the best combination then iterate and train. One person should be a coach (an OO) who solicits the team's commitment to the process and timebox and facilitates collaboration and adherence to the goals. Then the DTC is commissioned and sent off into the wild with fanfare and applause.

Now daily life begins. The DTC selects an approach for which they have the mandate and are committed. Multiple, and often parallel experiments with robust success criteria are performed, feedback from which may lead to further experimentation.

Daily feedback sessions report on progress and observations. Did the last 24 hours produce any insightful observations or new ideas for action and if not, why? Is there a need to change anything? It may be helpful to refer to the OODA loop thinking.

Those customers who respond positively and engage, are invited to discuss in more detail how their experience could be even better, including estimating the value of different possible products or service initiatives. This may reveal new objectives and perhaps strategies.

Following the timeboxed session, several things happen:

- The DTC organizes its findings and creates and presents proposals for initiatives to the wider organization.

- The organization evaluates the findings and does a comprehensive impact estimation resulting in the proposal of an impact matrix.
- The organization may implement some of the new initiatives, or send a team to a more targeted area.
- The DTC is then finally commended for its efforts and discoveries and then decommissioned.
- Before confirming a Liberating Organization approach and implementing Frontline Circles as described above, the organization evaluates the validity of the acquired evidence.

There are many methods and useful tools available for customer and product service discovery, here are a few:

- Collect *Micro Narratives* from customers with their self-assessment of why this is important to them.
- Use *The Future Backwards* in customer meetings to discover objectives and prioritize interventions.
- Discovery Circles can use the *Blackboard Pattern*[15] to visualize challenges, questions, and possible solutions.
- First responders in the DTC use *Actively Guided Interviews*[16] with customers. This is the same principle that applies later if Frontline Circles are implemented.
- Use *Online Estimation* to evaluate the value of proposed features (in meetings and privately).
- Use *Radar Charts* to visualize findings and show the balance of the findings.
- To facilitate optimal prioritization, use an *Impact Map*[17] to visualize the Why, What, Who, When, and Where of proposed initiatives.

---

15  Blackboard Pattern, read more in Chapter 7 *Everyday Life – The Practices* and *Appendix D - More Tools and Practices*.

16  Actively Guided Interviews, read more in *Chapter 7 Everyday Life – The Practices* and *Appendix D - More Tools and Practices*.

17  Impact Map, read more in *Chapter 7 Everyday Life – The Practices* and *Appendix D - More Tools and Practices*.

| What – Solutions | Epics level 1 | Epics level 2 | Epics level 3 | Done | Ease of use | Objective 2 | Objective 3 | Objective 4 | Objective 5 | Objective 6 | Cannot be maintained | Stakeholder 1 | Stakeholder 2 | Stakeholder 3 | Stakeholder 4 | Stakeholder 5 | Stakeholder 6 | 2020-04-01 | 2020-05-01 | 2020-06-01 | 2020-07-01 | 2020-08-01 | 2020-09-01 | 2020-10-01 | 2020-11-01 | 2020-12-01 |
|---|---|---|---|---|---|---|---|---|---|---|---|---|---|---|---|---|---|---|---|---|---|---|---|---|---|---|
| Getting new Content Management System (CMS) | | | | 50% | | | | | 100% | | | | | | | | | | | | | | | | | |
| Present case to editors, make decision | | | | | | | | | | | | | | | | | | | | | | | | | | |
| Commercial arrangement | | | | | | | | | | | | | | | | | | | | | | | | | | |
| Configure the CMS | | | | | | | | | | | | | | | | | | | | | | | | | | |
| Install ALH design | | | | 40% | | | | 10% | | | | | | | | | | | | | | | | | | |
| Configure access rights | | | | 20% | | | | | | | | | | | | | | | | | | | | | | |
| Instll cache solution | | | | | | | | | | | | | | | | | | | | | | | | | | |
| Move content | | | | | | | | | | | | | | | | | | | | | | | | | | |
| Review and move images | | | | | | | | | | | | | | | | | | | | | | | | | | |
| Review and move main content | | | | 20% | | | | | | | | | | | | | | | | | | | | | | |
| Review and move Posts and articles | | | | | | | | | | | | | | | | | | | | | | | | | | |
| Go live | | | | | | | | | | | | | | | | | | | | | | | | | | |
| Betatest with prime network | | | | | | | | | | | | | | | | | | | | | | | | | | |
| Back up old site | | | | | | | | | | | | | | | | | | | | | | | | | | |
| Go live | | | | | | | | | | | | | | | | | | | | | | | | | | |
| Add memership section with login | | | | | | | | | | | | | | | | | | | | | | | | | | |

# An Executive Initiated Reform

Sometimes it happens that the executives in an organization are convinced that they need to move in the direction of decentralization of decisions and more dynamic business processes. This is the way most of the Organizations that have adopted Beyond Budgeting (BB) have gone about their transformation – for a better understanding of this framework consult *Appendix B5 - Beyond Budgeting in 60 Seconds*. These organizations have not necessarily removed the traditional hierarchy, but rather softened it and granted more freedom to people in the details of execution.

The opening gambit for such a transformation is usually a replacement of the classic yearly budget process with three separate processes for setting *Targets*, making *Forecasts*, and agreeing on *Resource Allocation*. Very few like the yearly budget, it consumes enormous resources to produce, doesn't work, and people often game the system to comply. But most organizations continue to do it anyway. Not every organization needs to set targets, and some don't even make forecasts.

What everybody does need is some robust process for allocating resources to varied entities in the organization. Instead of agreeing on a budget 12-16 months ahead for expenditure, an iterative approach is adopted. Some high-level principles for spending resources are agreed on, and if unfolding circumstances should raise the need to reevaluate, it will be done. BB uses the phrase *"The bank is always open!"*. But it is not anarchy and chaos – there is still a due process for allocating funds and deciding on course adjustments. It is just more adaptive and flexible.

The key is to move the planning up, away from financial micromanagement, and review the Targets, Forecasts, and Resource Allocation each in its own cadence. Abolishing the yearly budget and replacing it with this approach sends a clear message to the organization, that the leadership is serious about granting freedom and being willing to operate more on trust. This does not necessarily mean changes to the accounting, which of course is regulated and compliance is needed.

There are also other processes that should be redesigned to convey trust and not just control, the most important being performance evaluation, compensation and rewards, and decision-making, which we have some proposals for in an Agile Lean Organization.

For this to really take root, leadership principles should also be addressed, just as we have done in this book. So, a journey toward a Constitutional Organization can start at the top with the executives, as long as they are consistent in communicating the intent of granting people a certain autonomy based on trust and that the processes and practices actually are coherent with that message.

# Details to Consider in Any Approach

In any organization, the most important value is a clear and worthwhile purpose. It has to be bigger than any individual and be more than just making money. If the stakeholders find the purpose worthwhile, it will bind people for the long term and create a unique identity.

The importance of creating an Organizational Manifest that clearly displays this purpose cannot be overstated. Everyone should be able to grasp and communicate its essence.

# The Value Stream

The Value Stream is the backbone of any Agile Lean organization because serving the customer is always the primary objective. The Primary Circles are the building blocks of the Value Stream. When creating and sustaining a Liberating Organization there are a few important, but perhaps counterintuitive, aspects to consider.

When designing the Circles in the Value Stream, it is important to consider the current status of the organization while projecting which outcomes would be ideal and which would be certain to make it worse. The ideal situation may not be attainable, and due to evolving circumstances it could change tomorrow, but it provides a purposeful direction.

Circle Manifests should be simple and clear. People instinctively choose the path of least resistance when trying to get things done, so if it is hard to comprehend what goes on in a Circle or how to use its services, it will not happen.

To avoid misunderstandings, delays, and other inhibitors of performance, Relationship Manifests should also be easy to understand. They are particularly important for Circles that delegate to other Circles because handovers are notorious for distorting information and producing sub-standard results. The transmission of information between two parties can diminish accuracy by up to 50% so it is important to keep delegations extremely simple and visible.

There is a strong case for at least one Service Circle where other Primary Circles can get help in such areas as accounting, legal advice, HR, and facility management. The adjustment from a traditional structure can be hard, but we have witnessed an organization where the CEO, CFO, HR, Legal, cafeteria staff, and receptionists were in the same Circle, and that worked well.

# Decision Making

Liberating Organizations are also different in the area of decision-making, using Resolution Circles to reach participatory and representative cross-circle decisions.

At first, this will seem strange to those used to "deferring" to a boss, but it is a great enabler of engagement. Especially in the beginning, be careful to use the language of invitation and inquiry, and not be too quick to close down the conversation with a conclusion; people have to get used to participating.

The biggest challenge in a transformation is for those who previously exercised power to restrain themselves, to be "aggressively patient" and not muscle in to make a decision when things seem to move slowly or be stuck. A mature OO is very helpful, especially when supporting the Strategic Resolution Circle.

Manifests for these Circles should be very clear so that those not normally in them know what to expect. Strive for robust feedback in the formative weeks of the new structure.

When a Resolution Circle is asked to intervene, it is a form of delegation called Escalation. The rules of engagement should be clear, about what can be escalated, the expected response time, and what should be prepared for the escalation. We want people to act responsibly and provide psychological safety to ask for help when needed. Help should be given without question in a spirit of collegial cooperation. Issues in this area should be resolved by the resident OO.

# Secondary Circles – Pillars of Competence

There is something great about being with people who share interests and passions and want to focus on achieving excellence in their field. To that end, Secondary Circles provide a place for people across the Primary Circles to address issues in the realm of their common competence. Other

Circles can delegate competence-related challenges to these Secondary Circles.

Participation in such Circles is extremely valuable, with many positive side effects, so people should be encouraged to participate. While the Primary Circles are central to the Value Stream, Secondary Circles provide a balance and means for people to achieve mastery and be proud of their accomplishments.

# Summing up

## When it just seems too Much

Even when any organizational transformation seems out of reach, there is always something that can be done. The book *Liberating Structures* contains a method called "*15% Solutions*[18]" which encourages people to think about small incremental changes that can be made within the boundaries of existing resources and mandates; it is often more than you think.

Even small changes in the right direction can have a ripple effect which eventually becomes part of the general culture. This is the ultimate Kaizen low road; separate what can be done from what can't, then focus on the former. Demonstrably positive results will spread to other teams and people.

## Issues often Encountered

### Geographically dispersed Organizations

When attempting change in a geographically dispersed organization it is clearly much harder to build trust and get everyone on the same page.

To build common understanding and trust, Circles should ideally be in one location. But, if this is not possible, consider bringing them together at least at the formation of the Organization and then perform regular re-alignments; it will be worth the investment.

---

18   15% Solutions: https://www.liberatingstructures.com/7-15-solutions/

In organizations where Circles are in different locations, delegations, and resolutions through Secondary and Resolution Circles all become harder. As a rule of thumb, the overhead or transactional costs are about double.

## Different Reactions from Different People

Any organizational change causes a reaction and so does this. Some people will be eager to participate, make observations, and offer solutions that contribute to the course of action. Others will be more passive and happily accept solutions that others come up with.

However, some will choose not to get involved, effectively disengaging themselves; work may be needed to draw them in and get their effective engagement in the new way of working.

Finally, there will be some who are outright against it and will try to stop it. Hopefully, this is only a small minority, but they may be very vocal or subversive. This has to be dealt with before it stifles or derails the process.

See if it is possible to find a way to offer them a spot where they can still contribute to the organization; or is it necessary for them to leave the organization? If the majority of the organization is on board, a small minority cannot be allowed to hinder progress.

*In this section, we found two ways of creating a Liberating Organization, the High Road to a complete change or one of several low roads of incremental change.*

*The full, High-Road implementation was described in detail to provide a solid foundation for the process.*

*There are several ways of taking a more incremental approach to an organizational transformation, we called this a Low Road.*

*A transformation can also be initiated by current leadership. In this case, it is very important that people are still included by invitation and have the opportunity chose to participate and commit.*

*We elaborated on the benefits of starting at the customer end of the organization. Something that makes sense to most organizations.*

*Remember, there is always 15% you can do.*

# Everyday Life – The Practices

*We now have a practical framework in place for a Liberating and Constitutional Organization; we have found plausible benefits, challenges, and pitfalls and have discussed various paths to such an organization. Now, let us look in detail at some of the practices and methods that have proven useful in everyday life. Taking action is key to working with complex systems. Knowledge is built up, and thought patterns are changed through the act of experimentation. David Marquet (former captain of the nuclear submarine Santa Fe) explains about his 'Intent-based Leadership':*

> *We call this act your way to new thinking, don't think your way to new action … Thinking about new actions doesn't build new pathways [in our brain], acting out new actions does. After repeating an action many times and receiving a positive stimulus each time, our new action becomes ingrained, and our habits change.* — David Marquet, blogpost July 23, 2019[1]

---

1    David Marquet: https://intentbasedleadership.com/acting-our-way-to-new-thinking/

We will examine helpful practices and methods from different angles. There may be some overlap, but such is a complex system; different perspectives reveal different fragments of the full picture. Practice overviews are described here, but for more detail and templates please see the Field Guide on the accompanying website[2].

# General Circle Practices

The Agile Lean Leadership framework has four organizational categories called Circles. They share many properties such as manifests, backlogs, retrospective sessions, and regular meeting intervals for planning and review, but there are also differences, which we will discuss below.

Teams are central to any Liberating Organization, so creating them is the first and most important practice. If possible they should be small and cross-functional. By contrast with the late modern idea of an almost absolute focus on the individual expert, teams provide a positive robust social structure that keeps people aligned, committed, and flourishing.

## Primary Circles

Primary Circles are the backbone of the Value Stream and include one or more Teams. They follow clearly visible practices which are described in the accompanying artifacts.

### Daily Coordination

To maintain a common understanding of the situation and progress plus a plan for the next day, there are short daily coordination sessions (max 15 minutes) where the Team and the Operations Owner (OO) exchange status, possibly challenges, and intentions for the next 24 hours. Sessions can be observed by anybody, but only team members speak.

In Scrum, this is called Daily Scrum, Kanban folks talk about Daily Kanban, and others use the term Daily Standup. In all cases, it is daily coordi-

---

2    Liberating Organizations, the website: https://liberatingorg.com/

nation or synchronization between the Team – the people who do the work and their OO or Scrum Master. It is a quick information exchange, rather than a meeting which implies coffee, small talk, and settling in. It is a valuable discipline, to make sure that nobody forgets to communicate with others. At the micro level, it is a great opportunity to communicate intent, set expectations, discover needs for help, and invite perspectives from others. When everybody participates freely, it is not a burden or a waste of time.

People describe what they have accomplished, what they intend to do next, and if anything is hindering their work. In Scrum such things are called *Impediments*, the OO takes action if the Team cannot resolve these.

It is an important aspect that everyone says what they *intend* to do next. This is an invitation to others to make suggestions, offer, or ask for help. Of course, these things happen throughout the working day, but the daily coordination ensures that the exchange of information is not forgotten.

### Backlogs, Planning, and Review

The Main Backlog which contains all Items slated for delivery or consideration, is visible to the public. This artifact can be a whiteboard with post-its, a spreadsheet, or a dedicated system to keep track of future work. This enables transparency, clarification, and prioritization.

The Circle will choose a tactical approach; typically some sort of iterative process like Scrum, Kanban, or a combination thereof. A Tactical Backlog, again board, spreadsheet, or system, is used to display the things currently worked on, the progress, and any challenges encountered.

There are Regular Planning and Review Cadences where items from the Main Backlog are selected and moved to the Tactical Backlog, possibly being further decomposed into Tasks, the smallest unit of work.

* Almost all Agile and Lean frameworks adopt this approach, variously called Sprints, Iterations, Cycles, or Cadences. There is a great benefit to having these at regular intervals so everybody, stakeholders in-

cluded, can participate; they provide a rhythm and a helpful sense of order.

- Review sessions are where accomplishments are demonstrated and feedback solicited from the appropriate stakeholders; in Scrum, this is called Sprint Review. This cadence can follow the Planning Cadence but can be run longer to minimize meeting overhead. Relevant stakeholders should participate, but it is useful to publicly announce these sessions so that anyone with an interest can attend.

- Make sure that the relevant people receive their invitations in good time. Some stakeholders may not be able to attend, but it is helpful to document proceedings, especially the review sessions. People should know that information is available and that they can get it if it is important to them. The Circle or Team should be transparent but invite people to look for themselves. Team members should participate to hear the discussion firsthand, but also to receive recognition for their work.

- It is good practice to have refinement sessions where the Items approaching the Planning stage are discussed, refined, estimated, and designed; often stakeholders are invited to participate in these activities.

The Planning Cadence is often one to four weeks depending on the rate of change and unfolding circumstances. Two to three weeks is ideal, one week is too short and four weeks may seem a bit too long, as it is hard to maintain focus on a goal that far in the future.

More long-term, strategic planning of larger deliverables or collections of smaller ones should occur at intervals of two to six months. About five to six tactical iterations per strategic iteration seem to fit. The Circle may choose to maintain a roadmap illustrating the longer view.

**Process Review**

- Process Review Cadence sessions are typically held at the same interval as the Planning sessions. We prefer the Scrum term Retrospective, others call it After-action-review, debriefing, or post-mortem.
- Everybody in the Circle reviews the last interval and reflects on how it went, what they were happy with (to amplify these things), and what could be better (to discover improvements). Then, it may decide to make changes or conduct experiments to gain new knowledge.
- In many ways, this is the most important practice, the hub around which everything revolves. There are many recommendations, templates, and tools to be found, and everybody has an opinion, but teams should find ways to do retrospectives that suit them and are sustainable. It should not end up being boring or too time-consuming. People often over-constrain Retrospectives with too rigid or complex procedures that ruin the spirit.
- Maintaining an Improvement Backlog, where potential improvements to the collaboration are kept, refined, and prioritized, is recommended.

The Daily Coordination is simply an implementation of the OODA loop; the Team Observes what is going on, Orients themselves, maybe reacts intuitively, or defers to the longer planning cadences and reviews for the Decide-Act part.

The Planning and Review cadences also close the Plan–Do–Study–Act Deming Cycle, focusing on deliverables and outward customer needs. By contrast, the Process Review cadence closes the Deming Cycle with an inward focus on the process and the collaboration in the team.

# Resolution Circles

In essence, Resolution Circles are a replacement for the traditional hierarchy, operating with representative decision-making instead of rank-based decisions at each level. Each Circle has one person called *The Chair*, who acts as mediator or arbitrator in case of deadlock. The Chair will often take primary responsibility for the Circle's Main Backlog, much like a Strategy Owner (SO or Product Owner). The Circle may choose their Chair but sometimes there are constraints demanded by law or the owners that dictate certain roles. Each Resolution Circle will have an appointed OO to be the facilitator and the one reminding the Circle to stick to its agreed process and mandate as documented in the Manifest.

Sometimes very quick decisions need to be made, for example in a crisis (a sudden drop into Chaos). In such cases, it is common practice to let the Chairs of the three Resolution Circles make that call, as a kind of executive committee, but this is for exceptional cases, not the norm.

### The Tactical Resolution Circle

The Tactical Resolutions Circle (TRC, previously called Scrum of Scrums) may not be necessary. If the Primary Circles can handle their daily interaction bilaterally, there is no need to invent more meetings and overhead. There is always an OO associated with a TRC.

Here are some helpful practices if a TRC is beneficial, typically because everybody needs an opportunity to hear the issues and the resolutions.

- When the Primary Circles have conducted their Daily Coordination, one of the team members may join the TRC session. It may not be necessary to do this every day, we have often implemented it on Tuesdays and Thursdays.
- Each Circle reports its important experiences, discoveries, or issues relevant to others. Questions are posed and answers are given in rapid-fire mode.
- This session should also be timeboxed to max. 15 minutes, to avoid creating an unproductive overhead.
- If anyone in a Circle needs to clarify something with other Circles, they normally go to the TRC, but if there are no special needs, it is normal practice to just take turns so that everyone gets involved. Other-

wise, there is a tendency to develop a de-facto team lead that represents the Circle.

- It is not necessary to appoint a Chair of the TRC, but sometimes it is helpful; the person may be designated as the Technology Owner (TO, similar to CTO).
- OOs may discover a need to hold TRC sessions if there is frustration or a lack of insight into progress.
- It is normal practice to let this meeting be open to all, but only the actively participating Circle members and the OO speak.

### The Strategic Resolution Circle

The Strategic Resolution Circle (SRC) is similar to what was once called a Scrum of Product Owners; it exists to deal with cross-circle-cutting concerns of customers, prioritization, and allocation of resources. Its members are the Strategy Owners from the Primary Circles and an OO who is often the Chair of the Operational Resolution Circle. The SRC has a top-level Main Backlog and an accompanying Strategic Roadmap or Impact Map.

- The SRC has a cadence of regular meetings at anything from weekly to monthly intervals, depending on how fast circumstances unfold. In between they can convene quickly if a need for a resolution arises. If an ultra-fast decision is needed, the three Resolution Circle Chairs normally act as first responders. The ability to react quickly is critical to preventing the SRC from becoming a slow-moving bureaucratic body[3].
- If two Circles cannot resolve issues of prioritization bilaterally, they can escalate the matter to the SRC. The SRC's Manifest should be clear about what is required and how it is tackled.
- If the situation is fast-moving, the Strategic Roadmap or Impact Map may be reviewed, monthly or quarterly. A new period will be intro-

---

3   At RiksTV in Norway at one point the SRC gave the rest of the organization the commitment that they could respond within 24 hours, which was a great boost to morale.

duced with established goals and the previously planned period will be reviewed and adjusted as necessary.

- The SRC Main Backlog, which is a public artifact,[4] contains large Objectives and deliverables for the whole Value Stream. The SRC constantly works to clarify and prioritize these, this is an important part of the SRC's role. Often other people are invited to participate in these discussions, as nobody expects the SOs to be experts on all matters, not even collectively. It is also good practice to delegate research, analysis, or experiments to Primary or Secondary Circles.

- Delegation to other Circles happens once an Objective or Strategy has been decided. If it cannot fit into an existing Circle, a Transient Circle may be commissioned to work on it.

- Often, the allocation of resources, in particular money, can be an issue; a Circle may experience the need for more investment or manpower. The SRC oversees the allocation of resources and the Beyond Budgeting principle of: "*The bank is always open*" is recommended. This still requires a forecast of financial development including the spending and investment, but appropriate and timely responses occur as circumstances unfold.

- Many of the items on the SRC Main Backlog are *wicked problems*[5] where no solution satisfies everybody. Where consensus cannot be reached, decisions reflecting the "common good" may offer an acceptable compromise.

- Occasionally a deadlock may occur, but the cost of delay is so great that a quick decision is vital. In this case, the Chair has the authority to allocate time for people to reconsider their position and perhaps suggest new approaches. If no acceptable solution is achieved after the time has expired, the Chair switches from mediator to arbitrator and

---

4    There are obviously some matters that require a certain amount of secrecy, such as personal matters, sensitive customer information or mergers and acquisitions.

5    A wicked problem is difficult to solve because requirements are incomplete, contradictory, and changing, read more here: https://en.wikipedia.org/wiki/Wicked_problem

makes a decision. This looks like the old-fashioned way of giving orders, but in times of crises, non-action may be the worst option[6].

It is important to understand that the SRC is not just a collection of department heads under the supervision of an executive. It is an assembly representing decentralized self-governing Circles, aiming to make decisions for the common good.

### The Operational Resolution Circle

The Operational Resolution Circle (ORC) is similar to the former Scrum of Scrum Masters. It deals with cross-circle matters like collaboration, Circle and Team composition, personal development, and conflict resolution. It comprises the Primary Circle Operation Owners with its Chair acting as facilitator. Its focus is a top-level Main Backlog of cross-circle improvements and impediments. The ORC operates like SRC but looks into the organization, instead of out towards the customer. A few extra practices can be helpful.

* If two Circles and their OOs cannot resolve a challenge bilaterally they can escalate it to the ORC. The ORC Manifest should be clear about what is required and how it is tackled.
* If team members have issues with the resident CO, it is good practice to let them go to another OO who is obliged to help.

## Secondary Circles

Secondary Circles (SC) deal with cross-circle concerns revolving around a certain set of competencies or skills, for example, design, architecture, quality, security, etc. SCs consist of relevantly skilled people from multiple Primary Circles and sometimes from customers and suppliers. An SC has a Main Backlog, a Chair chosen by the participants, and an associated OO.

---

6   A crisis can be thought of as a sudden drop in chaos. According to Dave Snowden, *"Chaos is always transient, it will stabilize. If you do not intervene, probably to your disadvantage!"*

- SCs have a regular meeting cadence of between one and four weeks. If something urgent comes up, they may convene in between, or allow the Chair to handle it through consultation with other relevant parties.
- Items can be delegated from other Circles to be tackled by those with special expertise in the SC.
- Items can be delegated from the SC back to a Primary Circle and displayed on that Primary Circle's Tactical Backlog. Normally an SC does not have a Tactical Backlog, some work may be accomplished directly when the Circle meets, and other work will be delegated.
- The Main Backlog of an SC often operates like a Kanban board, showing progress and information about where an item came from or where it is delegated.
- The SC is a form of representative influencing and decision-making forum, but the question of who participates does not have a simple answer. In principle, members should be volunteers who have the approval of their Primary Circle. Normally a Primary Circle sends only one person, and no person should be in more than two SCs, as the work in their Primary Circle is their main focus.

This differs from the old matrix organization where a person may report to two different people, in the line and project organization. Instead, it preserves the functional groups found in hierarchies, where people get support and sharpen their skills.

## Transient Circles

No matter how well-designed an organization is, there will always be unexpected situations. Minor challenges may be absorbed and dealt with in an agile way, by "inspect and adapt", but larger disruptions and drops into Chaos may require more concentrated effort. In such cases a Transient Circle, or task force is commissioned, to stabilize the situation and return to normal operation, possibly with changes based on what has been learned. Most disruptions are negative, but there are sudden unexpected opportunities. Here are some observations about using Transient Circles.

- An event in or outside the organization triggers a potential drop into Chaos. The Resolution Circles assess the situation and decide if it is necessary to commission a Transient Circle. In extreme urgency, the Resolution Circle Chairs have to make the call.
- The very best individuals are assigned to the Transient Circle, typically two to five people. Organizations may have contingency plans for some outlier events; perhaps a trained *crew* that can hit the ground running when the outlier event occurs. Otherwise, those with the best intuitive expertise will be urged to volunteer for the job. TC members choose their approach and how to make their own decisions.
- An OO is attached to the Transient Circle to liaise and compel cooperation with the rest of the organization. To allow the experts to focus fully it is necessary for someone to take this role.
- The Circle has a clear Manifest (sometimes called a charter). It agrees to be transparent about its work and progress, and how the rest of the organization will back up the team members. The Circle has an extraordinary mandate just to do things, and others support and provide assistance when asked for it.
- This will disturb the normal operation, as key people are drawn out for special work in the Transient Circle. OOs are hard at work to facilitate the best possible ongoing operation of the organization.
- To create a common view of the situation and drive appropriate action, Transient Circles typically use a Kanban task board.
- The OO keeps track of developments and unfolding circumstances, harvesting useful knowledge, and monitoring emerging stability.
- When the Resolution Circles and OO consider the situation to be stable, the organization reverts to normal. TC participants are shown appreciation, and the Circle is disbanded with no residual authority.

- Harvested knowledge may be used to introduce permanent changes to the organization. One option is to form a new Secondary Circle to digest the new information and make recommendations.

A Transient Circle should be short-lived. If its function is expected to last longer than three to six months, it is better to form a Primary Circle with full-time team members, or a Secondary Circle if the workload is expected to be lower than full-time.

# Transparency and Artifacts

Radical transparency is the foundation of the Agile Lean way; it is the antidote to politics and covert operations. To create maximum coherence inside the Circle and help the organization understand, Circle artifacts should clearly state their common understanding, who they are, what they do, why they do it, the stakeholders they serve, and any time-related constraints or commitments. Physical artifacts are more effective communication tools, but it may be necessary to rely on electronic artifacts. In all cases, it is important to make artifacts easy to access and understand; otherwise, there is a risk that they will not be used and information is lost.

## Manifests

The Manifest (or Charter) is a self-declared statement from the Circle about themselves and their commitments. It is a message to the outside world but also a means to keep Circle members aligned. Some elements of the Manifest are recommended:

- A top-level statement of the Circle's unique value proposition, stating the vision and mission of the Circle, its goals, and its *Raison d'etre*.
- Who are the *customers* of this Circle, those they serve, the beneficiaries?
- Why does the Circle do what it does? What value does it create for the beneficiaries?

- What are the services offered by the Circle? How to acquire the services, what should be included in a service request (delegation) for the Circle to accept it. Are there other constraints?
- When will the Circle deliver and what rules apply to get its services? What are its prioritization principles? If the Circle is a service provider, this may include average and guaranteed response and lead times.
- The Circle's public artifacts, how to find and use them.
- The Circle's activities and meetings, how to join, get information, and participate. Some Circles choose to record their review sessions so that people not able to participate can catch up.
- The people in the Circle, key players, the SO, OO and any specialist the outside world should know about. It is good practice to include a Competency or Asset Matrix, displaying the competencies and other assets individuals can provide. It may include a statement about Circle competencies and competencies needed. Are people OK with the work they are delivering?

## Main Backlog

The Main Backlog is a prioritized list of *Items*, everything the Circle has to deliver or do, whether large or small. It is helpful to distinguish between the following categories of backlog items:

- **Stories** are deliverables of a reasonable size, which can be completed within one cadence or iteration (2-4 weeks).
- **Epics** are just big stories that are too big to implement in one Cadence and therefore need to be decomposed before structured work can begin.
- **Objectives** are goals currently without an implementation strategy or solution, or which require contributions from other Stories and Epics.
- **Analyses or Research** are deliverables that produce knowledge through analysis or research.

- **Experiments or Probes** are deliverables that produce knowledge through hypothesis and experiment.
- **Improvements** are steps the Team will take to improve their work.
- **Other** items not directly related to main deliverables like company meetings, training, etc. but which still require time.
- It is good practice to include a **Timeline** of the most important constraints:
  - **Deadlines** that come from the outside and are non-negotiable.
  - **Milestones** that the Circle has defined as important dates.
  - **Delivery-Out** milestones where something has to be delivered, often in order to get a future result.
  - **Delivery-In** milestones where deliveries are expected.

The SO owns the Main Backlog, anybody can add items to it, but the SO has the responsibility to prioritize and secure the refinement of the items.

## Tactical Backlog

Circles choose their own approach to getting work done, it may be Scrum, Kanban, or some other way. They will always have an artifact illustrating the progress of the tactical work. It is good practice for the Tactical Backlog to include stories broken down into Tasks (the smallest unit for work) lasting less than a day. This is the main place to see the progress of the work, both for those in the Circle and those external to it.

The Circle Team (Developers in Scrum) own the Tactical Backlog. Only they can add items, prioritize them, decide how to split the work between team members, and make deliveries.

## Improvement Backlog

We recommend that Circles maintain a list of potential improvements that have been discovered during the course of their work and from their Retrospectives. This may be related to processes, skills, or tools to acquire, or changes to the environment. It is good practice at each Retrospective to examine and prioritize improvement opportunities for improvements, and then select those which are believed to have the most impact.

The OO (Scrum Master in Scrum) owns and prioritizes the Improvement Backlog. Most of the work is done by the OO, but sometimes other team members may contribute; in which case, it is good practice to reflect the items on the Main and/or Tactical Backlogs.

## Other Artifacts

More artifacts may be needed to develop radical transparency and help people in their daily work. Some common ones are listed here, but be careful not to create unnecessary bureaucracy:

- Impact Map is a matrix showing the relationship between the **Why**, **What, Who, When**, and sometimes **Where** (expected delegations). This is very powerful when properly maintained and updated.
- A visual architecture of solutions. A common understanding of complex solutions is most easily achieved through illustration.
- Burn-up and Burn-down charts showing progress and remaining work. These exist both at the tactical and strategic levels.
- Cumulative flow diagrams are used in Kanban to inspect flow and delivery rates.
- Chart of currently outstanding issues.
- A statistical control chart to detect if a process is in statistical control, if the variation is stable, improving, or degrading, and if outlier events are happening. This is for processes mostly in the Obvious or Complicated domain, not the Complex.

# Enabling People to Flourish

Every Circle relies on the strength of its people; the OO is the cornerstone, facilitating an environment where people experience fulfillment, grow, and flourish – i.e. become the best version possible of themselves. Daily life is a constant journey of learning and improvement.

## Retrospectives

The practice of regular, disciplined Retrospectives is central to all liberating organizations; it is a well-known practice in high-performance sports, rescue teams, etc. It is the key event for the OO to facilitate discussion about people's experience, and how it could be better, faster, of higher quality, or more enjoyable. It should be something to look forward to, not a drudge. To keep the Retrospective useful and enjoyable, one must not lose sight of the true purpose or regress into a scripted set of procedures. It should be absolutely clear that the Retrospective is not a blaming event where people are attacked. Difficult situations may be discussed, but disciplinary action does not take place here.

There is an abundance of resources and ideas about the discipline of Retrospectives and possible approaches. Here is a commonly used outline, a-step approach:

1.  Perform a security check. Is everybody OK speaking openly about the work just concluded? The facilitator (typically the OO) may try different approaches to discover people's true feelings, including an anonymous vote. The process should not proceed without a commitment to openness. Retrospectives require mutual respect, openness, and trust, otherwise they fail and may backfire. Typically the OO tries to discover the source of the resistance; mostly due to residual fear, maybe of a domineering person.

2.  A timeline of the last iteration is drawn up and people are requested to come up with short, unvarnished narratives of what was important to them during the iteration. Narratives can be discussed, noted on yellow Post-Its, and put on the timeline with agreement that they are roughly in the right order time-wise. Everybody now has a common understanding of the situation, of what actually happened. An

important side effect occurs when people recount what was important to them; they show something about their value system. A little more openness and trust has developed, and the Team nudges closer to each other.

3.  Ask: *"What were you happy with?"* People write green Post-its or place green marks on the existing yellow ones. This is a small celebration of success, reinforces the positive experiences, and amplifies them in the next period.

4.  Ask: *"What could be improved?"* people write red Post-its or put red marks on existing ones. People try to focus on the improvement angle and not on what went wrong, although it may certainly be necessary to clarify the exact nature of the issue.

5.  Ask: *"Who can improve what we just found?"* The findings are divided into those that the Circle can deal with locally and those that require outside intervention. The former are dealt with by the Team, larger items may go on the Main Backlog for refinement and prioritization, and smaller ones are just dealt with. The findings that require outside intervention end up with the OO who will work with the rest of the organization to find solutions.

6.  Finally, ask: *"What is the best improvement we can do now?"* The Whole Team prioritizes and makes a decision. They commit to making at least one improvement and to making it visible, perhaps by posting it on the wall. They also discuss the priority of the items on the Improvement Backlog.

## Personal Sustainable Work

Many people in an organization do not work in an idealized team setting where common backlogs are sufficient to manage their work. They often combine working in a team with working alone, while being available to help others. Circle SOs and OOs are examples of this. They each work with the Team but have things to do on their own. They are also generally available for the Team and for outside actors as liaison officers. This is common in Service Circles (primarily assisting other Circles). We call these roles "Service Workers", any leadership role should be considered a Service Worker.

How can this situation be structured to avoid frustration, loss of concentration, or meltdown of the person in the hurricane's eye? We recommend a Personal Sustainable Work[7] approach inspired by several writers and concepts, among which are *Getting Things Done*[8] and the *Pomodoro Technique*[9], but the main thinking is from John Boyd's *OODA Loop*[10] and Daniel Kahneman's *Thinking Fast Thinking Slow*[11]. Here is a quick overview of this micro-framework that can be followed unless sudden drops into chaos occur, in which case fires just need to be put out:

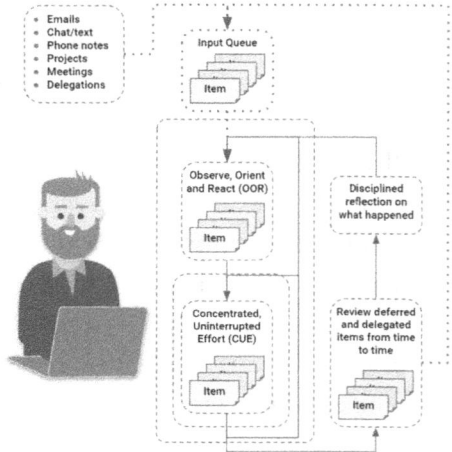

- The fundamental idea is to separate concentrated, focused work from interrupt-driven, fast-responder work; which don't mix well. No one can stay focused while being frequently interrupted, and those expecting a quick response get annoyed if they don't get it. By time-boxing the activities, space is created for both types of work resulting in more met expectations and less frustrated service workers. This is achieved by thinking the OODA way: *Observe, Orient, Decide, and Ac*t.

---

7   Read more in *Appendix B14 - Personal Sustainable Work in 60 Seconds*
8   Dave Allen's Getting Things Done (GTD), https://todoist.com/productivity-methods/getting-things-done
9   Francesco Cirillo's Pomodoro Technique, https://en.wikipedia.org/wiki/Pomodoro_Technique
10  John Boyd's OODA Loop, https://en.wikipedia.org/wiki/OODA_loop
11  Daniel Kahneman's Thinking Fast Thinking Slow, https://en.wikipedia.org/wiki/Thinking,_Fast_and_Slow

- Create an Input Queue for items coming from the outside, emails, chat, phone, meetings, and incoming delegations. Then sort them according to urgency (urgent means a large cost of delay).
- The working day is defined by a pattern of the two modes of operation followed by reflection and review.
- There is the Observe, Orient, and React, fast intuitive action loop (OOR)

  - **Observe** – What has entered the input queue?
  - **Orient** – What needs to be done with the item at the top?
  - **React** – Do it now, *Defer* (do it later), or *Delegate* (get someone else to do it)?
  - Keep looping until the input queue is empty or the timebox expires

- Then there is the Concentrated, Uninterrupted Effort loop (CUE)

  - **Decide** – Prioritize the items to be processed.
  - **Act** – Work on the Item prioritized.
  - Keep looping until the timebox is up, or a sudden drop into chaos appears. Results from the *Act* phase may produce new items in the Input Queue.

- **Reflection** – At regular intervals, preferably with other involved colleagues, reflect on how things went, looking for improvements or potential changes. At this time the Deferred and Delegated items are revisited.

Consult *Appendix B14 - Personal Sustainable Work in 60 Seconds* on the topic for more detail and to better clarify the principles, artifacts, and activities.

It is amazing how much efficiency and peace of mind can come from following this simple script. However, it does require some discipline on the part of the Service Worker; distractions must be resisted to allow interrupt-free focus on the work at hand. This is not always easy as today's environments are not designed for it. On the contrary, devices and applications are pinging newsflashes and updates to get our attention; we are continuously exposed to distractions of one sort or another.

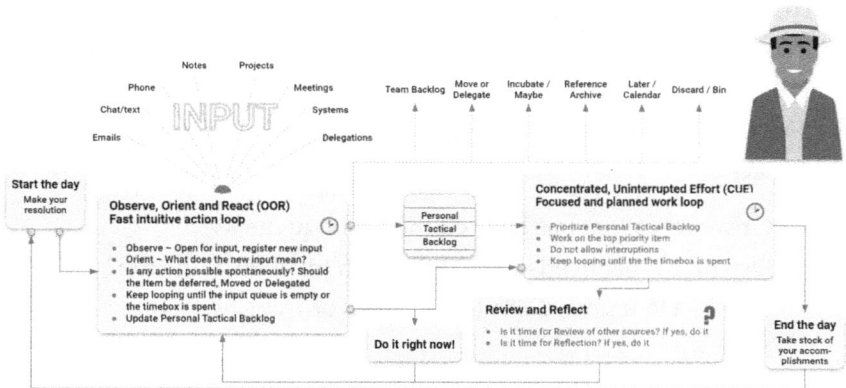

As Service Workers, we are often guilty of violating our own commitments by succumbing to the fatal attraction of outside distractions that force us to task-switch and fall out of flow. We must build barriers to protect our focus within the defined timeboxes.

## Liberating Structures

In any organization, there are many interactions between people beyond the activities and practices described here. A great inspiration is the book and the website *Liberating Structures*[12]. Like us, the authors reflect on why organizations are filled with what they call *"disengaged workers, dysfunctional groups, and wasted ideas."* Similarly, they conclude that the root cause of the situation is that the practices they have learned to follow will stifle inclusion and engagement.

Building a Liberating Organization on the Agile Lean Leadership framework provides the macro-structures necessary to create and sustain liberty and engagement in an organization. It also offers some excellent supplemental mini-structures for different tactical interactions. Here are a

---

12  Keith McCandless, Henri Lipmanowicz 2014: https://www.liberatingstructures.com/

few of our favorites, but please take the time to familiarize yourself with the greater body of work.

- **Impromptu Networking** – for quickly sharing challenges and expectations and building new connections, for example when a new group comes together. First, everybody is asked two questions: *"What big challenge do you bring to this gathering? What do you hope to receive and gain from this group?"* Then each person finds someone else with whom to share the answers to these questions. There are three rounds with different pairings of 4-5 minutes each. This helps introverts engage and find someone they can be at ease with; the aim is for everybody to feel involved and heard.

- **1-2-4-All** – This is for engaging everyone simultaneously to generate questions, ideas, and suggestions. We open all our training classes this way to gather a backlog of what the participants really want from the course; this structure has never failed to work. Here is the flow:

    - Pose a challenging question like *"What do you expect to get out of this class?"*
    - Everybody reflects alone on their response and jots down ideas (1 min.).
    - Next, they pair up and share their thoughts (2 min.).
    - Then they form groups of four and produce some written responses (4 min.).
    - Finally, each foursome presents a maximum of 3 or 4 discoveries to the whole group. Defer judgment, and make ideas visual.

- **TRIZ** – This is designed to make space for innovation by stopping counterproductive activities and behaviors. It is inspired by the Russian engineering approach *Teoriya Resheniya Izobretatelskikh Zadatch*[13]. It is somewhat counterintuitive but works really well.

---

13  In English, *The Theory of Inventive Problem Solving*.

- Identify and explain the topic, project, or situation discussed. Brainstorm the worst plausible results imaginable.
- Using *1-2-4-All* ask the group to make a list of activities that would ensure the worst result imaginable.
- Then ask the group to go through each item to see if there is anything currently being done that even remotely resembles those items, use *1-2-4-All* and build a second list, be brutally honest.
- Then ask the group to go through the second list and identify what steps could be taken to stop these now-discovered undesirable activities or behaviors.

## Nourishing Psychological Safety

We know that Psychological Safety is vital, especially during Retrospectives. Consider how much time and resources could be saved if organizations engaged and empowered everyone (especially those from traditionally underprivileged groups) to share their ideas and contribute their whole selves. Here are a few practices that can amplify the sense of Psychological Safety.

- Be open and approachable: communicate consistently that it is okay to speak up and share ideas, concerns, and questions; actively listen to what others say. Nobody should worry about getting shot down when speaking up. We may meet opposition, but that is OK if it sharpens the discussion and leads to a better result.
- Be human and humble: Admit when you do not have all the answers or when you make a mistake. Being open about slip-ups makes it easier for others to feel safe doing the same. We are in the real world, fragmented knowledge and imperfection is the nature of things.
- Be aware of biases: Make sure everybody gets a chance to participate, perhaps use Liberating Structures. We each have deeply engraved biases, and only by testing assumptions with others is it possible to balance them and prevent skewed decisions. If you spot issues with biases, tackle them firmly but respectfully.

- Develop a spirit of support: In my dealings with different healthcare groups, one feature that stood out was their willingness to help the younger or inexperienced, they said *"It is very easy to get help around here"* which gave them the confidence to take on new challenges. That was a huge thing.

- Ask honest questions, don't fake it: People feel appreciated when somebody wants to hear their opinions and proposals. Avoid cheap techniques to manipulate people into feeling appreciated. It is especially helpful to ask *why* – maybe several times – to try to understand motives or root causes. Prepare questions that demonstrate interest by researching people's situations beforehand. Similarly, when you meet again, try to remember what they said before. Maintain eye contact during conversations to show interest and engagement. Failure to do so implies disrespect and signals passive-aggressiveness.

- Don't rush to seemingly conclusive statements. To create an air of superiority people in power may think they must appear all-knowing, strong, and decisive, but this just shuts down others and compels them to disengage. Instead, ask *"I wonder why…"*, anybody is allowed to wonder; it is not threatening, but inviting. Or try *"Can you tell me more?"*, *"I didn't quite get that, can you give a bit more detail?"* or perhaps *"I never thought of that! But how does it fit in?"*

- Avoid criticizing or talking down a person's initiative. There is an old saying: *"Beware of the yes-but people"*. When you propose something and are met with *"Yes, but …"* giving a bucketload of reasons why this would not work but go badly, you feel rejected and shut down. They did not say *"How could anybody be so stupid to suggest that?"*, but you probably heard it that way. Try instead to say *"Yes, and…"* suggest an improvement that signals affirmation of the person's input and invites dialog.

- Communicate intent. This idea comes from David Marquet's *Intent-based Leadership*[14]. There is a lot to learn from that, but the key thing is this: If possible, develop a practice where everybody at every level communicates what they intend to accomplish and do. We understand that there are times when there is no time for this sort of thing, but there are lots of benefits to Intent-based Leadership:

  - It is a way of starting with the *Why*, it eases the cognitive load on the recipient and improves the likelihood of them actually absorbing the message. If they subscribe to the intent, they are more tolerant towards the actions.

  - Clear intentions are easy to react to. Obscure communications lead to vague responses.

  - Communicating intent shows respect for others.

  - It sets expectations, and when fulfilled it amplifies trust.

  - It provides early warnings to other people so they have time to intervene if the projected course conflicts with what they do.

  - Presented in the right way it invites others to suggest a better course, ask for, or offer help.

  - This should also happen at the Circle level. A Circle that intends to change its ways of working should communicate the intent to the other Circles; it is especially to inform those that are directly affected, but also inform the broader organization. Other teams may have experienced similar challenges and have great ideas for their resolution.

- Together time. A study at the Massachusetts Institute of Technology[15] found that teams that took regular 15-minute breaks together had 18% more interactions than other groups. Furthermore, annual staff turnover was more than 25% lower among teams that held collective

---

14  Intent Based Leadership: https://intentbasedleadership.com/
15  Alex "Sandy" Pentland, quoted in: https://thesumisgreater.wordpress.com/ 2016/10/14/fika-the-case-for-having-coffee-breaks-together/

breaks compared to others. Regular breaks and informal interactions significantly enhance team performance. These breaks allow team members to share information, build social cohesion, and re-energize, which improves overall productivity and creativity. The amount of time team members spend together in face-to-face communication positively correlates with their ability to collaborate effectively. Frequent and high-quality interactions lead to better information flow and problem-solving capabilities. There is a purely social aspect to being in a team, connecting at the basic human level. Chimpanzees have grooming sessions to make the troop bond, we need to interact around ordinary activities and experience the small positive strokes from other people to develop strong relationships.

# General Organizational Practices

We looked at helpful practices at the Circle and team level, some of which apply to the whole organization, but on that level, there are some additional ones to consider.

## Organizational and Relationship Manifests

As the Circle Manifest expresses the *Raison d'être* of the Circle, so does the Organizational Manifest for the whole organization. It is more high-level, with fewer details, but expresses the vision and mission and most importantly the organization's common values. Liberated people are bound together with common goals and values framed by a set of enabling constraints that provide the checks and balances that curb the abuse of power and hold a steady course.

The main statements of the Organizational Manifest should apply both internally and externally, providing an umbrella for The Circle Manifests which should align with the Organization's overall values and goals.

Relationship Manifests detail the interaction between Circles, especially where Primary Circles delegate deliverables (Backlog Items) to each other. Other Relationship Manifests outline the exchanges with Resolution and Secondary Circles. Delegations to Resolution Circles are often called Escalations, as they represent cases where Circles on their own, or bi-laterally, cannot resolve a situation for the common good. This must be clearly defined so that a balance is struck between overburdening the Resolution Circles and not getting to meaningful and timely action. The relationships to Secondary and Transient Circles usually do not need much work as most of the principles are in the Circle Manifests.

## Ownership

How can and should owners act if they want to build a Liberating Organization? We have already discussed challenges relating to owners, but here are a few extra hints:

- The owners should examine their own motives. Are they really behind the idea of a Liberating Organization and believe it will create great results, or are they only in it for shareholder value? It is better to be clear and transparent because insincerity will be discovered and backfire. Sometimes owners are just in it for the money – it is an investment. If the organization is a publicly traded company or owned by a capital fund, that will be the case. It is better to know and it is still possible to create a great organization. Another special case is if the organization is a public institution or dependent on politically allocated funds. That can be really difficult as politicians like to exert power and change things willy-nilly to appear forceful and polish their profile, and central bureaucracies believe in central planning and control. Very good examples of success do exist though. In Norway the government agency NAV has had great success in allowing decentral offices to be self-governing, this has reduced costs significantly and improved people's job satisfaction.
- The owners are responsible for the legal bylaws and potential shareholder agreements. They should be transparent and consistent with the Organizational Manifest.

- The Owners appoint or employ Board Members or executives. In doing so, they should look for character, not just their factual skills or professional track record. They should ask the question, *"Are they capable of deciding for the common good according to our values?"*

- Finally, owners can decide to distribute shareholder value with a form of profit sharing. In a company we know well, very positive effects were seen over a number of years where the family owners gave bonuses when the company performed well. Unfortunately, it recently backfired as the bonuses became skewed towards management, creating resentment from the other workers.

- We have always liked the idea of giving people the opportunity to acquire shares in the company they work for, sometimes approaching the idea of a *Cooperative*. It is ideal if everybody takes responsibility for the well-being of the organization and also shares in the upside when available. In Denmark, having shares like that unfortunately has become rather difficult due to an incomprehensible and unpredictable tax system.

## Setting of Goals and Allocation of Resources

Typically a Liberating Organization adjusts its goals and decides how to invest its resources (money, time, talent, etc.) in the Resolution Circles, predominantly the Strategic one. We recommend following the outline of *Beyond Budgeting*[16] (BB) for this. Very simply, instead of the classic budgetary discipline, BB separates goals, the allocation of resources, and sometimes the setting of targets. In BB the allocation of resources is dynamic, they say: *"the bank is always open"*; meaning that unlike static traditional annual budgeting, allocation and reallocation can be considered as circumstances unfold. An initial framework can be proposed:

- On principle it is good to revisit the allocation of resources regularly, quarterly seems to be the preferred interval, but in fast-moving situa-

---

16  For more information see *Appendix B5 - Beyond Budgeting in 60 Seconds*.

tions, a monthly cadence may be more appropriate. This is called an Ordinary Allocation Session.

- Any Circle can request consideration of allocation if unforeseen circumstances have developed. This is called an Extraordinary Allocation Session.

- When preparing discussions about the allocation of resources it is good practice to use a standardized form for presenting the case. We like to use an *ALL Canvas – The Business Case* based on the *Lean Canvas* (see later). The great benefit of this approach is that it gets directly to the point and its standardized layout makes it easier to compare with others.

| 1. Why - Challenges | 3. What - Solutions | 2. Value Proposition | 7. Because - Rationale | 1. Who - Beneficiaries |
|---|---|---|---|---|
| | *3-5 key elements?* | | *Why are the observation and solutions coherent and plausible?* | |
| | 6. How - to Measure | | 4. How - to Introduce | |
| *What is the "trigger"? How are the challenges overcome today?* | *Early indicators of success or failure?* | *A short, clear and attractive statement.* | *Ways to inform, involve and rally people, getting their cooperation* | *Who could be the first to benefit?* |
| 5. Cost Expectation | | | 5. Value Expectation | |
| *Expected costs and investments.* | | | *Plausible and visible, preferably quantifiable, benefits and values.* | |
| A. Constraints, Milestones, Risks | | | | |
| *Any existing and typically external limits to the options.* | | | | |

- In an Ordinary Allocation Session (consisting of at least two meetings) let every Circle with proposals present their canvas, followed by a quick feedback round, preferably based on Ritual Dissent (see later). The Circles then go back and refine their Canvas as needed. Next time quick presentations are made (highlighting changes made since the last time), the group tries to consolidate the input into an Extended Impact Map (EIM, see later) to provide an overview, after which deliberation of a decision should be possible. Sometimes one or more OOs take responsibility for consolidating input and building the EIM to save time for the Resolution Circle.

- An Extraordinary Allocation Session is a compressed version of the above. The Circle that initiated the session presents its case and the process is followed.

## People and Employment

It is essential that the Circles have a mandate to make decisions about personnel selection and how optimal working conditions are created. In this way, the Circle can create a workplace that attracts the right people. From first-hand experience in the healthcare sector, I have observed highly popular organizational units and other units in the same institutions that could not retain staff.

It is very expensive to onboard new staff, often taking six months before new hires have contributed what has been invested in them. There are good reasons to create a low turnaround environment; as we saw earlier it hinges on engagement.

This is not an easy freedom to acquire. Central administrations like finance and HR do not want to give up their power. Circles may need help from a central HR service, but HR should never take over the hiring process. They should be advisors, not enforcers. It is especially dangerous when centrally issued budget cuts hit. That will be the time to fight.

If there is a need to reduce manpower in a Circle, it must be dealt with swiftly and with transparency. Delaying action, causing rumors to spread is even more damaging. The OO is a central player in this situation. Here are some recommendations that have worked in various organizations:

- Perhaps there are vacancies elsewhere in the organization, and some people might consider moving there.
- Perhaps some people want to take leave for educational purposes for example, or simply reduce their work hours. This is particularly relevant if the slump in activity or demand is expected to be a temporary one.

- It has been seen that people have agreed to reduce their salary by a certain percentage to avoid laying off colleagues. Sometimes those with the highest salaries took the deepest cut. When this happens, team bonding can be greatly amplified.

- Finally, when there is no way around it, the number of employees has to be reduced. It is important to consider very carefully how the Circle can retain most of its capabilities and competencies – both factually and socially. There is a tendency to look only at the factual skills affecting the deliveries in the short term. That may be necessary in a crisis – after all, survival is the first priority – but it may not be optimal. We have seen OOs or Scrum Masters being dismissed because *"they do not contribute to deliveries"*, in which case the situation gravitates towards the old top-down management style with a single boss. The consequences of different people leaving should also be considered. I have known people who volunteer to leave because they would not suffer as badly as some of their colleagues; that requires a very special character.

- Occasionally, people are wrongly assigned to a position, the error can be on either side of the employment agreement or internal transfer, but no matter which, it is important to approach the situation respectfully and look for positive solutions, whether it be re-transfer, education, coaching, or even finding a better life elsewhere.

## Compensation Schemes

How to compensate people is an important question and one without a simple answer. Everybody would like to have more – and should be allowed to want that – but available funds are always limited, so it is a *wicked* problem. Money will drive some people, but it is not the attractor on which a Liberating Organization focuses; it may not be possible to retain these people long-term if the argument of freedom and intrinsic motivation does not appeal to them. It is also the case that what sometimes looks like greed, is really envy. People do not necessarily want more in absolute terms, but more than the next person to boost their self-esteem and apparent status. It is a potentially harmful need to feel superior to others. People do not normally admit to envy as it is not considered an attractive character trait. Some helpful guideline ideas:

- Most importantly, the Circle is in charge as much as possible. To protect freedom the decentralized unit (the Circle in this case) must have a mandate to operate. Only at the very local level is it possible to have a true understanding of circumstances and special conditions. The Circle should be allowed to develop local compensation schemes if that suits their conditions and people. The freedom to determine compensation is always controversial. Central bureaucracy does not want to give up its power to set compensation and it can be a problem in unionized or government-controlled organizations.
- If the Circle has the freedom to administer compensation, it can be helpful to let people determine how the available funds are split; some have even tried to let people suggest salaries for others – not themselves. If the maturity level is sufficient, this can create a positive atmosphere in the Circle.
- If the organization has a variable bonus split among Circles, a similar approach can be chosen. All Circles suggest bonuses for other Circles. Inside the Circle, it is good practice to split the bonus equally.
- Pay at the market rate. People should be compensated sufficiently so that lack of money does not create pressure to find a better-paying job; all the positive sentiments in the world do not pay mortgages. Because of this, it is important to be consistently profitable, and consequently have the resources to pay people appropriately. Constant improvement and innovation are necessary, how can value be added to products and services? How can customers be upsold or new ones discovered? All that to increase profit and available funds.
- Avoid schemes that create competition between people because they dampen teamwork and sow the seeds of envy. It can be OK to bench-

mark Circles, but the aim should be to find ways to improve, not to punish.

- It can be helpful to link compensation to assumed special responsibilities. In an Agile Lean Organization, the SO and OO roles - plus those that participate in special Circles, eg, Resolution, Secondary, and Transient are candidates. One area often overlooked is that of technical expertise; it is good practice to pay people extra for building and maintaining key areas of expertise. A good example is that of a scheme promoted by Google. On being hired straight from university a person is placed in a compensation bracket, but if that person acquires expertise and assumes responsibility in an area of value to Google, they will be moved up a level and this can happen two or three times.

- What about people with special needs? There are some people with special needs who may need accommodation within the organization to allow them meaningful opportunities to contribute. How should these people be handled in terms of payment? First, it is important that the Circles agree to take on people with special needs, understanding that there may be adjustments, including financial ones. The rest of the people will typically make a sacrifice of their own convenience to create space for such a person, but that is the kind of service-oriented attitude necessary in a Liberating Organization.

- People with young families may also need flexibility to deal with their children's sick days, doctor's appointments, school, and special events. The Circle needs to be transparent and flexible about it, with a desire to make it work, but it is a *wicked problem*. Those who need extra latitude must be aware that others are pulling a heavier load in their absence and show appreciation, and perhaps volunteer for something extra at times. If it develops into a sense of entitlement, it creates resentment. I have experienced people with families and some who volunteer for nonprofits having the attitude that everybody must understand their needs and that it is effectively OK to slack off.

This question of compensation is intrinsically linked to the next one.

234

# Reinventing the Career Path

Traditionally, people's career paths are linked to moving up in the classic hierarchy, *"You either move up, or you move out!"* Paychecks grow accordingly and exponentially as the top is approached. Understandably, people in mid-career may see an Agile Lean Organization as a threat to their career prospects.

It is crucial for an Agile Lean Organization to value and properly reward the different roles and encourage those who seek more responsibility. It may require a new way of publicly acknowledging the contribution of people, teams, and Circles, which is in contrast with the more sensational way imperial CEOs are either lauded or lambasted by the media.

In a recent firsthand healthcare situation, I was very impressed that everybody's contribution was appreciated, even the normally less regarded cleaning and service staff, *"their work is the foundation for keeping this place free from infections."* Everybody worked for their team, sometimes taking on tasks that might be considered below their status, including the surgeons who I often heard saying, *"Anything I can help with here?"*

There are special areas where technical expertise is revered – academia and research-heavy organizations for example. This needs to be developed in other organizations. The people with the competencies, vision, and innovative capabilities need to be appreciated also in monetary terms. Those who are cornerstone experts, perhaps being chairs of Secondary Circles are exceedingly important and need to be recognized as such.

Starting with character, career paths should work towards increased competence, responsibility, and service to others, with the aim of being able to make recommendations and decisions for the common good – not increasing power, money, and status.

## Working in a Team

Teamwork has been variously defined for the last 50 to 60 years, so there are plenty of resources and recommendations. Here are some observations that can help identify a well-functioning team:

- Everyone on the team talks and listens, and they share the bandwidth fairly equally, keeping contributions short and sweet, and with a propensity for listening.
- Members face one another, and their conversations and gestures are energetic.
- Members connect directly with one another, not just with a perceived leader.
- Members carry on back-channel or side conversations within the team.
- Members communicate intent and are keen to interact with others concerning the next steps, including offering help.
- Members periodically break out, explore outside the team, and bring information back.

It is a generally accepted fact that individual reasoning and talent contribute far less than most believe. The best strategy for building a great team is not to select highly profiled experts, but to find individuals who appreciate the fabric of teamwork and are able to follow successful communication patterns. In complex scenarios it is not necessarily the experts who win, but those who can discover and share knowledge in communication with others.

## Radical Transparency

Radical transparency is an essential fuel for running a Liberating, Constitutional Organization. People cannot act on what they cannot see. However the classic organizational hierarchy implies that knowledge is *on a need-to-know basis*, so it is a hard sell to traditional management who want to preserve their status and power over others and use a certain amount of *fact-spinning* to achieve desired results.

However, people generally respond positively to transparency. We have found the discipline of maintaining top-level, transparent backlogs for the Resolution Circles especially helpful. This is particularly powerful when combined with open reviews for people to ask further questions. A variation of this is a high-level Extended Impact Map highlighting the most important objectives, deliverable activities, stakeholders, and events on a timeline. Another helpful artifact is a *Blackboard* where questions in search of answers, or objectives in search of strategies can be posted. These are covered in the next chapter.

# Special Cases that need Attention

## Divisions and Super Circles

The standard framework of Primary Circles, Resolution Circles, etc. works up to about 150-250[17] people, about the size of a *Company* in the military. We shall refer to such a unit (a network of Circles) as a *Division*.

What about larger organizations? Attempting a full-blown transformation in a very large organization will most likely require some innovation and trial and error. It is also likely that the structure above the Division level will retain its traditional form, in which case the discussion about *Free Zones* later in this chapter applies. However, here are some helpful principles and practices to follow:

- Resolution Super Circles – it makes sense to have Strategic and Operational Super Circles that resolve the challenges that are not possible to resolve at the Division level. There is normally no need for formal Tactical Super Resolution Circles here, as tactical matters must be possible to resolve in the Division. It is pretty much the same with ordinary

---

17  Studies have indicated that humans are best able to maintain stable relationships in a cohesive group with between 100 and 250 members,

Resolution Circles, the challenges will be bigger and the meeting cadence longer. However, it is important to maintain the ability to respond quickly to challenges. Often larger changes in resource allocation need to be addressed in the Super Circles, and *The bank is always open* principle from Beyond Budgeting is maintained. It is common practice that the chairs of the Resolution Circles in the Divisions are those participating in the Super Circle. Sometimes just one Super Circle is implemented to handle both strategic and operational matters.

- Secondary Super Circles. Some of the topics dealt with in Secondary Circles may need to be addressed for the whole Organization. In such cases, there is a call for Secondary Super Circles, because the challenges are bigger, and meeting cadences are longer.

- It is important that Super Circles avoid the temptation to deal with very detailed issues that belong to the individual divisions. Likewise, the Division should be granted as much authority as possible to protect its independent operation mandate. There should be no need for Divisions to be accountable to a central administration, especially for finance, legal, HR, and IT. These service functions should be placed within the independent Divisions and coordination within the whole organization should happen via the Secondary Super Circles. There may be exceptions, like cafeteria, facility management, delivery service, etc. that are impractical to distribute to Divisions, so they may be placed in one division, which "*sells*" its services to the others.

- Each Value Stream should exist within one Division, but that does not mean that a Division cannot use the products and services of another. Transactions are more like those with external suppliers, not as close as Delegations within a Value Stream. It follows that such products and services should be standardized and possible to specify, i.e. complex deliveries should not cross Divisional borders.

- Occasionally it is necessary to commission a Transient Team comprising people from across Divisions. That is the case if a sudden drop into Chaos triggering the intervention is not local to a Division.

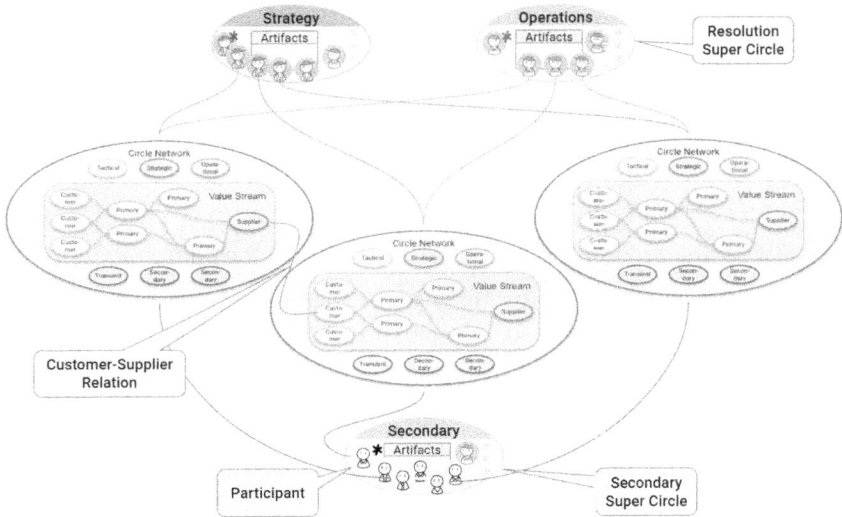

These principles may seem foreign to people used to traditional structures. However, an organizational architecture that reduces dependencies among organizational units produces great benefits. In our investigations, we have found that much of the delay in getting things done is due to dependencies that take a long time to resolve, and sometimes organizations end up with circular dependencies that make everything grind to a halt.

Another area where these principles can be applied is when smaller organizations cluster or network for a greater impact in a market or in a society. Sometimes it involves co-ownership like a cooperative, and sometimes a looser federation bound through agreements and a manifest defining the constitution. The principles and practices described above are directly applicable to this scenario. What we define as Divisions will then be independent organizations that have granted some authority to the federation to decide for the common good.

# Special Circles

We have discussed the core types of Circles in the Agile Lean Leadership framework, but sometimes a variant is required. Let us look at the more common ones:

### Scaled Up Circles

Sometimes the amount of work on the Main Backlog combined with the required competencies and time constraints requires more people than can be realistically crammed into one small cross-functional team. One solution is the *Scaling Up* pattern; there is still one Main Backlog and one SO, but more than one Circle Team, each with its own Tactical Backlog and possibly its own OO.

This is an alternative to *Scaling Out* by delegating to other Circles in the Value Stream. Scaling Up is preferred if the deliverables are predominantly in the Complex domain, Scaling Out is helpful if the deliverables delegated are in the Obvious or Complicated domain.

The Circle Teams work in parallel iteration after iteration, dynamically deciding together the best way forward and who does what as circumstances unfold.

Examples of situations where Scaling Up has been helpful come from large software or complex construction projects. But it has also been seen in situations where the customers served by a Frontline Circle require more interaction than one small team can accommodate.

A few things change when using the Scaled Up pattern, here are some recommendations:

- During the Refinement of Backlog Items, the Teams allocate work; sometimes this is self-evident based on competencies, sometimes it has to be discussed, or maybe items are split into parts that fit better. Teams pull from the Main Backlog prioritized by the SO.

- That same pattern is followed during the planning process where the split of work is finalized.
- Daily Coordination is conducted in each Circle Team. The Teams may find it helpful to have a mini-tactical resolution session after this, but often it is overkill. Another strategy is to stagger the time of team sessions so that team members can visit other teams. Under all circumstances, there needs to be discipline to capture impediments or blockers.
- Review sessions can be conducted using the *Turkish Bazaar* pattern: First, everybody gets together and each Team makes a very short presentation of the main accomplishments and findings during the last iteration. The attending stakeholders make notes and when this part is over, the teams go back to work, and the stakeholders follow their main interests visiting Teams in the Turkish Bazaar.
- Retrospectives are held individually for each Team (the SO cannot be present everywhere). After that, all Teams get together and share their respective findings including potential impediments and possible solutions.

A scaled-up environment is more complex and should only be used when necessary. It is always better if the bulk of the work can be split into pieces and worked on by one small cross-functional team. Instead of one big project think of two smaller ones with high internal coherence and little external coupling.

**Scaled Down Circles**

In other situations, we find a need to use the *Scaled Down* pattern. Here there is just one Team, SO, and OO, but there are multiple inputs, multiple customers perhaps, effectively leading to multiple small backlogs. It now becomes the Circle's job to prioritize the order in which to execute the requests, no small job as every customer wants full and immediate attention.

Normally, such a Circle needs a published strategy (on the Circle Manifest) for how prioritization is done. The simplest is to work First-come-first-serve, with the possibility of an expedited queue where deliveries cost more.

These Circles are often found in the middle of the organization's Value Stream, where they serve multiple other Circles. Scaling down is also common in circles that serve many outside customers with special work, for example, developing websites or smaller building or construction jobs. Almost all small to medium-sized companies experience this in one form or another, for example:

- A request for delivery comes with a desired delivery time, making it harder to juggle multiple time constraints. It is recommended that the Circle aligns on milestones where delivery can occur, so they are not overwhelmed with multiple deadlines. This could be a specific day of the week. It is also recommended to give customers commitments in a range, like: "*We expect to deliver on such-and-such a date, worst case one week later.*"
- Refinement will be different, the different stakeholders should only attend the discussion of their items, so it will probably be less structured and more *Inspect and Adapt*.
- Planning will take different time commitments into account, so this is a bit harder.
- Daily coordination may have to be in closed session if the Circle is working with external customers, it is normally not a good thing that they hear about each other's deliverables.
- Reviews may also have to be conducted separately for external customers. It is common practice to let one or two team members do the review with a particular customer in order not to introduce too much overhead. If the customers are internal, it can help to give each one a time slot where their deliverables are being reviewed, they don't necessarily need to be there for everybody else's stuff.

Scaled Down Circles are harder to work in, with more complexity due to the rather unrelated stakeholders or customers, but it is an issue that many have to solve.

## Service Circles

Service Circles are special internal Scaled Down Circles that almost always service other Circles that have special skills and competencies in short supply. This can be assistance with finance, HR, legal, facility management, catering, etc.

These kinds of Circles often don't work as Teams in the best sense, there is too little overlap and cross-functionality, for example, there may only be one Legal Adviser, so other team members may not be able to help with legal challenges. It is still better though, to let them be together in a Circle as there is always something to do that does not require deep expertise. For example, if the legal expert is not available, someone else may be able to take a request from another Circle, record some facts, and still give this Circle a sense of great service.

It is common practice in such circles to take turns as the *Fast Responder* to requests from other Circles, whose perception of the quality of service and positive attitude is highly influenced by responsiveness.

*Lead Time* is an important factor in requests for help. Some – and often quite a lot – can be resolved on the spot, while others may take more time. It is good practice to give the requester an expected lead time with a worst-case if there is uncertainty.

Service Circles will typically develop some sort of Kanban board to keep track of the requests for help. It is helpful to use the principles from *Personal Sustainable Work* described above.

## Circles of Travelers

A *Circle of Travelers* is an even more specialized scaled-down pattern that we have used in situations where there were Circles with a majority of inexperienced people. This can be seen in organizations going through rapid expansion.

The experienced people are placed in a Circle where they work as *Travelers* visiting other Circles, teaching, and helping out. Travelers get parachuted down into other Circles.

- Prioritization of Traveler time is crucial, and often a source of contention.
- This should be clearly stated in Traveler Circle's manifest along with other rules of engagement: What does the Traveler bring and do? What is expected of the receiving Circle?
- For the individual Traveler, concentrated uninterrupted time when on a mission is very important. While on a mission, the Traveler reduces interrupts to a bare minimum, to get out again as quickly as possible. Others have to respect that. Getting things done without delay is crucial so that the Traveler can move on
- In between missions Travelers can loosen up and have more *Observe and Orient* time of their own. There should be time to sustain the relationship with other Travelers, get their feedback, and learn.

**Production Circles**

Production Circles are units that can regularly deliver fairly standardized goods, which means they deliver mostly well-known things, in the Obvious domain. They often take orders from many sources, but it is less of an issue, due to the standardized nature of work. It means that it is easier to define the process for prioritizing orders and projecting deliveries.

In a Production Circle, processes should be under statistical control, some variation is present, but normally constant attention to the principles and tools from Lean can lead to constant improvement. It is not always the best solution to work in small agile Teams with constant interaction, it may not be necessary due to the more standardized nature of the work, but do invite people to participate to find the best structure.

It is always important to keep the feedback loops going, there should also be a review cadence of deliverables and processes, where perhaps up to 20 people can do these together.[18] This is the original PDSA Cycle from Lean.

Planning in these Circles is mostly well-known from Lean; however, we would like to highlight the benefit of having a clear Manifest so that other Circles know how to interact with it in the best possible way. How are orders placed, how are they prioritized, and what feedback and transparency are offered to the customers?

## Engineering Circles

In organizations with a high content of research and innovation of complex and complicated products, there is often a need for a special Circle of experts that can develop special parts, modules, or algorithms. This can be mechanics, electronics, chemistry, software, and math among other things. Some people really shine in such a lab environment, and this can help them flourish.

By nature, it is a Scaled Down Circle and follows the standard pattern. Due to the complexity of the deliverables, it typically requires a lot of interaction with those who delegate work to it.

Those who work alone in an engineering Circle will benefit from following the *Personal Sustainable Work* previously mentioned. Under all circumstances keep the feedback loops (Review and Retrospective) going as these are the foundation for all learning and improvement.

## Dual Mode Circles

Transient Circles can be commissioned when sudden drops into chaos occur, but there are many scenarios where a Circle as part of its normal operation has to be able to deal with emergencies.

---

18  In an ordered environment with well defined deliverables a rule of thumb is that we can work with up to 20-25 people, this is similar to what we believe we can handle when teaching a class.

An obvious example is a hospital department where the normal routine of patient care is punctuated by a crisis, calling for a different form of engagement and decision-making. It actually switches to *Red Alert* and operates more like a Transient Circle, with intuitive decision-making by experienced people and others mostly following orders; there is no time for extensive deliberation. When the situation is stabilized, everybody reverts to normal. An emergency room is an extreme form where the arrival of each new patient triggers a Red-Alert cycle.

Similar situations exist among firefighters, rescue services, security services, police, and the military. They all rehearse the scenarios like *crews* and know how to play their part once the Red Alert goes off. Quite often different people lead in normal and Red Alert modes. An interesting parallel exists to the ways the native American Cherokees were organized with a White Chief and a council of eight normally in charge of the village in peacetime, but a Red Chief would be given authority in times of war[19]. When the crisis was over everything reverted to normal.

**Innovation Circles**

Finally, organizations sometimes need to enter into the zone of Radical Innovation, this is a voluntary small step into chaos, removing the majority of constraints and letting people run multiple parallel probes and discovery processes to unearth radically new ways of serving customers or building products and services.

This is a Transient Circle, typically commissioned and funded by the Strategic Resolution Circle. The best people are invited to join for a specific timebox, only a small number (max five) should be in such an edge-

---

19  About the Cherokee, see for example: https://nativeamericans.mrdonn.org/southeast/ cherokee/government.html and https://www.coretexts.org/old/cherokeelessons/ unit3/downloads/ Woodward%20Cherokee%20Women%20and%20Deliberation%20Units%201%20and% 203.pdf

of-chaos Circle. They may find it helpful to use the *Idealized Design*[20] pattern.

They will hold regular review sessions where the rest of the organization can follow progress and provide corrective input if the process develops in an undesirable direction.

## Special Organizational Constructs

In real life, it is not always possible to achieve a fully Liberating Organization, at least initially. Organizations are complex organisms due to the presence of humans, so it may be necessary to settle for incremental evolutionary steps. Some advice can be offered on how to deal with various hybrid situations.

### A Free Territory Under a Traditional Organization

If a Free Territory based on freedom is established under a traditional hierarchy, some practices are helpful to protect it in the long term. All of these practices have to exist within certain constraints in the overall organization. A balance has to be struck, with enough freedom to reap the benefits of the Constitutional Organization, and enough compliance with the surrounding traditional organization to prevent it from trying to blunt the freedom.

The concept was already discussed at length in Chapter 6. However, it is important to highlight the importance of being transparent on both sides. It is easy for people on either side to slip into them-and-us thinking, which is another example of a classic culture clash – openness and a constant mutual display of respect is the recipe for keeping the balance.

Regular reviews, retrospectives, and communicating intent from both sides are key to getting the benefits and protecting the longevity of the Free Territory. Sometimes an investment must be made in extra information and review sessions to develop and keep alignment.

---

20  Idealized design, please consult Appendix *B10 – Idealized Design in 60 Seconds*

Another practice that has proven helpful is for the Free Territory to send one of its OOs as a liaison officer to help out at a critical spot in the traditional organization, which can really boost respect and trust.

## Keeping the Line Organization in Place

As a variant, several organizations have tried to implement some form of Agile Lean organization with Agile Lean teams, while still keeping the Line Organization intact. We have seen it work for a while at least, and it requires the line managers to concentrate on supporting people in teams on matters of competence. In this case, the line organization takes the place of the Secondary Circles. Matters of collaboration, onboarding, and offboarding should be left to the agile lean teams. In one example the team members spent about 80-85% of their time in the teams and the remainder on line-organization activities. That worked well for quite a while until for other reasons the hierarchy abandoned the self-governing teams.

Experience shows that this is at best a transitional phase where the idea of self-governing teams settles and matures. It is unstable in nature, always with a little uncertainty about people's primary loyalty and who makes the ultimate decisions. The classic matrix organization – now largely abandoned – is a way of trying to make this structure permanent. Often the finance department is a third shadowy force that operates like politically appointed commissars in the Soviet Union who could show up at any given time and start exercising authority.

## Small to Medium-sized Businesses

During our investigation, many of the positive experiences with freedom in organizations originated in small to medium-sized businesses (SMBs). This normally means no more than a few hundred people with a maximum of three, and often only two layers of traditional hierarchy.

In such organizations, the owners are directly involved, either because they are founders actively managing the organization, or because they have employed a CEO to act as their *steward*. Whether the organization provides freedom to its people or not, is very much up to the owners or their steward. They must choose the constitutional organization, grant people freedom and mandate, and demonstrate it in practice. They have the right to intervene, and pull rank, but if they want people's true commitment they should only do so in the case of a deadlock or disaster.

In this case, it is a good idea to organize the value stream in Primary Circles and with Resolution Circles for decision-making, with the CEO (and sometimes the CFO) employed by the board to represent the owners. Under most jurisdictions there has to be at least one person (director, CEO) who is legally responsible for compliance with the laws, etc. The CEO can be in a Service Circle together with others who help the other Primary Circles in different situations. The CEO in such an organization is very often an outward-oriented person who needs to help Primary Circles close deals with key customers and generally represent the organization publicly. The CEO would also be part of the Strategy Resolution Circle, and often be the chair of that Circle.

If the CEO is committed to the Constitutional Organization and there is a mandate from the owners, it can work really well. Such a CEO is a leader working to create an environment where everybody can grow and take on more leadership work. He or she can then focus on the outside world and the long-term sustainability of the organization.

Ideally, there should be a senior or chief Operations Owner (OO or COO) whose constant focus is on collaboration and culture. Do not fall for the temptation to combine this with another role, or the traditional power structures will creep in. There must be checks and balances accepted by the CEO and the owners who must not fall back onto the exercise of unilateral power. If the CEO is more inward-oriented, as happens with some owner-leaders and founders, there must be a senior Strategy Owner to chair the Strategy Resolution Circle and focus on the outside world and customers.

Startups, often dominated by a single charismatic person, are usually hectic and turbulent. The evolution to a larger organization is always challenging, especially finding a balance between structure, freedom, and the founders' egos. Static models never work. A deeper discussion of the whole topic of startups will be deferred to another book.

**Public Sector Organizations**

In public sector organizations not primarily driven by profit, one would imagine that Agile and Lean ideas would thrive. However, it turns out that in most cases, the idea of a Constitutional Organization with decentralized freedom seems too foreign. Instead, the organizations conform to a rigid, detailed rules-based centralized system where following plans, and compliance are absolute. We know this will cripple the capability to deal with complex matters, hence the exponential growth of large-scale catastrophic failures of public initiatives.

Something good can still be achieved, noting the previously mentioned Norwegian NAV institution and several health care institutions. In all known cases where a liberating enclave has developed, there has been a strong leader who wanted this to happen, believed in it, and dared to put their reputation on the line. They have been willing to commit to the long haul of taking the time to develop the right culture, keeping bureaucracy from getting out of hand, and resisting damaging political micro-management and rigid budgets.

**Non-profit Organizations**

Non-profit organizations are obvious candidates for liberating principles of leadership. One can argue that since many of them operate with volunteers, they have to work this way. After all, if volunteers don't like the work conditions, they just go home, and nothing can be said about that, as they are not paid.

We believe that it is extra important for people in leadership roles in non-profit organizations to exhibit servant leadership and institute freedom out of respect for those served and those who serve others. Since there usually is a body of donors involved in setting the future course, high levels of transparency and engagement are essential.

Some non-profit organizations unfortunately develop sprawling bureaucracies – often publicly funded. They often maintain the self-righteous demeanor of *The Good Guys* because they are not profit and power-driven. This combination can create even less freedom and very subtle pressure to comply with *the system* because it is indisputably *good*. We have seen this in trade unions, religious organizations, and relief organizations just to mention a few. You can usually spot these organizations by the fact that centrally employed staff clearly are *upstairs* compared to the local people who often are volunteers.

# Looking back on the Everyday Practices

In a liberating constitutional organization, many practices will differ from those in a traditional hierarchical power-based organization. The practices we mentioned have either a theoretical or experiential foundation, some come from our own experiences, and some from all the people we interviewed in the process of writing this book.

There are several workgroup methods that we collected from various sources that proved extremely helpful in creating an environment of psychological safety, engagement, and transparency, some of them have been mentioned before. We will just mention some briefly here, for a more comprehensive description please consult *Appendix D – More Tools and Practices*:

- 1–2–4–All – A method from Liberating Structures for starting a workshop or similar, improving the engagement of the people participating, and getting an improved agenda.
- Poker-Chip Voting – Write a number of value items or objectives on paper and place them on a long table, give people some poker chips, and let them place these on the items according to their assessment of their value.

251

- Estimation Poker – Use a deck of planning poker cards to estimate effort, cost, or value collectively in a team.

  - First, the team builds up a common understanding by discussing the item being estimated and getting the known facts on the table.
  - Then the team performs an independent estimation, everybody shows their estimate at the same time.
  - Then the team discusses the estimates and people defend their estimate.
  - With the improved information the team re-estimates.
  - After two or three rounds of estimation, the team goes with the majority.

- Lean Canvas – Build a quick A3-sized business plan showing: the customers, their challenges, the unique value proposition, the main components of the solution, the channels to reach the customers, the expected value and costs, the metrics to follow progress, and the reason why this team can do it.

- The Future Backwards – Build a wall of a team's or group's understanding of the current situation regarding a specific situation.

  - First, the team makes the best description of the current state.
  - Then they discuss and display events leading to the present situation.
  - Then they describe where they really would have liked to be now.
  - And where they would hate to have ended up.
  - Then finally the team tries to make a plausible path of events from each of these hypothetical states back to points in the past.

- Blackboard Pattern – Find an emerging solution to a question where nobody sees a clear path.

  - Post a question or a challenge.
  - Let other people post questions, other potential challenges, and solutions.

- Interact and see if the discussion converges toward a solution.

- Ritual Dissent – One team quickly presents a proposal to another one, who then criticizes the proposal, the presenting team does not discuss or defend themselves, but makes notes. After two minutes, the team goes back and refines their proposal.

- Roadmapping – Build a roadmap consisting of a number of columns representing months, typically 18-24 months, and a number of rows displaying events in different categories starting with market expectations, the features, infrastructure, and external events. Potentially more rows can be added.

- Impact Estimation – Develop a matrix showing objectives and strategies and how the latter contribute to the former, including stakeholders and their relationships to Objectives and strategies.

- Micro Narratives – Ask people to tell a small story about the desired topic, and then ask them to self-assess why this story is important to them, positive or negative.

- Actively Guided Interviews – A series of conversational states are described and the events that mark transitions to other states. In each state, the interviewer has a collection of prepared questions at his disposal, some answers will trigger a change-state event. The script is prepared with a visual representation and rehearsed.

- Impact Map – Estimating and visualizing the relationship between the Why, Who, What, When, and Where of an initiative to facilitate prioritization and decision-making.

- Confidence Vote – Before closing a decision, ask everybody how confident they are that all important aspects have been covered. Let them use for example a scale of 1, 5, 20, 50, 80, 95, and 99 percent confidence. Occasionally an outlier is captured this way, someone who perhaps was not heard in the discussion.

- Personal Sustainable Work – Combine the OODA loop thinking with traditional agile and lean practices, effective operation in two modes:

Observe, Orient, React (OOR) and Concentrated, Uninterrupted Effort (CUE).

*General practices in the different kinds of Circles.*

*The need for transparency and the artifacts used.*

*Enabling the flourishing of people, psychological safety is a cornerstone.*
*– Facing reality and the complexity of it.*
*– Accepting cognitive bias and noise – and trying to mitigate it.*

*General Organization practices in different situations.*

*The need for Super Circles in large organizations.*

*Special kinds of circles to use if the context calls for it:*
*– Scaled up and down Circles.*
*– Service Circles and Circles of Travelers.*
*– Production, Engineering, Dual Mode, and Innovation Circles.*

*A host of practices for specific contexts:*
*– For creating an environment of engagement.*
*– For building up common understanding and knowledge.*
*– For creating radical transparency.*

# Everyday Life – The Situations

*Now having built a Liberating, Constitutional Organization either in the whole organization or a specific territory of it, daily life begins. As we saw earlier, upholding any democratic organization based on the freedom and good citizenship of the individual requires constant attention and work and occasional adjustments. Daily life in such an organization is a constant learning and adaptation session as circumstances unfold. We refer to this as the Organizational PDSA Cycle.*

*An excerpt from the preamble of the Swiss constitution can serve as a starting point:*

> *… in the knowledge that only those who use their freedom remain free, and that the strength of a people is measured by the well-being of its weakest members…*

In this chapter, we discuss situations that arise in organizations as they pursue their purpose and suggest ways to handle them within the framework of Agile Lean Leadership values and principles. It is important to remember that when dealing with complex matters, context is everything. Therefore, the following are not recipes, but ideas on which to elaborate in context.

# General Situations to Get Accustomed to

Working in a Liberating Organization based on Agile Lean Leadership principles feels quite different from a traditional organization; many situations require different patterns of behavior. Most have been used to traditional hierarchical and power-based organizations and can easily succumb to the habitual reactions in that environment.

In a traditional hierarchy, superiors may use a carrot-and-stick approach to manage their subordinates. In a Liberating Organization solving complex challenges is achieved through engaged people who take responsibility and have a mandate to operate. This is very different and not easy; developing and maintaining human relationships can be challenging and requires attention and interaction.

In a Liberating Organization, there is an ongoing balancing act involving: intrinsic motivation, psychological safety, competence building, clarity, character, humility, a serving attitude and finally the absence of status as a tool for exploiting others.

## Working with Teams and Volunteers

Most people will claim that they work in teams, and the word can be used in different ways. What people normally mean by the word *team* is a group of people under the same superior. In Agile Lean Leadership a Team is defined as: *"A group of people with complementary and supplementary competencies, with a common goal and commitment to help each other to reach it."*

256

The Team is a critical element of the foundation and one that has to be right for everything to keep working well. If the teams don't work as they should, all the other structures in the organization will fail. The functioning of the team relies on the attitude, behavior, and choice of the individual as a free agent. It only works if the individual wants it to and volunteers to contribute, engage, and take responsibility. It cannot be forced upon unwilling people. James Madison[1] said the same in 1788, structures are not enough, they rest on the goodwill of people:

> But I go on this great republican principle that the people will have virtue and intelligence to select men of virtue and wisdom. Is there no virtue among us? If there be not, we are in a wretched situation. No theoretical checks – no form of government can render us secure.
> — James Madison, Virginia Ratifying Convention 1788

It is therefore important to maintain the goodwill of people towards the organization and others, but mostly those closest, the team members. If the organization loses the goodwill of its people, they leave. If the team loses its goodwill with its people, it is no longer a team just a group.

At the Team level within a Constitutional Organization, the Operations Owner (OO, Scrum Master in Scrum) is the one who tills the Team soil enabling goodwill to grow. Sports team coaches work to help their Team become the best possible version of itself. This focus on the human aspect was what attracted me to Scrum and Agile 20 years ago.

The OO works to raise the individual's understanding of and commitment to the principles and to ongoing education and adaptation as circumstances unfold.

> A well-instructed people alone can be permanently a free people.
> — James Madison

---

1   James Madison, one of the founding fathers of the US and the fourth president: https://en.wikipedia.org/wiki/James_Madison

Knowledge sharing between team members is fundamental to solving complex challenges. Dave Snowden said, *"Knowledge can only be volunteered, it cannot be conscripted!"* Complex challenges require people to engage all their capabilities voluntarily.

Non-profit organizations are aware of this: a person we worked with said: *"People are volunteers here, if they don't like it, they go home. And what can we say to that, we don't pay them to be here!"* – correct. Many organizations have the same experience, if they lose the goodwill of the individuals critical competencies can be lost. One of the best investments an organization can make is to ensure their Teams are healthy.

## Avoiding the Boss Syndrome

There are many reasons to avoid slipping back into the classic boss role.

- True communication only occurs between people who consider each other of equal value. If there is a power distance, subordinates will adapt their expressed views to accord with their superiors, distorting the communication.
- The SO and OO are perceived as leaders, even though everyone has the opportunity to lead by showing the way to others. However, they are at risk of sliding back into the classic boss role unless they have the character to display humility and patience and to create space for others. Within a radically transparent team, there should also be naturally occurring checks and balances to provide additional safeguards.
- The dark side of humanity breaks out from time to time – wanting domination and power. We have all experienced it, we think we are acting in a non-self-serving way, but suddenly "The silver-tongued devil[2]" appears and starts to manipulate and exercise power over others. Hopefully, people around dare speak up.

---

2    From *The Silver Tongued Devil and I* album from 1971 by Kris Kristoffersen.

Everybody with some authority, formal or otherwise, must exercise self-restraint, be willing to serve others and create space for others to engage. One of the best pieces of advice and a way to invite dialogue is to habitually announce intent and ask others to do the same. Another is to force yourself to look at poor results as a learning opportunity while showing a genuine desire for the insights of others. Finally, although hard, make your communication an invitation for input, avoid starting confrontational, and by all means, do not signal superiority; René Figgé (one of the trainers in our Network) famously starts all difficult conversations with "*I wonder why…*", anybody is allowed to wonder, that is not threatening.

## Understanding and Using Complexity

Surprisingly few think consciously about complexity, although we deal with complexity intuitively all the time when non-familiar situations arise. We have painted ourselves into an organizational corner, assuming that all knowledge is available, because we are accustomed to getting direction from further up the hierarchy. That might work in obvious or even complicated situations, but it cannot work for truly novel issues with no precedent. The world is rapidly becoming more uncertain with few guiding examples of prior knowledge; more than ever before we are operating in uncharted territory.

It is good practice to estimate the complexity of work, either explicitly or by asking simple questions:

- Start with: "*Do you know how to solve this?*" – "*Yes, we have done it before*", then it is probably *Clear/Obvious*.
- If not: "*Do you know where to find the knowledge to solve this?*" – "*Yes, we know people to ask, or we can do this or that research*", then it is probably *Complicated*.
- If not: "*Can you come up with an experiment that will shed light on how to solve this?*" – "*Yes, we have this or that hypothesis we can test*", then it is probably *Complex*.

- If not then: *"Have any of you seen similar challenges?"* – *"Yes, we have had other cases that might have a bearing on this"*, then it is probably in the Chaos domain.
- If not, then they are probably clueless, and in Disorder and Confusion, the situation must be described better or new aspects discovered before the assessment is resumed.

Working with experiments and hypotheses in the complex domain requires a special dedicated approach. It is very different from analyzing and researching things where knowledge is believed to exist already. Those with authority, waiting for results need patience and to accept that not every experiment leads to a desirable result; then it would not be an experiment.

> *By definition, when investigating the unknown, you do not know what you shall find!* — Derek Barton[3]

However, experiments should be planned and carefully conducted. The experimenters should commit to a high standard of transparency and acknowledge that others need to follow progress and perhaps provide insights.

When specifying and planning an experiment it is good practice to define early signs of success and failure upfront and what success or failure means in practice. It is helpful to reference any outside inspiration for the experiment and possible side effects. Finally, experiments must be coherent and consistent with the known facts.

## Battling Bias and Noise

Daniel Kahneman pioneered research into how cognitive bias and noise affect our decision-making, his books on the subject are highly recommended reading[4].

---

3   Derek Barton: https://en.wikipedia.org/wiki/Derek_Barton
4   Please see *Appendix B9 – Cognitive Bias and Noise in 60 Seconds*.

Kahneman deals with many cognitive biases, we will just highlight a small set here:

- **Confirmation bias**. People have a pronounced bias for information or experiments that justify or corroborate existing convictions – it feels more comfortable and affirming.
- **Substitution bias**. People often subconsciously substitute a difficult question with an easier, related one – which they answer, believing that they answered the original.
- **Anchoring effect** or the **Focusing illusion**. The first piece of information people get before being asked their opinion, always limits how they answer. The first aspect of a challenge usually dominates judgment.
- **Sunk cost fallacy**. When people have sunk cost or effort into something, they are much more prone to interpret results positively and continue to invest in it.
- **Loss Aversion** or **Status Quo** bias. To protect against an unpleasant experience, people react more strongly to the possibility of a loss than to a gain, leading to more conservative behavior than is warranted by the facts. We have an emotional attachment to the current state of affairs, even when change could lead to better outcomes.
- **Shared information bias**. People in a group tend to spend a disproportionate amount of time on what is already common knowledge, instead of what is only known by a few.
- **Conservatism**. When new information is presented, people tend to change their convictions and behavior, but too little in proportion to the new data.
- **Planning fallacy**[5]. People grossly underestimate the time needed to do their own jobs due to insufficient consideration of past experiences and historical data. In a famous experiment, students were asked to estimate when they were 50%, 75%, and 99% done with a major as-

---

5    The Planning Fallacy: https://en.wikipedia.org/wiki/Planning_fallacy

signment. When the time came, they were in reality only 13%, 19%, and 45% done. In another experiment, students estimated the number of days required to complete their thesis, their average best-case estimate was 27.4 days, the worst-case was 48.6 days, the overall average was 33.9 days. The actual completion time was on average 55.5 days, with only 30% of the students completing their thesis as predicted.

*The mother of all biases* hovers above all biases according to Kahneman, who says: *"What you see is all there is!"* – our ability to ignore our ignorance is equivalent to our ability to ignore complexity and believe that everything is already known.

The question then becomes, how to counter these damaging biases; here are a few suggestions:

- Psychological Safety allows people to speak up when they expect that others may not have seen the complete picture.
- Teams and transparency make it possible.
- Humility and a genuine commitment to seek and react to feedback.
- As conclusions are being reached, conduct a Ritual Dissent[6] exercise, and challenge others to come up with alternative interpretations of the facts and conclusions.

Noise is different, it is about how external factors obscure our view of the situation – sometimes randomly – and lead to divergent interpretations and decisions. Noise refers to the differences in decisions or assessments made by others, or even by the same person at different times when faced with the same information. Kahneman distinguishes noise from bias, which is a systematic deviation from accuracy. While bias consistently leads to errors in a particular direction, noise is the inconsistency in judgment that adds variability and error without a predictable pattern. Kahneman says that noise can lead to unfair and unreliable decisions, impact-

---

6    Please see *Appendix D - Tools for the Constitutional Organization.*

ing more or less all fields. Strategies for battling biases also have an impact on the mitigation of noise, here are a few key strategies to consider:

- Clear Decision Criteria: When well-defined criteria for making decisions exist, consistency is improved. When decision-makers follow specific guidelines, it reduces the influence of subjective factors and personal biases. Algorithms and statistical models can be helpful where applicable, so can checklists and standardized procedures.
- Feedback and calibration: When decision-makers receive regular feedback about their past judgments it helps them calibrate and improve consistency. Understanding where their judgments have varied can help them become more aware of potential sources of noise. Retrospectives are a perfect place for this.
- Aggregated judgments: When aggregating multiple independent judgments noise is somewhat averaged out. Combining independent decisions reduces the random variability found in individual judgments. It is important that judgments are independent so that people are not influenced by others' opinions.

# Situations Relating to Employment

An organization's people are its main asset but also the principal source of its challenges; there are always personality issues, agendas, and issues of suitability and competence to deal with. It is therefore not surprising that this section is rather large compared with others.

## Upholding Relationships – Respect and Forgiveness

The core of a Liberating Organization is the positive relationships between those who commit to truth, transparency, and honoring commitments. It rests on mutual respect and the conviction that personal dignity cannot be violated, exploited, or abused. Open collaboration will not develop unless that is the case, and power and control will prevail. This is a conviction and a worldview that people must share.

But even if this is the case, relationships break down for many reasons. The dark side of humanity occasionally surfaces and people will wrong, abuse, or take advantage of others.

When someone is wronged, damage is done, and there is a cost to bear. Either the assailant pays a price, or the cost is absorbed by the one being wronged. Our natural response is retribution, but that never restores the relationship and only furthers the escalation and polarization. Unfortunately, that seems to be the preferred approach in many public and political interactions these days.

Forgiveness is an option if a restored relationship is mutually desired. But the concept is often misunderstood. Forgiveness is not a therapeutic exercise, where you manipulate yourself into believing that the offense didn't matter; that just turns the pain inward and damages yourself. Forgiveness is also not real if it is only given when the offending party apologizes and crawls in the dust, may also be just another way to punish the other party.

The true forgiveness with the potential to restore relationships follows a specific pattern:

- First, there is an inward commitment to absorb the cost and pain yourself and not retaliate. However, you still seek justice and correction, not out of revenge but to prevent damage to others and perhaps help the culprit alter their behavior.
- Secondly, respectfully confront the offender and explain the damage that has been done. Discuss your possible role in the issue and aim to work together to avoid repetition.
- In the case of an unfavorable response, take a mediator with you who can assess the situation without prejudice and point out faults on both sides. If this does not help, you may need to involve more relevant people, but starting in private leaves more room to restore the relationship.

On the path to restoration, both parties must commit to truth, transparency, and honoring their commitments. A good practice is to announce intent to the other party and genuinely request their feedback. Then slowly trust can be rebuilt, relationships restored and sometimes even improved after such a crisis.

## Attracting and Retaining People

Attracting and retaining the right people is of increasing importance. As awareness of the demands of complex work becomes clear, organizations are making a serious investment, particularly in young skilled people. It is very expensive to attract talent so it is critical that the investment is not wasted and the new hires stay with the organization for a long time.

The structures of the Liberating Organizations can help. Small teams and Circles and Relationship Manifests make it easy to communicate purpose and practice, which makes it easier for applicants to see if they would like to be there and make a choice for the right reasons.

Because OOs are close to the Team, they are aware of developing situations and can help ease tensions. The OO leads by demonstrating respect and appreciation for people, slowly building a culture of responsible freedom. The OO is cultivating the soil for intrinsic motivation to grow: Purpose, autonomy, good relationships, and mastery.

A special challenge exists in attracting and working with the young generation (gen-z), many of whom are not career and money-dominated, but want a fulfilling life in balance. This can be mostly positive but occasionally manifests itself as ego-centricity or selfishness. Then the concern for the team and the organization disappears. An organization cannot be sustainable and resilient with that attitude, there has to be a balance of freedom and responsibility. The young generation must also see that fulfillment comes through contributions and accomplishments with and for others – not just getting personal privileges.

Whenever onboarding people, take care of their needs, and help them quickly feel appreciated and able to contribute. Good practice is to appoint one existing team member as a *buddy* of the new person, the buddy is there to explain, help, and advise. Existing team members should exhibit patience and not signal irritation over having to spend time helping the new person. The new person should conversely realize that this is about making a contribution as quickly as possible.

## Hiring and Firing

This is an area that is very hard for the traditional organization to relinquish. It is so deeply ingrained that decisions about hiring and firing are made by executives or experts in an HR group often without reference to those doing the work.

It is clear that for freedom to survive the Circle or team must be able to determine the kind of people they need. To ensure that they share a common vision and have the right competencies, teams must have the final say when taking on new team members.

It can be helpful to use a competence and value matrix to let applicants self-assess how well they fit in a particular team. It is a good practice to invite existing team members to meet applicants. It is good to have a central HR service to assist during the hiring process, to ensure that rules are followed, and to use their interview expertise.

It is usually a positive situation to expand with more people, it is a lot harder to face a headcount reduction, or if a person has to be reassigned due to *irreconcilable differences*; books have been written on this topic, but we will only touch on some of the principles here.

If the team has to reduce staff costs for economic reasons, it is best to be transparent and ask the team for ideas. There are many examples of people volunteering to absorb financial inconvenience if they are truly committed to the team and the organization. Some have reduced their hours and used this spare time on private projects, some have taken early retirement but would return if the situation improves. There are many examples of teams being creative, perhaps finding cost savings or new income sources. Creativity is triggered by need and enabled through the freedom to act. If people have to be let go, it is important to help them find another position and welcome them back if circumstances improve.

The hardest challenge is when, even after attempts to improve, someone just doesn't fit in and work out, for whatever reason. The OO cannot let the team descend into mediocrity and must assume the responsibility for deciding what to do after consultation with all relevant parties. The OO has the ultimate responsibility and should avoid making team members feel guilty. It may be helpful to solicit HR help to ensure that proper procedure is followed to avoid future problems.

A particular gray zone today is that of *non-commitment*. Increasingly, there are those for whom work is a lower priority than family life, sports, entertainment, and non-profit engagements. The scale of the challenge surprised us during our recent series of interviews with senior business people. Several said that they actively screened for it in the recruitment process, but others seemed to possess the attitude themselves.

There is nothing wrong with prioritizing other activities over work. I would always argue that people's first priority is their families, but that does not mean that all family activity takes precedence over any company activity. It's fine to have special priorities, but that should reflect the type of employment chosen. I know someone who delivers food from his small truck, which leaves him plenty of time for activities that are more important to him.

The problem is those who feel entitled to work whenever and wherever they want, but still be lavishly compensated, which can cause deep resentment among their colleagues, *"They are having the fun, we are pulling the load!"* Working in teams helps maintain a culture of commitment. The team members are your immediate social circle; most people don't let down people close to them so a sense of responsibility develops naturally,

*"They are my buddies!"* Remote work is a challenge as it is much easier to slide away from a sense of responsibility and commitment if you only see people occasionally on a screen. Extra effort is required to uphold that sense of responsibility for the team when most of the work is remote.

## Compensation

This is perhaps the hardest area for the traditional organization to let go. But as with employment, and as each decentralized Circle or Team works to create an environment that is conducive to their goals, they must have a mandate to determine the details of the compensation scheme, albeit within organizational and economic constraints.

First people should be paid at a fair market level so that money is not an issue. Tensions over money make people look for other opportunities.

Secondly, the way money is allocated should be known to the team, not necessarily in detail, but in outline, and it should be accepted as fair; the younger generation reacts strongly if they experience something as un-fair. We mentioned Google's responsibility-based compensation scheme in the previous chapter. Others use years of experience, total and in the company in determining a bracket of pay.

Finally, in the case of variable incentives, bonuses should be shared among the team, not directed at individuals, because individual rewards turn team members into competitors. Where such incentives are deemed acceptable to a Circle or Team they should be based on transparent and real metrics like revenue or profit over an extended period. All such schemes are susceptible to gaming and distort intrinsic motivation, so be careful what you ask for, you might get it.

A variety of this is so-called *sweat equity*, especially common in startups. People work without full pay to accumulate future benefits, such as stock or profit sharing. The individual regards it as an investment, and it may increase the level of commitment. But it has to be by invitation with transparent metrics. In many places, the taxation or unemployment systems can get in the way of such flexible solutions.

A popular approach is for teams to publicly set aside a sum to reward the extraordinary achievement of a member nominated by their peers. Team members may not nominate themselves.

It should be noted and respected that not everyone on the team has the same needs. Those with young families struggling to pay rent, car, and expenses relating to children may not be as flexible.

## Conflicts between People

We use the term conflict for emotional situations that block normal goal-oriented behavior. A professional disagreement about a solution or approach is different.

Conflicts happen and should be tackled respectfully as early as possible. The OO is responsible for uncovering such conflicts and individual team members are responsible for alerting the OO if they feel that they cannot get any further bilaterally. Conflict spreads like a weed, other people start taking sides, and a team can fracture quite rapidly.

As mentioned, reconciliation, forgiveness, and restoration of relationships are vital. To diffuse further tension, the OO must respectfully prevent escalation and retaliation. More details are at the end of this chapter.

## People with Special Challenges

Most theories about teamwork assume perfect competencies, personalities, values, and life circumstances. In reality, ideal situations are very rare. Special challenges are often present, which come in many varieties.

- There are ordinary things like the special needs of young families with kids that are sick from time to time, need support in school, etc. Flexibility is needed here.

- Some people have to take care of elderly parents, a sick spouse, or similar.
- There are people with various disabilities. Physical conditions may have to accommodate such needs. One area close to my heart is people on the autistic spectrum, they may need an especially quiet environment and much order and structure in their everyday life. Accommodating these people in a team requires the understanding, respect, and collaboration of the rest of the team.
- People who have been out of work for a considerable time, or just entering their work-life also need special attention and catering for their special needs.
- Currently, a lot of people are struggling with stress-related disorders. It is still a bit of a mystery why this is so bad, I suspect a combination of a lack of experienced psychological safety. It is quite a job to get someone on the team with a history of blacking out due to stress, it is very hard to see what exactly the triggers of stress-related anxiety are, and therefore difficult to create the right environment. As much openness as possible is good, but the person in question may struggle with this perhaps due to a sense of shame, and may prefer being open only to one or very few people.

In all of these situations – and many more probably could be thought of – it is important that the team volunteers to handle it, the team should not feel penalized by having these people on board, and others should show appreciation for their efforts. In all things avoid patronizing people with special needs or letting them know how much everybody else suffers for their sake. On the other hand, the person with special needs must pay attention to contributing and not playing the victim card, justifying their reduced contribution. As in all things, there is a balance to be found for which there is no detailed prescription; respect and honoring the dignity of people are the guiding principles.

Each organization must decide how far it is going to accommodate people's special needs. Commercial businesses have to survive and make a profit, they are not public social institutions funded by taxpayers' money, but their engagement in providing a meaningful existence for those who for some reason or another are marginalized, cannot be overestimated. People don't just need donations, they need to feel that they are contributing and respected for that.

Some organizations have gone the extra mile, creating services in support of their colleagues. This ranges from cafeterias, kindergartens, and daycare to special transport arrangements, shopping services, and more. In some jurisdictions, organizations can get a tax discount if they arrange such services or support people otherwise at risk. Maybe that concept could be explored further; in our rigid tax system, it is certainly difficult to be creative.

## Upgrading Team Competences

In a situation of flux and unfolding circumstances, the team that had perfect competencies for the situation yesterday does not have it today. The traditional way, overly focused on experts, is to replace people with others allegedly better suited. This is a misunderstanding when working with complex challenges. It is not the extraordinary experts that win, but those who can communicate, collaborate, and build new knowledge.

At every level, a Liberating Organization must have a disciplined approach to building the right team for each situation. It is important to invite people and get their commitment to entering new knowledge territories.

It is helpful for the team to collectively identify new knowledge and skills needed, and decide who takes charge. The others will then take more of the day-to-day stuff to create space for the investigation. The OO needs to be aware of those who might aim to grab all the fun jobs while others work the treadmill.

## The Human Sensor Network

A Liberating Organization has Psychological Safety and is engaged in creating a human sensor network on the lookout for unexpected or unusual things which aid a timely reaction should they prove significant.

In the Obvious and Complicated domains, statistical methods can be used, but in the Complex domain much less so, only human beings can uncover novelties and looming outliers. This needs to be nurtured. Retrospectives are good for discussing new discoveries and potential responses for intervention or further investigation. The OO encourages people to look out for the unexpected.

One practical method is to use the Blackboard[7] pattern mentioned in the last chapter; where a person posts an observation or a question, where the interpretation or answer is not known. Everybody can then post comments, questions, further observations, or proposed resolutions. Sometimes this process converges on a solution no one imagined to start with.

# Ownership and Executives

Occasionally there is a change of ownership or managing executives, which represents a special set of challenges and opportunities, depending on how the new players are disposed to freedom, Agile, and Lean.

One of the more challenging situations is when a company is taken over by a private equity fund. Most of those have a default mode that is solely focused on the finances, quickly "improving" the balance sheet to make the company look a lot better than it is, and selling it off to the next buyer in the chain. They reduce costs, lay off people, and flip the organization before the bad consequences become clearly visible. The only remedy is to make them brutally aware of the risk of the collapse of the organization, the loss of customers, and the numbers going south. Such bad news is seldom appreciated, but appeasement only works if you accept apathy

---

7   See *Appendix D - Tools for the Constitutional Organization*

as a solution, and stay under the radar while continuing to collect a salary.

Sometimes a new executive needs to quickly justify their appointment to the board or the owners. This can lead to random initiatives, just to show decisiveness. Every effort should be made to make them aware, in detail, of the real situation before major changes are launched. We have often seen this cause great frustration for and sometimes exodus of key people.

Fortunately, there are also positive experiences where new executives or owners present an opportunity to change things that were not possible under the older regime. But often people have invested so much of their prestige in a certain way of doing things that it is fundamentally too hard to give it up, it will feel like a loss, and we all dislike the feeling of losing.

Under all circumstances, approach the new situation decisively and confidently, presenting a way of quickly bringing everybody new on board up to speed regarding where the organization really is, where we would like to have been, and where we would hate to have ended up. Take the approach or choose to serve them, but insist on the facts and truth, not just politically correct behavior to appease the new owners or executives. Sometimes this candid approach backfires, but better to find out sooner than later, who you are dealing with.

If the owners are distant, if institutional investors are only concerned about the money, or if the organization is effectively controlled by banks, do not expect any engagement with them. If you can create an interface where they see what they need, and the organization can do what it wants internally, then it can work. But be careful to establish very precise rules of engagement and establish boundaries so that they do not slip in and start affecting people and customers. Very often the CEO and CFO bear the brunt in a situation where there is one image toward the owners and one toward the organization and the customers.

# Organizational Strategies

At the organizational level, different strategies can be deployed to achieve resilience and sustainability. The first three points below deal with improving orientation towards the customers – the only source of income for the organization. Then we look inward at changing some of the inner mechanisms and finally take a look at the special opportunities and challenges for smaller companies and startups.

## Customer Awareness

Most companies today suspect that they don't know what their customers are up to, and what they really want. This lack of understanding is probably the number one reason for losing customers – certainly in non-commodity businesses. Customers do not feel appreciated or taken seriously. In one of our interviews, a very compelling story surfaced: after a recent change in leadership the company was able to finally get the right experts out and talk directly to customers and their advisors, not just salespeople. That changed the customers' perception dramatically, their product was and still is very complex, and there was no way you could guess the customers' real needs at a distance.

First, make sure the organization is ready to have a dialogue with the customer, the hotline should always be open. For years organizations have drifted in the opposite direction In the name of *operational efficiency*, they created long, tedious queues to talk to somebody, or irritating chatbots and incomprehensible IT systems as replacements for direct dialog. If we want the customer to trust that we care about his challenges and not just his money, we should stop making our service as cumbersome as possible. Complex challenges are seldom solved through one-size-fits-all solutions, dialogue is required. Organizations have to provide an easy way for qualified dialogue, it sounds trivial, but it isn't!

Organizations have to develop new methods for engaging with existing customers. Clever, easy-to-use feedback and dialogue systems can help a lot, however, people need to be on top of them and keep the communication flow going, or customers will lose interest.

It is also necessary to come up with new methods for finding new potential customers. We call this the Customer Discovery Process. Creativity is called for here. Regarding modern online possibilities, the surface has barely been scratched. Some have tried to use the idea of an online shop or even a shopping arcade, where potential customers could drop in and engage in the discovery process with a combination of artifacts and real people.

Our suggestion is to have dedicated, cross-functional front-line circles (Agile Customer Circles) directly in front of the customers to increase the likelihood of good responsiveness and rich dialogue.

## Products and Service Discovery

Closely linked to the previous topic is this one of product and service discovery. The question is how to discover the best possible product-market match. In times of rapid change, the best you can do is to be prepared for change and look for the evolutionary potential in the present. Some new – or rather old and rediscovered – disciplines can help:

* Be available. The biggest obstacle to discovering what customers prefer and need is that it is just too hard for the customers to get in contact with the organization. There is good evidence that if it is easy to get help, it increases Psychological Safety for customers, and has a direct bearing on their willingness to engage in honest conversation.
* Interviews. There is good evidence that if you ask people for help they will give it. One effective way is to ask permission to interview people for a particular occasion, such as an article being written, some research, or a speaking occasion. Another avenue is to ask people to give an account of their experiences of a certain subject; most respond very favorably to such requests.

- Micro narratives[8]. Ask people to tell a short story about what is, or was important to them, then self-assess the story and say why it was meaningful; it provides nuanced information about them. It is also a good way to frame an interview, it reveals more than just answering the interviewer's questions or filling in a questionnaire.

- Deep dialogue. If there are customers willing to invest a bit more in the relationship, it can be rewarding to include them in high-level review, planning, and estimation sessions related to different approaches to the products or services they are interested in. We are especially enthusiastic about including customers in estimating the value of future options for products and services. Several excellent techniques[9] exist to estimate the relative value of product features and qualities producing direct information about what drives customer decisions.

- Roadmapping. Customers react positively and deepen their trust when kept abreast of future plans. If customers only get short-term information, they may suspect that they are being sold something, transparency is normally greatly appreciated. The best roadmaps should be viewed from the customers' perspective, without distracting internal details.

## Innovation and Creativity

In most organizations, perpetual innovation should be part of daily life, with built-in slack to innovate and test ideas. Over-optimization and efficiency drives can kill innovation and creativity, which need the freedom and time to explore ideas and inspirations to develop. Keywords are slack, freedom, and psychological safety. The Japanese call this activity *Kaizen*, a process of constant improvements and minor course adjustments.

---

8   Micro narratives, read more in *Chapter 7 Everyday Life – The Practices* and *Appendix D - More Tools and Practices.*

9   For more on estimation, please refer to Appendix D - *More Tools and Practices.*

Occasionally, organizations realize the need for a larger revamping of products or services due to changing circumstances or sub-optimal performance. We recommend that a dedicated cross-functional task force or transient circle be commissioned and given a lot of space to innovate with as few constraints as possible, as Deepak Chopra[10] said *"If you want people to think outside the box, remove the box!"* Although Chopra is a controversial new-age personality, this statement is nevertheless true. Frame the charter for the transient circle as *"If we didn't have anything today, what would we want to achieve and how would we build it?"* and iterate from there. Russell Ackoff describes this in his book *Idealized Design*[11]. The keywords are Concentration (both opportunity and ability), freedom through removal of constraints, and time and space for multiple iterations. The Japanese call this activity *Kaikaku,* a radical and big change.

It is also possible that something really earth-shattering has to happen, like a reorganization or a change to another market. A more comprehensive process is then called for to include everybody and do everything to get the broadest perspective and the best common understanding possible.

In Chapter 6 we described the *High Road to a Transformation* as a series of steps designed to give everybody a fair chance of being heard and able to influence the future. The High Road is not a recipe but can serve as an inspiration for a process in a given set of circumstances. In our opinion, it has to start with an unconditional invitation to participate from the beginning with as few constraints as possible.

The most common error is to let experts or managers predefine too much of what could be possible. That is over-constraining and invokes anchoring, *"The Box"* is reintroduced and all thinking will gravitate towards conformity. Another effect is that when someone with apparent authority is

---

10   Deepak Chopra: https://en.wikipedia.org/wiki/Deepak_Chopra
11   Please see *Appendix B10 – Idealized Design in 60 Seconds*

heard, the natural reaction is to only come up with ideas and suggestions that align with that authority.

The keywords to likely success are invitation (of the honest kind), freedom to choose and psychological safety to express views and ask questions. The Japanese call this a *Kakushin*, an innovative or transformative change.

## The Internal Processes of the Organization

There are some processes and practices that are used in most organizations, they have become ingrained, something that is done, because it has always been. Such processes and practices often get in the way of liberating people to take responsibility, change is called for.

### The Annual Budgeting

The annual budgeting process is one of the most common practices in organizations, yet, it is also one of the least appreciated. The yearly budget tries to combine forecasting, allocation of resources, and the setting of goals, into one master detailed plan. The common perception is that this doesn't work in today's complex environment, the budget is outdated as soon as it is agreed. The process is usually long and arduous with conditions often changing along the way. Oddly, many don't believe in the budget and tweak both its inputs and the reporting on the budget follow-ups, just to comply and stay out of trouble. It has become "*form over content*". Traditional budgeting aligns with the following quote:

> "A good deal of the corporate planning I have observed is like a ritual rain dance; it has no effect on the weather that follows, but those who engage in it think it does. Moreover, it seems to me that much of the advice and instruction related to corporate planning is directed at improving the dancing, not the weather."                                                   – Russell Ackoff

But there are alternatives, the most comprehensive and well-known framework is Beyond Budgeting[12] (BB), which is much more than just budgeting. For the current discussion it suffices to note that BB splits the activities mentioned above into three independent ones:

- **Forecasting.** This is the process of trying to predict something about future development, most typically to see if all ends meet financially, especially cash flow. But other aspects of forecasting, such as market and technology changes, need to be addressed to achieve the best possible result. The process needs to be repeated periodically and if major assumptions change.

- **Allocation of resources.** Any organization has limited resources, there has to be a process of evaluating the needs and opportunities and then prioritizing how best to spend the available money, time, and competencies. The big difference is that here *"the bank is always open"*. If a need or an opportunity is discovered, the organization must respond quickly and see if priorities need to change and appropriate decisions made.

- **Setting of Goals.** An organization needs to set visible goals, to achieve alignment. While the setting of goals is good, it can be misused. First, they are often too granular and detailed, based on the mistaken belief that knowledge is more stable than it is, i.e. in reality things are more complex than usually perceived. Secondly, goals are set centrally and pushed down on people, which does not result in a commitment but rather in creative ways to game the system, producing the desired result in obscure ways. Finally, goals are sometimes so lofty or out of reach that people shrug their shoulders and disengage. Good goals need to be developed with the people who are supposed to work on them, only then can true commitment be achieved; the effects of people's actions on the goals need to be visible as quick feedback; finally,

---

12 Please see *Appendix B5 – Beyond Budgeting in 60 Seconds*

the goals need to be open to revision regularly or if any major change in circumstances occurs.

## Standard Operating Procedures (SOP)

Best practices and standard operating procedures are great if circumstances and knowledge are stable, i.e. if the work is in the Obvious/Clear domain. In talking to those with first-hand experience SOPs are a very common source of grievance in their organizations. The problem usually occurs when someone in the bureaucracy believes work to be obvious while those doing the work know it is not. This leads to conflict and loss of transparency as people work around the procedures to get anything done. In the worst case work becomes so over-constrained by SOPs that the *Zone of Complacency*[13] is entered, where everybody adheres blindly to the rules and catastrophic failure ensues if circumstances change.

SOPs tend to be implemented rigidly in deep bureaucratic hierarchies. Those at a distance from the real action assume the work is simple and suitable for central planning and regulation when it is not. This has to be confronted as the assumption of simplicity only applies to the most simplistic production environments and markets these days.

For ordered (Obvious, or Complicated) work, SOPs can be used if people have the flexibility to discover and implement improvements without huge managerial overhead. Once improvements are discovered, a feedback loop must be in place to review and refine them for inclusion in the standard SOPs. This practice is often used by surgeons when they encounter a patient whose organs are arranged in a slightly non-standard way. This information is updated in their SOPs so others can be better prepared.

If it is believed that the work is mostly complex, i.e. where only fragmented knowledge exists, then there will be a lot more experimentation.

---

13  Please see *Appendix B6 - Complexity in 60 Seconds*

Any form of SOP should use enabling constraints, defining clearly what knowledge exists, and which tools are available to conduct experiments.

## Yearly Performance Review

The yearly performance review for employees is another unhelpful practice that does more damage than good. First, it is typically conducted in tandem with a salary review by a superior who is entitled to pass a verdict. This immediately signals a power relationship, inducing fear on the employee side that is not conducive to improvement. Secondly, the cadence is way too slow, feedback needs to happen more often to be meaningful.

In an Agile Lean organization, performance review happens continuously in a non-threatening way. If work is done in teams, feedback happens between peers who respect each other, not by a boss with power over people. In a good team, feedback happens every day, it then happens in more detail at the end of an iteration at a Retrospective meeting – one of the most important practices to uphold. The OO is responsible for the feedback loop working properly. It is good practice to have a regular, quarterly, or half-yearly low-key one-on-one between the OO and the other team members, to catch the more personal aspects that need to be addressed. Under no circumstances should the feedback be directly coupled to compensation. It is quite legitimate to bring up the question of compensation in these conversations, people may want to earn more, and they can explore the avenues with the OO for making that happen.

It is also legitimate to have mechanisms and metrics for evaluating performance and improvement. The key is that the metrics are accepted and perhaps proposed by the team. Teams should be prepared to be transparent about their performance.

## Stage-Gate project models

Stage-gate models are often used in companies that primarily think in terms of projects. This is a special kind of SOP focused on the execution of a project. It defines a number of project stages from cradle to grave with gates in between signally when the project can move to the next stage. A simple example could be:

1. Initial idea
2. Concept definition
3. Specification
4. Initial plan
5. Phase 1, 2 … etc
6. Verification
7. Closure

In principle, there is nothing wrong with this if the project is straightforward and circumstances are stable. But it is often enforced on highly complex and volatile projects, and then it becomes a ball-and-chain that the project team drags along. We have witnessed countless situations where a team spent disproportionate effort on tweaking numbers and documents in order to pass the next gate. The model easily becomes an inward-looking bureaucratic exercise, another rain dance as Russell Ackoff would call it.

Drawing the process as a line immediately leads people to think that there is only one predetermined path to success, which implies that specifications can be written in complete detail upfront, and verification can be done at the end.

Another flaw is that the conditions for passing certain gates revolve around written documentation and that is reviewed by decision-makers far away from the details of the project, leading to focus on form over content. In this situation, complex details will be lost, and people will tweak the documentation to suit those who have to approve and credit it.

It is good to have a framework for projects, a set of enabling constraints, defining how to get started in a rational way, and how to conduct regular reviews to see if the project is on an optimal track. However, the purpose has to be constantly to determine the best possible way forward, not to secure compliance with a plan.

# Adapting the Organization

An organization is never static, perhaps semi-static for a while, but sooner or later circumstances unfold or some discomfort occurs that demands change. We will take a brief look at a few typical categories of adaptation or change.

## Need to Change Circle Composition

Customers change, new technologies have to be adopted, people have left, or an idea for improvement of the value stream was discovered. All sorts of things can trigger the process of updating operational units, Circles. Changing a Circle's personnel is a major step and has to be done with care.

One option is what we call the "High Road", as described in Chapter 6. The important thing is to invite people to participate so maximize their commitment to a new model. We recommend the following:

- Ask all Circles to use the Future Backwards[14] exercise at their next retrospective to express their opinion of the current, ideal, and undesirable paths the organization has, or could have taken.
- Make the findings visible and invite another team to critique, adapt, and improve.
- The OOs collect the input and try to consolidate the findings into one common mental model. A meeting is convened where everybody is invited to discuss. Improvements are made. By now the objectives of any change should be clear.
- At their next Retrospective, the teams are asked for proposals that would improve the Circle structure.

---

14 Please see *Appendix D – More Tools and Practices – Future Backwards*.

283

- The OOs collect input and consolidate proposals. A meeting of everyone is convened and a solution is chosen, if possible. Otherwise, issues have to be resolved first.
- Facilitated by the OOs, people are asked to volunteer for the teams in the new Circles; it typically takes a while before an acceptable solution is found.
- The new structure can launch and start iterating – Plan-Do-Study-Act.

This kind of process can take some getting used to. Those who have lived in a traditional hierarchical organization will expect their superiors to present a new model and perhaps ask for feedback. However, if people want freedom, they also have to take it, along with the responsibility and the work.

A simpler situation exists if a new Secondary Circle is needed. It is normally quite straightforward to invite people to participate. The OOs will help define the Manifest and one of them will facilitate proceedings and participate in its meetings.

Another scenario is when the workload in a Circle increases, and more team members are added. At some point, the limit of 9 plus SO and OO is passed, and increasing discomfort creeps in. It may even result in a *de facto* split into two sub-teams. Then it is time to scale up, that is, two teams with their own tactical backlog, but just one Main Backlog and SO. It is also possible that this triggers a large change in team composition, but we recommend exploring this avenue before enlarging the value stream with more Circles and Delegations. When scaling up, let the Teams suggest the best team composition, perhaps explore the Tandem Teams[15] approach: we have found that helpful and a relatively easy way to grow.

---

15  Please see *Appendix D – More Tools and Practices – Tandem Teams*.

# Need to Change Relationships and Delegations

A host of different events and discoveries can trigger a need to reconsider Relationships and corresponding Delegations, as described in Manifests. It is normally simple when the people involved in the work are allowed to define how to work together effectively. OOs should facilitate conversations and focus on decisions, preventing the team from being distracted by things best left to others. Do not spend time on detailed, fixed, and brittle rules when there is only fragmented knowledge.

A special and more complicated case exists about relationships with an external Circle, such as a supplier. It is not safe to assume that they each share the same goals, due to their different commercial interests. An experienced OO or a person from a Service Circle with negotiation skills may help negotiate a Manifest for this relationship. If possible, let those doing the work on both sides be involved, as this is the best way to achieve true commitment.

Sometimes suppliers will not participate in such discussions taking an adversarial attitude in an attempt to get the upper hand. Why would you want to work with such a supplier? If trust is not an option, then only control remains, why would anybody want that?

Under all circumstances do not let a central purchasing department or individual have authority to close such agreements and just push it on the Circles and Teams in question. There are countless examples of broken relationships and bad behavior resulting from such an approach.

# Need to change Team Composition

When Teams need a different array of competencies let the Team be part of the solution. Develop a Competency Matrix to create a common understanding of the need compared with the current status; it is an excellent illustration and a useful tool when trying to attract new people.

First, see if the desired competencies can be found internally. The OO is normally in charge of this process. Here is one way to do it:

- The need will be made public in the organization.
- People can show their interest or ask the OO questions; the fewer formal requirements, the more people will come forward.
- The OO will then conduct discussions with the applicants.
- At some point, the OO of the person's current Circle will have to be involved, and a way forward negotiated.
- When there is a realistic path forward, the Team should be involved, and everybody has the opportunity to explore details and ask questions.
- Then a decision is made.

Things may happen through informal conversations like over lunch, which is good, there is no need to invent procedures.

If it is concluded that a new hire has to be made, we suggest following the same plan. It is good practice to involve someone with some expertise in dealing with employment matters, for example, an HR person in a Service Circle.

## Need to Downsize and Lay off People

This is the hardest part. Markets can disappear, supply chains can fail, and bad luck can strike. The result is that the size or rather the cost structure of a Team cannot be sustained in a commercially responsible way. In such situations, some Teams managed to find solutions: sharing the work and money available, some taking leave to focus on other things and then coming back when the situation was better, and others taking early retirement. Such an extraordinary commitment and sense of responsibility is rare but beautiful. If possible the Team should be involved in finding a solution to the challenge of unsustainable costs. In the end, it may not be possible to reach a solution with reasonable consensus, and the OOs may be left to make a crisis decision.

First look for spots in other Circles, then re-training possibilities so people can acquire the skills that fit the needs of another Team.

Finally, there may be no way around letting a person go. The aim should be to treat the person with respect and to provide them with the best possible opportunity of finding a new position. This is perhaps self-evident but nevertheless often handled sub-optimally. People who are terminated often feel belittled or treated indifferently, as many either distance themselves or come across as insensitive when dealing with their loss. This does not have to be so. Inexperienced OOs may need the help of an HR person in a Service Circle and the organization may help people find new positions, this is normally well received if the options are served respectfully.

# Problems with People

We touched earlier on conflicts between people. No matter how positive the environment, how little stress, and how carefully teams are built, problems with human relations are sure to pop up. There is no basis for romanticism relating to human behavior. Although we have stressed the need to create freedom and trust enabling people to engage, create results, and take responsibility, sooner or later someone will try to take advantage at another's expense.

The organization cannot afford to let one person ruin it all. Trust, psychological safety, commitment, and intrinsic motivation are delicate and can easily wither. As a rule of thumb, one negative event takes five positive ones to restore the balance; restoring trust may take longer.

Failure to be truthful and not recognize reality is the most damaging character trait. Some people will blatantly lie or put a spin on everything, *"Presenting the truth in its most favorable light"*, as I learned in the US; such people destroy trust. Unfortunately, it has almost become accepted and expected behavior to make it up as you go along, which reduces everything to a power game. Trust in society and consequently in organizations is in decline. This trend has to be forcefully opposed if freedom has to be achieved and sustained.

If someone is clearly in the wrong with negative consequences for colleagues, customers, or suppliers, intervention is called for. In a Constitutional Organization, there are negotiated agreements, enabling constraints, etc. Everybody has to uphold the agreements, and special responsibility rests with the OO.

Intervention must aim to restore relationships and trust, it cannot be about retaliation or retribution. Read about this earlier in this chapter *Upholding Relationships – Respect and Forgiveness* . True forgiveness has the potential of starting to restore relationships.

Moving forward on the path of restoration, both parties have to commit to truth, transparency, and honoring commitments, a good practice is to announce intent to the other party and genuinely request their feedback. Then slowly trust can be rebuilt, relationships restored and sometimes even improved after such a crisis.

A special case exists if the problem is with one with a perceived higher authority or status. In this case, many people will choose not to react out of fear of consequences. Especially in this case, it is very important that the OO step up and muster the courage to deal with the situation. In case the problem is with the OO, we have normally recommended that anyone is allowed to go to another OO they feel comfortable with, if they have an issue of their own.

# Small and Medium-sized Organizations

We already discussed the special practices often needed in small to medium-sized organizations in the previous chapter, here we will just look at a couple of situations that are more prevalent in these organizations. Most situations are actually just a lot easier to handle because everybody knows each other to some extent.

In such a small environment, challenges and disappointments tend to be more personal and not directed at some remote impersonal system or bureaucracy. The OOs attention will be more directed towards working on personal relationships than improving processes and procedures. It requires more personal self-reliance and not just a technical understanding of processes.

In small organizations, sometimes owners or executives start to think of the organization as their family and themselves as the patriarch or matriarch to whom allegiance is owed. It then becomes difficult to accept that people have other priorities, their own families for example. It is important to have checks and balances here as well, that someone is willing to talk to such owners or executives and explain what is going on.

Finally, sometimes small organizations grow, and with that comes the need for more structure, everything is no longer just tackled at the coffee machine. This will be a series of rapid transformations, each having the potential to cause disruption. Each step should be handled with the involvement of people, signaling intent, and using invitation. Inspiration can be found in the recommendations in Chapter 6. A special challenge rests with founders and owners, how do they transition from a situation with very few involved in decision-making to one with many involved? For everybody, there is a challenge in transitioning to a situation where influence cannot be direct anymore but hinges on delegating mandates and using representative decision-making. People have to be able to trust those who make decisions on their behalf.

# Looking back on the Everyday Situations

Our investigation of everyday situations, calling for a different approach than a traditional hierarchical power-based organization, has been a broad sweep. The situations highlighted come from personal experiences and the comprehensive interviews of witnesses, who have experienced their own particular challenges and need to act differently.

We have come to the end of the gathering of evidence and recommendations, a few bullet points will capture the essence of this chapter.

*Some general situations are very different in a constitutional organization:*

*– The whole area of working with teams and volunteers instead of giving orders.*

*– Facing reality and the complexity of it.*

*– Accepting cognitive bias and noise – and trying to mitigate it.*

*The relationship between the owners and executives takes on a special dimension.*

*Many organizational strategies will be different in and Agile Lean Organization:*

*– Interaction with customers to drive the value stream optimally.*

*– Several common processes (e.g. yearly budgeting) will take different shapes.*

*There has to be constant attention to adapting the organization to the unfolding circumstances, nothing is static.*

*The necessity of dealing with people violating agreements, checks and balances must be upheld.*

# Closing the Case of Freedom

*We have come to the end of our investigation, consisting of research, interviews, and the establishment of models and hypotheses. We are now ready to present the closing argument.*

*In the process, many plausible cause-and-effect relationships were uncovered. Furthermore, many patterns and templates were discovered or re-discovered resulting in a comprehensive repertoire of interventions to pursue when traveling the road less traveled toward freedom in organizations.*

*But, we also found a considerable amount of anti-patterns — practices that should be avoided. Many organizations feel that general patterns and principles would not work for them, they see themselves as one of a kind. Once again, we lean on W. Edwards Deming:*

> *A common disease that afflicts management and government administration the world over is the impression that 'Our problems are different.' They are different, to be sure, but the principles that will help to improve quality of product and of service are universal in nature.*
> *— W. Edwards Deming: Out of the Crisis, 1982.*

This book is an investigation into the "cold case" for freedom. Everybody wants and talks about it, but few do anything practical to create an environment where people can engage, flourish, and create value.

When we speak of freedom, it is not just freedom from constraints and outright oppression, it is also freedom to choose, contribute, and become the best possible version of yourself.

# The Status of Leadership and Collaboration

We conducted comprehensive interviews with witnesses to get many different perspectives on the status of leadership and collaboration in organizations. We also had our own testimony from witnessing situations inside many organizations over the years.

The situations described were very different, including very positive experiences of people taking up freedom, and demonstrating initiative and responsibility, even in the face of outright despair with incomprehensible bureaucracies. The most positive perspectives came from executives but that tapered as we descended the traditional hierarchical ladder. The most positive views came from smaller organizations and the most negative from the larger ones.

A common trend in the witness accounts – especially from Scandinavia – was that executives talk a lot about empowerment, empathy, and work-life balance, but the policies and practices in everyday life lag behind. In fact, many say they are currently experiencing a trend toward more centralization and control, not freedom for the individual. This is oppression mostly by bureaucratic or expert control, not so much by old-fashioned macho, hard-line giving of orders. This gap between communicated intent and actual practice is apparently widening with an increasing distrust of executives as a result. Many have told us stories about how executives and managers try to empower people but retain the prerogative to reverse any decision. There is a fear of losing control, even though what they have is only an illusion of control.

Across the board, there is a struggle to develop a common mental model of the work. Senior people, especially in large organizations, see the world as orderly, plannable, and measurable with simple KPIs (key performance indicators), at least that is what their subordinates report. The lower ranks, on the other hand, understand that the world is increasingly complex, that uncertainty reigns, and that quick adaptation is needed.

There is also tension between the tendency to look at one's own identity, self-actualization, self-staging and actually getting things done in an organization. In particular, executives find it hard to create an environment where younger generations are motivated to participate and contribute. In Western Europe especially, there are challenges with people mentally checking out, the phenomenon of quiet quitting; something that is also documented through Gallup's research.

We are all hope-based creatures, without it we wither. We firmly believe that the evidence points to the fact that we all need the freedom to act as independent actors, choose to engage, take responsibility – also for others – and flourish, growing and creating value. Everybody needs freedom to participate in building the positive organizations and institutions that are pillars of society. This gives us hope for a better future.

# The Main Culprit

In trying to understand what brought us to the present situation, several lines of inquiry were followed, but eventually, all lines brought us back to two fundamental problems:

- The use of power to control others. This can also take the form of a rather invisible control by a bureaucratic system.
- The lack of trust that people will stand by their commitments. This can also take the form of avoiding commitments, which is strongly correlated with a lack of engagement.

This is what every school of self-government or self-management says: Don't use force against others and honor your commitments.

This points to the dark side of humanity where the quest for power rears its ugly head if there are no checks and balances. When power and the struggle for it becomes the most important thing, honoring commitments to others is less important and truth becomes whatever you can make followers believe.

The main culprit in this investigation is the classic power-based hierarchy, traditionally used as the management backbone. The purpose of the hierarchy is to secure compliance and predictability. At every node in the hierarchy the person in charge plans, delegates, monitors, and controls, to keep the subordinates in check. As in many situations in life, *"Beware of what you ask for, you might get it!"* The same goes for the hierarchy, compliance and predictability will be promoted, most of the time with predictably substandard performance, at the detriment of adaptability and innovation. There are discernable consequences of a pronounced hierarchical organization, we shall just enumerate a few:

- People inevitably focus on the power game. Moving up the hierarchical ladder provides freedom, status, and certain privileges, so that is what people go for.
- Where power prevails, fear is present, and according to W. Edwards. *"When there is fear in an organization, the numbers are cooked!"* People will please upward for self-protection.
- Transparency and truth suffer as people "green shift" (put a positive spin on) information when delivering it to superiors, in a deep hierarchy the people at the top are left with very distorted information for their decisions, frequently making bad ones as a result.
- The middle of a hierarchy becomes a bureaucracy, neither close to markets, people delivering products and services, nor owners. A bureaucracy has the power to say no to everything and yes to almost nothing. The easiest solution is to make sure nothing happens. At one

of our large clients, the four middle layers in a seven-layer organization were unashamedly referred to as the "permafrost".

- Russell Ackoff talks about how *"sins of commission"* are visible, whereas *"sins of omission"* rarely are so, hence the former can be punished, the latter not so. In a hierarchy, it is therefore the safest bet to do as little as possible and just make sure that you are not to blame for anything.

- The hierarchy demonstrably creates upstairs and downstairs thinking, resulting in a very stratified organization. Those in the lower layers of a hierarchy frequently resign to being downstairs and may find other ways to engage, quite often in confrontational, undercover activities of undermining the efforts of those upstairs. Even in Scandinavia, where we pride ourselves on low power distance, the upstairs and downstairs stratification is highly visible.

- In a hierarchy, if the boss is the customer, who takes care of the real customer? Highly hierarchical organizations become focused on the inner workings of the organization and are typically not capable of catering to their customers very well.

- A pronounced hierarchy, where permission is required for everything, is very slow to react to anything extraordinary, or not covered by the standard operating procedures.

These examples will suffice for the closing argument. These days the hierarchy is always accompanied by a bureaucracy, doing much of the compliance control, with its own set of challenges as previously documented.

We traced the origins of the current management style going all the way back to medieval feudalism with its aristocracy, via the organization of armies, e.g the Prussian army, and leading to the works of Max Weber, Henry Fayol, F. Winslow Taylor, Henry Ford, Alfred Sloan, and the rather obscure Robert Michels.

Of these, F. Winslow Taylor became the most influential and well-known, mostly because business schools adopted his theories (or rather the interpretation by his followers, as his writing was scarce). After WWII, American business schools produced a flurry of MBAs and other thoroughbred managers, who had no actual domain knowledge, but just knew how to *manage*. This growth of management as a separate discipline is perhaps the most damaging of all the evidence we found. It sometimes goes by the name of Neo-Taylorism in honor of its father F. Winslow Taylor. It often relies on very simplistic theories, metrics, targets, and KPIs. Many of the underlying economic and management theories have been proven to be bogus, for example by Nobel laureate Daniel Kahneman and W. Edwards Deming, but these facts have been largely ignored.

We do not claim that authority should be abolished and replaced by a romantic idea that by removing boundaries, good things will happen. There has to be a structure and checks and balances to prevent a drift, either into oligarchy or anarchy.

We also distinguish between smaller (two or three layers in a traditional organization) and larger organizations with deep hierarchies. Our argument covers the latter, the big organizations. In the smaller organization, the owner is very visible and normally present, the state of freedom in this case is highly dependent on how the owner (or the executive who is his steward) conducts himself. This person can liberate people and abstain from playing the power card in all situations of normal operation.

However, there is a strange reverse trend to be seen in the attitudes of many people working in organizations. It is that of expressive individualism, seeking the constant manifestation of one's own identity by always looking at one's own needs in the moment. This often gets in the way of collaboration, commitment, and willingness to serve others. It is a concern often expressed in our interviews, especially with younger people, many of whom struggle to find a balance. We believe that both the power game in classic hierarchies and this claim of instant self-gratification go back to the problem of putting oneself above everything else and not balancing one's needs with the needs of others.

Finally, there are situations where classic command and control is called for. If a sudden drop into Chaos is experienced, those with the highest intuitive skills are granted the authority to tell everybody else what to do to stabilize the situation. It is important to dissolve this power structure as soon as a stable condition is reached, otherwise, this power structure will stick and freedom will suffer. There also might be a call for command and control if the people are incapable of self-governing due to a lack of competency, clarity, or character.

# A Call for a Verdict

We contend that the traditional power-based hierarchy is the primary guilty party, locking organizations in a perpetual quest for power. This results in substandard performance and people working in a permanent condition of servitude, preventing them from engaging, flourishing, and creating value.

The hierarchy is not alone in the dock, there are associates and accomplices:

- Bureaucracy will spread like an invasive weed and consume more and more resources while further alienating people.
- The underlying theory behind the conventional management paradigm – Neo-Taylorism – is an accomplice with its over-reliance on the so-called cult of the expert.
- The isolation of the managerial class into an upstairs compartment, distanced and isolated from the real work and the real customers, reduces transparency leading to an echo chamber of managerial speak and sub-standard decisions based on poor information.
- Along the same line, the separation of thinking and doing, exemplified by the creation of a class of pure managers without domain knowledge, degrades decisions and alienates people causing them to disengage.

- This leads managers to be distant from the real work and to regard it as clear and obvious, or plannable and controllable; when in fact, as those directly involved know, much of it is complex and uncertain, requiring knowledge building and experimentation.

All these factors – and a host of lesser ones – interact dynamically and cannot be addressed in isolation. But, we will argue that the traditional power-based hierarchy is the main culprit and should be removed from the equation, allowing the other factors to be addressed in due course.

# Now to the Sentencing

If the evidence so far is clear, what are the repercussions? What shall we do with the hierarchy, its sidekick the bureaucracy, and its many unhelpful practices?

We ask that the traditional hierarchy be taken into custody and then deported to a remote island; Saint Helena has worked before. Please note that we refer to the institution of hierarchy, not necessarily the people in it.

We ask that the hierarchy be replaced with value streams composed of self-governing units with representative decision-making, united by common goals and values. This will keep a sharp focus on the external world of real customers and will provide a fertile environment in which people will engage, flourish, and create value.

The exhibits and evidence presented in the earlier chapters presented examples of how a constitutional organization with mutual agreements could be built, with plausible and simple ways to start. The main elements are:

- A clear Manifest describing the purpose and values of the organization.

- A Value Stream of self-governing units, called Primary Circles. It starts with the customers and works its way backward, potentially including strategic suppliers.
- Circles are based on small self-managing teams with specific competencies, roles, and responsibilities for strategic prioritization and operations.
- Normal collaboration between Circles is handled through mutual agreements called Manifests. Deliverables can be Delegated from one Circle to another.
- A set of Resolution Circles handles cross-circle issues through representative decision-making by people from all primary Circles.
- Secondary Circles handle cross-cutting concerns, typically around certain competencies such as quality assurance or design.
- A principle for handling exceptions when the unexpected hits with force, using Transient Circles, temporarily commissioned to stabilize the situation.
- A cadence of feedback, reviews, and retrospectives to enable constant dynamic evolution of the organization, its products, and practices.

If the organization has an elaborate bureaucracy, it is not enough to deport the hierarchy, the power vacuum created will likely be filled by bureaucracy, which will extend its control further. Suppression of this tendency can consist of the following:

- Clearly state the mandate and responsibilities for individual Circles. Go through the rules and control mechanisms and prune those that are no longer needed or replace them with simpler ones.
- Reduce and continue to monitor central administrative planning, especially budgeting. Replace the yearly budget with less detailed forecasting, resource allocation, and goal setting, open to frequent review. Let Resolution Circles deal with resource allocation as needed instead of following a fixed budget.

- Transfer authority to the Primary Circles for employment and compensation – within boundaries of course.
- Ask people in administrative positions if they would rather contribute in a Value Stream Circle.
- Ask the remaining administrative people to form one or more Service Circles assisting the other Circles when needed, this would include finance, legal, HR, facility management, internal service staff, etc.

This may be traumatic for those in the bureaucracy, and some will decide to leave. It is important to respect and demonstrate the value of the administrative staff to everybody and present them with a carrot, not just a stick. But it must be clear that over-administration is a waste that needs to be dealt with.

Once this is dealt with, other unhelpful structures will start to wither, but further adjustments may be necessary as circumstances unfold.

# Ready for a Constitutional Organization?

Empowering people with some autonomy may sound risky; we have often heard statements like *"There is no telling what people might do!"* or *"Nothing will get done then, they will be off to the beach!"*. The current leadership is afraid of losing control, even when that control is illusory. It requires a mind-shift toward trust and away from control. In the end, there are only two options when dealing with people, you either trust them or control them.

What we are promoting, leans on the following quote:

*Push authority as far out as you can find someone who can carry it.*
*– General Stanley McChrystal[1]*

Later, McChrystal said that one should grant people authority and mandate all the way out to the edge of one's comfort zone – and then one step more. Nevertheless, one should always assess readiness for this sort of freedom.

## Preconditions for Leadership

We found that people assuming leadership authority should score high on the following parameters:

- **Competence** – nobody wants incompetent people walking around and pushing buttons. There is no substitute for comprehensive competency.
- **Clarity** – a deep understanding of objectives and the direction in which to move. Nobody can make decisions without knowing where to head.
- **Character** – ability, and willingness to make decisions for the common good. Anybody making decisions affecting others needs to be trusted to look beyond themself.

If people's capabilities in these three areas are evaluated on a scale from 0 to 100% and multiplied together, the resulting number is a pretty good measure of the probability of success. It doesn't matter how clever or visionary a person is, lack of character just makes for an even more dangerous person.

---

1    As a curiosity, searching for who originally is to be credited for this quote, an interesting situation with three different AI tools surfaced. When asked who said it, one claimed Cyril Ramaphosa, the President of South Africa, another general H. Norman Schwarzkopf, the last AI tool could not identify the source. On the other hand, when asked if this or that person said so, they happily attributed the quote to the two people mentioned earlier, Stanley McChrystal and David Marquet. It certainly shook me up a bit to discover the true nature of AI tools as discussion partners.

## Are People Willing to Participate?

During our interviews with eyewitnesses, we often heard people say that they found it hard to get people to actively accept freedom and its accompanying responsibility. It seems that some people prefer to stay in their comfort zone, being told what to do, and not bothering with the outcome.

A special case of this was often mentioned concerning working from home as opposed to being with others. In the post-Covid period, a narrative about working from home being better and more efficient has spread, and apparently, quite a few have come to think that they are entitled to work where and when they want. It follows that in this case there is some disregard for the necessity to be physically with others to find solutions to complex challenges This is sometimes highlighted in the expressive individualism of the Gen-Z who occasionally put self before community.

If a significant majority of people in an organization do not subscribe to the idea of freedom and are willing to work for it, it will not work.

## Are there External Inhibitors?

When contemplating a journey toward freedom, it is wise to consider the nature of the external stakeholders in the organization, especially those that could block the road to freedom.

Will higher authorities in a large organization suddenly intervene? Will they reserve the right to institute more heavy-handed control in a crisis? If the probability is high, the journey is probably a non-starter.

A special case may exist where owners suddenly demand drastic measures including the replacement of executives. Be especially aware of private equity funds. Firstly, most of them are purely finance and legally focused, hence deeply ingrained in Neo-Taylorism. Secondly, they may unexpectedly flip the company which may find itself in the hands of totally different management.

In some instances, external constraints like compliance demands are so draconian that any attempt to introduce freedom will fail. We have met several such situations in the public sector where people are resigned to the fact and joined the ranks of the disengaged and disgruntled. In some cases the central bureaucracy imposed harsh new rules, causing the best people to leave. The situation also occurs in commercial organizations, commonly in those owned by private equity firms.

## Is it Worth the Risk?

Some witnesses have decided not to pursue freedom further, as the bureaucratic hierarchy would never tolerate it and they do not want to risk their current comfortable lifestyle and handsome paycheck, by challenging it. Instead, they quietly sub-optimize what they can within their sphere of control, and try to create a localized oasis of freedom for the people they work with.

A few mavericks enjoy a good challenge and decide to tread the road less traveled toward freedom, without securing permission. These may be like those who jump out of airplanes without a parachute, convinced they can borrow one on the way down. They often anticipate achieving visibly positive results before the bureaucracy discovers what is going on. They typically broadcast their success so abrasively that the process is hard to reverse. It has worked in some situations, but not all.

## Ready for the Rewilding?

Occasionally one might see a video of animals raised in captivity being released into the wild with either comic or tragic outcomes; the former often being where the animal comes back because it would rather stay with its familiar cage and food bowl.

It is the same with people who have lived the insular life of the power hierarchies, being told what to do and being fed at regular intervals. Before starting the journey, consider if a life of freedom is worth it. Is fulfillment, autonomy, mastery, and strong relationships worth the effort required? Is there a willingness to accept responsibility for others amidst the challenge of unfolding circumstances?

Remember the preamble to the Swiss Constitution:

*In the name of Almighty God! The Swiss People and the Cantons,*

*mindful of their responsibility towards creation, resolved to renew their alliance so as to strengthen liberty, democracy, independence and peace in a spirit of solidarity and openness towards the world,*

*determined to live together with mutual consideration and respect for their diversity, conscious of their common achievements and their responsibility towards future generations,*

*and in the knowledge that only those who use their freedom remain free, and that the strength of a people is measured by the well-being of its weakest members,*

*adopt the following Constitution*

And for good measure another quote from James Madison:

*Equal laws protecting equal rights, are found as they ought to be presumed, the best guarantee of loyalty, and love of country; as well as best calculated to cherish that mutual respect and good will among citizens of every religious denomination which are necessary to social harmony and most favorable to the advancement of truth.*

*– James Madison, letter To Jacob De La Motta, 1820*

# A Final Summary of Central Elements

Whether you choose to follow our path to a Constitutional Organization or have better ideas, here is a summary of important elements:

* Have a clear and well-understood purpose for the organization. Have frequent conversations about purpose and values to develop a common understanding. In complex environments, bind people with common goals and values, not power-based rules and regulations. Develop a visible manifest – a constitution – for the organization.

- Embrace the complexities and uncertainties of work and life. Multiple perspectives are needed to get a useful understanding. Avoid silos of competencies and groups of only like-minded people. Avoid long-term and centrally made detailed plans as they are brittle and can break catastrophically. Always have feedback loops to enable learning. Focus on people's engagement and intrinsic motivation. Work with self-managing and cross-functional teams with the freedom to act. Build up psychological safety, so people speak up – never use fear to control people.
- Avoid the classic power-based hierarchy as it makes the struggle for power an aim in itself. Maintain central bureaucracy at a bare minimum. Never use power to force somebody to do something. Have checks and balances to moderate the use of power. Have a different modus operandi for crisis and chaos situations and return to normal when the situation is stabilized.
- Use representative, consensus, and consultative decision-making.
- Honor commitments, and develop trust. Collaboration should be based on negotiated manifests – rules of engagement.

With this, we rest our case and suggest that you embark on the journey to freedom in organizations along the road less traveled, where there is the rule of law and not just the law of the ruler.

Our organizations, commercial or otherwise are the pillars of society. If we fail to give people a way to develop and experience freedom, we will also diminish their ability to participate constructively in the larger democratic and free society.

We will end this journey more or less as we started it with a quote from the grand old man

*It is not necessary to change. Survival is not mandatory*
*– W. Edwards Deming*

# Appendices

We uncovered a lot of extra material and information during the investigation of the Case for Freedom. This additional material has been collected in the following appendices. Only the first of these a summary of the interviews conducted is directly included, the other can conveniently be addressed on the accompanying website: https://liberatingorg.com.

*A – Summary of Interviews (included here, https://liberatingorg.com/a )*
A series of 90+ interviews were conducted to get many different perspectives on the Case for Freedom. The result of that exercise was many changes to the core content of the book, but this editorial summary of the findings was also produced.

*B1 – Agile in 60 Seconds (https://liberatingorg.com/b1)*
The concept and definition of Agile, including the *Agile Manifesto*.

*B2 – Lean in 60 Seconds (https://liberatingorg.com/b2)*
Lean originated from the Toyota Production System (TPS) but was in principle born during the American WWII war production, W. Edwards Deming was instrumental in this, he created the *Plan–Do–Study–Act* (PDSA) Cycle, also known as the *Deming-Cycle*.

*B3 – Scrum in 60 Seconds (https://liberatingorg.com/b3)*
A discussion of the core principles and practices of Vanilla Scrum and its enabling constraints: iterations, roles activities, and artifacts when dealing with complex challenges.

*B4 – Kanban in 60 Seconds (https://liberatingorg.com/b4)*
An agile framework for mapping and visualizing workflows, creating focus and transparency.

*B5 – Beyond Budgeting in 60 Seconds (https://liberatingorg.com/b5)*
A framework for an organization better suited for the present day, starting by abolishing the yearly budget in favor of a better way to forecast, set targets, and allocate resources.

*B6 – Complexity in 60 Seconds (https://liberatingorg.com/b6)*
In complex situations, we only have fragmented knowledge. Cynefin, the basic cognitive framework by Dave Snowden gives a model to think about this and act appropriately.

*B7 – Intrinsic Motivation in 60 Seconds (https://liberatingorg.com/b7)*
People need Purpose, Relationships, Autonomy, and Mastery so that they can and will engage, take responsibility, and flourish at work.

*B8 – Psychological Safety in 60 Seconds (https://liberatingorg.com/b8)*
People need Psychological Safety in order to engage openly. That means: Nobody is punished for admitting a mistake, nobody is punished for asking for help, and Nobody is punished for proposing a better way of doing things.

*B9 – Cognitive Bias and Noise in 60 Seconds (https://liberatingorg.com/b9)*
We often think systematically wrong and encounter a lot of noise in our information and judgment. How do we battle these systematic and random errors in thinking and judgment?

*B10 – Idealized Design in 60 Seconds (https://liberatingorg.com/b10)*
How to achieve radical innovation? Idealized Design is a way of defining the desired state and working backward to what can be done now.

*B11 – The OODA Loop in 60 Seconds (https://liberatingorg.com/b11)*
A discussion of how to combine the intuitive expertise-driven and the carefully reflected approach to engagement and decision-making?

*B12 – Value Impact Estimation in 60 Seconds (https://liberatingorg.com/b12)*
Prioritize cleverly. Quantifying objectives, values, and goals; then estimating the impact of available strategies in order to prioritize better. Getting your act together – Tom Gilb style.

*B13 – Constitution and Þings in 60 Seconds (https://liberatingorg.com/b13 )*
How to achieve federate and representative decision-making among free actors based on a commonly agreed set of core rules – a Constitution or a Covenant.

*B14 - Personal Sustainable Work in 60 Seconds (https://liberatingorg.com/b14)*
A practical framework for applying the Agile Lean principles associated with teams and organizations, when working alone  Many people do not work in a strictly team-based setting, they have to do things on their own from time to time, how to balance the need for concentrated effort and responsiveness to external requests.

*C – Neo-Taylorism and the Fatal Attraction to Hierarchy (https://liberatingorg.com/c)*
An account of how the medieval serf system and the command and control of armies of old, crept into the business world.

*D – More Tools and Practices (https://liberatingorg.com/d)*
A collection of tools, practices, methods, patterns, and templates that have proven helpful.

*I – Illustrations (https://liberatingorg.com/res/liborg1.0_ill.pdf)*
The illustrations in this book are rather small, for a better printable resolution, download them from this link.

# A. Summary of Interviews

*We were challenged during some early reviews of our manuscript to cast out the net a bit wider to secure a wider perspective through interviews with many people from wide-ranging backgrounds. We did that and found huge differences in the responses we got, but we believe that there are some commonly useful perspectives:*

> *A common disease that afflicts management and government administration the world over is the impression that 'Our problems are different.' They are different, to be sure, but the principles that will help to improve quality of product and of service are universal in nature.*
> — *W. Edwards Deming: Out of the Crisis, 1982.*

*So, here is a summary of the interviews put together in a thematic structure rather than recounting what every interviewee said, at the end is the list of people who contributed.*

# Interview Method and Questions

This series of interviews does not represent rigid academic research, but rather a heuristic gathering of input from the people we could reach on short notice. We have then made an – admittedly subjective – aggregation of all this input. This appendix is the result of that, and the interviews have significantly influenced the rest of the structure and content of the book.

We decided to structure the interviews around some of the ideas presented earlier in the book: Identifying as clearly as possible the current state of leadership and collaboration and how we got here, then uncovering where we would have liked to be. Based on that, what objectives would be desirable to seek? And finally, we asked if they had any practical advice on how we could move in the right direction.

## Selecting the Audience

We decided to follow a few different routes to get these diverse perspectives.

We targeted CEOs, COOs, managing directors, founders, and board members mainly in Scandinavia and associated with Scandinavian organizations through LinkedIn. This is where we are most well-known and we expected a reasonable percentage of responses to our request for help. In the same way, we also targeted project and program managers in a couple of very large organizations. At the time of writing about 10% of those approached in this way entered into a dialogue, although not necessarily ending in an interview.

Then we asked our contacts in various countries and found people who either are vocal about the subject matter, teach it or in other ways are perceived as authorities. Quite a few from the public sector contributed as well.

Finally, we drew on the contacts from our different encounters with teams, project managers, product owners, and scrum masters in the recent training sessions we have held.

All in all 60+ structured interviews have been conducted. There have also been about the same number of looser conversations about the same topics, relevant feedback from those has also been taken into account.

We ended up with valuable input also from Central and Eastern Europe and Asia, mostly through people who managed local territories or were suppliers to Scandinavian organizations. We took the attitude that those who decided to volunteer for the interviews were the right people. That probably means that we have mostly collected input from rather friendly sources, the people who vehemently disagree with the concept of freedom in organizations probably did not show up. We did not come across anyone who subscribed to the old-fashioned feudal hierarchy, they all wanted a workplace where people would thrive. So you can blame us for a spot of *Confirmation Bias,* but at least we are aware of it.

## The Actual Interviews

The interviews were timeboxed to 30 minutes and most were conducted using Google Meet, but some in person. We made recordings of many of the online sessions, which made it a lot easier – although labor intensive – to get back to catch nuances in statements later on. Background research of each person and their organization was done prior to the interviews.

When starting the interviews, especially with those who were not previous contacts of ours, we made an introduction, to establish a frame of reference, and why we were working on the book. Interviewees also presented their background experience.

Then we proceeded with five discussion questions, to give some common structure and comparability to the interviews. Finally, we wrote minutes of the interview right after the event.

## Interview Questions

We used the following questions to guide and direct the conversations, and a timebox of 30 minutes to have an enabling constraint and provide a certain sense of urgency:

- How do you perceive the state of leadership and collaboration in organizations right now?
- What do you consider the most important challenge for organizations today?
- What concrete objectives would you strive for? Which one is the most important?
- What practice or activity would you most of all want to stop, prevent, or dampen?
- Do you have advice (practical strategies) on how some of this could be achieved?

It did not always pan out exactly like that, some people went off on valuable tangents, and we found it more useful to collect those narratives than to force a particular scheme on them.

# General Takeaway from Interviews

A general observation is that people are mostly willing to help and contribute when asked. We had a much better response in this line of inquiry than anything we tried before. All interviewees were eager to contribute, which was to be expected – after all, they volunteered for it – and no one was coerced. So these were conversations in an amicable tone, where no one pushed the other side in any way, and people were supportive of the idea of getting a broad perspective on the issue at hand. In general, there was consensus that the key to better performance and job satisfaction is people's commitment.

The responses covered a very wide territory. Especially the assessment of the current situation of leadership and collaboration varied considerably.

The situation was experienced very differently from region to region, from top to bottom of the hierarchy, from old to young, and from large to small organizations. To a lesser degree, we observed some different cultural perspectives, but the focus of the interviews was on the Nordic countries, and people in other territories typically were associated or connected to an organization or person in the Nordics. Many struggled with how to handle the shift in attitude in society, perhaps especially in the younger generation, exemplified by the following quote:

> *I have spent years outside the Western hemisphere, and I think we in Europe and other Western countries tend to disturb our work environments with a pronounced focus on our own identity and status vis-a-vis others. I see a surplus of self-staging around. And I think the manifestations of this self-staging hurt our happiness and productivity.*
>
> *— Anne Sofie Allarp, lawyer, author*

In general, we heard mostly about leadership challenges in larger organizations but often challenges with satisfying the complex demands from staff in the smaller ones. Some said that over the course of the last few years, the demand for liberties and perks from staff had become out of touch with reality in many local and smaller organizations.

Remember, we spoke mostly with people at the top of the classic hierarchy in smaller organizations, where the people from larger organizations were somewhere in the middle; so there is probably a bias there. We did however hear from some people in larger organizations that they had managed to create "Free Territories" where their superiors protected independence and freedom and made sure the rest of the organization did not interfere negatively, which seemed to work very well. However, some also said that such protection was gone the moment the sponsor was promoted or got another job. In larger organizations there was also a pronounced effect of frequent change of superiors, resulting in certain shallowness of the leadership, as these people never developed a deep appreciation for what was going on.

So we found people who were indeed very satisfied with the present, some who were below the line of despair, and any shade of grey in between. But there were some general observations that we dare to present as general trends and conclude on.

# Status and Challenge Observations

## A Growing Push for Freedom

The trend may not always be framed as freedom, and that may seem too radical a word to use. Empowerment and involvement are more popular words. In any case, there seems to be a clear movement towards flatter hierarchies and greater opportunities for people to influence things. The workplace moves toward greater inclusion and taking care of individual needs. Most executives stated that this is the case in their organization, they express a genuine desire to provide people with a more satisfying workplace. They have initiatives in place, have stated their goals, and are trying to implement the change. Most younger people further down in traditional hierarchies said that as employees what mattered was flexibility in when to work and where, so that they could pursue the whole gamut of interests that they nurtured.

Some reflected on the situation with their customers, some of whom were quite advanced in liberating people, transforming their culture to one of engagement. These customers were ready to seek trust-based relationships and not just contract-based ones.

However, the people in the lower ranks were not so convinced that freedom was growing. In particular many expressed concern that the stated purposes were not followed up with practices. There was often an experienced disconnect between words and practices, often in the form of a bureaucracy that just kept churning the way it had always done or a deepening hierarchy that had to be satisfied.

One frequent public speaker at management events explained how he often ran a questionnaire session that revealed this discrepancy between what people said they were doing and what was actually happening.

But there was a lot of encouraging input from smaller companies that had managed to create a culture that encouraged people's engagement and they responded by taking the initiative and responsibility. Many founders, owners, or CEOs seemed to generally work in this direction. One challenge that a few of those mentioned was to be patient and remember that while they had an extreme passion for what they were doing, other people might not share that intensity, and that was OK.

## Stifling Bureaucracy

Almost without exception when asking people about something that they would like to dampen, bureaucracy came up. The only exceptions were some people at the very top of larger organizations; they did not experience the burden of the bureaucracy. In smaller companies, the grief was mostly expressed at strangling demands from government institutions, large customers, unions, or the European Union. The issues were not so much something happening internally; that makes sense, in a small company everybody is facing the brute reality of customers and real work.

Many felt the pressure of over-administration and financial micromanagement. They were project managers, middle managers, and managers of divisions reporting to some corporate headquarters. Some said that micromanaging had been increasing over the last 15 years, and permission now needed to be asked upstairs for very minor things, this especially happened in situations of rapid growth and actual success – apparently, the hierarchy and bureaucracy were allowed to deepen, and develop extensive internal procedures and documentation for everything. Following Standard Operating Procedures (SOP) became the most important thing. Reports in large quantities were required although nobody remembered why this particular report should be made, but other documents referenced its existence, so it could not be abandoned.

Interestingly a similar effect was experienced for the opposite reason, crisis. For many the pandemic presented a sudden drop into chaos, and the response was a demand for more procedures, more control, and less freedom to decide. Once these extra compliance measures were institutionalized, they were almost impossible to dispose of again.

> Many want to build an engaging organization but are stuck in goal control, KPIs, and OKRs. The effort becomes half-hearted, and they do not understand that these mechanisms of control prevent self-management.
>
> – Bård Kuvås

If people could dampen one thing, bureaucracy would be it. Some believed around 50% of their time was spent on reporting and administrative procedures, they did not see any reason for this at all.

## Hierarchy of Experts

Somewhat similar to the growth of bureaucracy, people in larger organizations said that the hierarchy had deepened considerably over the last years with the addition of hordes of academics, PhDs, and the like. These people were never in real contact with those actually doing the work and never out where the action was, but stayed in their offices or worked from home on reports and theoretic inward-looking exercises.

The effect observed was that everything slowed down to a snail's speed. Things that could be solved on the spot before, together with the people doing the work downstairs, now required the involvement of multiple experts, meetings, and written reports upstairs. Many experienced that for whatever reason, approval is now required from many more people and for ever smaller matters.

So a collection of experts can also morph into another body of bureaucracy whose main purpose – albeit subconsciously – is to spread as much as possible.

The organizations in question were successful Scandinavian operations. People were exasperated with the slow execution, several said that it was not so in East Asia where things could be accomplished in days or weeks, but here it would take months or years. This all happened in good times with plenty of profit, leading to the sense of urgency being lost. One person reported that some years ago where there were 5 or 6 middle managers there are now close to 50. And they all need something to do so they invent work for each other. The people downstairs in fact often said to executives: *"Please do not employ more people, we don't have the time to be in meetings with all these folks!"*

In the public sector, this occasionally reaches absurd levels. In one city the local child-care institutions were starved of people on the floor working with the children, and instead, 35 experts and consultants were employed to sit in offices, have meetings with people on the floor, and tell them what to do. The rationale for this was that quality needed to be improved. Not surprisingly, people are leaving their jobs in child care in droves. A similar effect was reported in many healthcare institutions.

## Generational Tensions

A rather surprising outcome of the interviews was how widespread the experience of tension between generations was, exemplified by Gen-Z entering the job market.

The younger generations tend to experience organizations as oppressing and limiting their opportunity to choose paths, pursue their goals, and express themselves. They want to see a purpose in what they do, to engage, and are very concerned about justice and fairness, and don't want anybody to tell them what to do.

The older, perhaps more experienced, people currently in leadership positions find it very hard to accommodate the younger people and get the necessary stuff done. They typically want to give the young people room for decision and development, but they are aware that it requires competence, sometimes hard earned through experience. They often experience that younger people expect to do what they want, when and where they want, and to be able to immediately enter senior positions.

In a way it is not a new situation, there have always been elements of this tension, and we just find that it is very pronounced now. The young people very easily get disappointed and check out mentally or perhaps leave. They are more driven by the need to express themselves individually, feel emotionally aligned, and get approval for everything than I have experienced before.

The older generation has – perhaps because of the crisis due to Covid, war, and other things – retracted into more bureaucratic rule setting and control. Although they claim to want to dispense freedom and empowerment, their practices show otherwise. This lack of authenticity is quickly picked up and distrust develops. Some have given up trying to understand the younger ones and have stopped trying to employ them; it is just too difficult to deal with.

A quote from a Gen-Z: "We want something different in our relationship with work, and it's going to be built on more flexibility, choice, transparency, and control of our own situation.'"

> *"There is a gap, a disconnect between the way management is executed and the desire to empower employees. Practices get in the way."*
> — *Bjarte Bogsnæs*

## Remote or Hybrid Work

Although this may seem like a small specific topic, the question of remote or hybrid work was nevertheless a recurring topic in almost all the conversations we had. This was a common theme across almost all boundaries, but it is fair to say that the biggest challenges were experienced in smaller organizations. The Covid pandemic of course changed the landscape and accelerated the move towards remote work. The ripples from this are still settling.

Many leaders experience significant difficulties in finding a balance between accommodating people's desires and actually getting work done. Many employees now regard it as their prerogative to work where they want, whenever they want, and some with whatever they want. Many executives understand that being physically together often is necessary in order to find solutions to complex challenges, and they are disappointed that people don't see that but think that their needs always take precedence. This is especially pronounced with younger people.

Much hype around the benefits of remote work has led many people to think that there are only clear advantages. It is true that working alone remotely can be more efficient if there is one large body of work to be done by just one person, and it is always nice to avoid the commute. However many of the softer parts of collaboration suffer. People mentioned a number of challenges:

- Building team commitment, building mutual trust, and getting help from team members.
- Teamwork suffers, everyone sits on his or her own little island and does their thing.
- Communication suffers, it takes more to call people online at home than to step over to their desk.
- When physical meetings are necessary, it takes a lot of effort to plan this, often with irritating delays as a consequence.

Some people – also younger ones – had really experienced the negative consequences of not being able to be together. If they could change one thing they wished for people to be co-located.

## Hierarchy and Politics in Large Organizations

Very few of our interviewees had experienced brute force power display in their organizations. Their challenges were more due to complex bureaucracy or incomprehensible decision-making in the mesh of experts involved – as described above.

But, large organizations were generally reported to be held back by internal politics. Some had direct experiences, and some felt it in relationships with customers. People often experience a pronounced paralysis regarding decision-making and taking any sort of risk in a hierarchy. People spend much time protecting their position and turf and making sure they are not attracting blame. This dampens transparency and hence the possibility for trust to be the backbone of collaboration. Much effort is dispensed in this turf protection or in vying for position.

People said that the existence of the hierarchy and the status connected with higher positions often results in a wide gap between the upstairs and the downstairs. For some, it was a minor annoyance, for others the source of intense exasperation. "Why can't we reach those people with our message?", and it went both ways. But once there is this gap, then behavior from upstairs is often interpreted as patronizing or paternalistic by the people downstairs. Seen from the upstairs position, the behavior of people downstairs is often seen as unprofessional, immature, or an outright expression of insubordination. This drive to get higher up in the hierarchy makes everybody competitors instead of collaborators.

> *"How can we stop the middle managers' constant quest for upward career moves, which makes everybody competitors instead of collaborators?"*
> — Geir Amsjø

## Managing only through Financials

Many people close to customers and the real work struggled with management that had purely financial or legal approaches without a real understanding of the actual customers, products, and services. This of course often coincided with the effect of the bureaucracy mentioned above. It was especially prevalent in large companies, the financial sector, and the public sector.

In some organizations, one or more layers of financial middle management seemed to have developed into a permafrost layer where nothing could change for fear of being non-compliant upwards, and an almost total risk averseness had developed. Consequently, the people below stopped trying, flew under the radar, and in some situations just made sure that the upstairs only saw what they wanted to see. There was a pronounced desire to stop the practices of trying to control everything with simplistic numbers.

This particular observation was typical for larger organizations, in smaller ones reality forces itself on everybody. However, being ruled and managed by people who have little understanding of the actual circumstances and work is a strong demotivational factor for most. Some organizations had dissolved the rigid reporting structures, some used Beyond Budgeting and others had just generally loosened up to react faster.

*"Life in the boardroom is very different from the executive management practice, often reducing the detailed financial walkthrough on board meetings, instead having maybe monthly or bi-weekly reviews prior to the board meetings, and then focusing on the actual strategic decision-making in real board meetings."*                    *– Torben Ballegaard Sørensen*

## Reality Crash

A few interviewees mentioned how external events had triggered major changes, some of these were going back to more control and tighter budgets.

However, especially one reported how a significant shift in an emergent market had transformed the organization to one that was much more customer-oriented, working on discovering the customers' real needs, which were by no means self-evident. It has also enabled a change in executives' behavior, where they now participate in reviews and standups to learn about reality from the people actually working on products and services. Before, things were more speculative and geared toward showing growth potential and attracting funding.

There is nothing like a good dose of reality and a certain sense of urgency to make people change, in this case for the better. I believe it worked because there were talented people to act as pilots in the uncharted waters the organization had to enter into.

## Some Other Observations

Here is a collection of observations that were mentioned to a lesser degree than those above, and a few interesting outliers:

- Many companies are internally focused and not looking at the customers or the world around them.
- Many in management positions have no clue where to go in this world of rapid change. They are not geared for change or innovation, they are administrators. Many expressed the wish that their owners and boards would invest the time in understanding why modern leadership principles pay off.
- Global Teams work better as people are forced to take on multiple perspectives and show respect and concern for each other.
- Many organizations do not work on creating the right conditions for innovation and resilience, they only look for operational efficiency.
- People have a tendency to stay in their comfort zone and not really be committed and engaged. There must be a certain sense of urgency in getting something done and not just sitting around discussing big plans. "Done is better than perfect".
- As a leader who wants to empower people, it is difficult to find the balance between freedom, responsibility, and control. One person expressed that, "After all, we have to deliver, if I intervene it is often labeled micro-management."
- The value of traditional reporting is limited, in the fast-moving world reports are obsolete when they are printed.
- Some people who claim to want to create progressive organizations for engagement are unconsciously incompetent – they don't know what it means, they only recognize the buzzwords.

- Middle managers are so far removed from either end of the hierarchy that they de facto are reduced to carriers of papers up and down.

*"The biggest challenge in our part of the world is the lack of speed. In East Asia, things are up and running in a week, here it takes months or years!"*
*– Martin Ågerup*

# Objectives

Perhaps the previous section seemed overly negative, but it is important to note that the first and most dominant trend was that people in general agreed on a push towards greater freedom, engagement, value creation, and growth. It was also clear that the interviewees were not just passive complainers and whiners, they had specific objectives that they considered worth pursuing in order to improve. Many of these objectives are of course somewhat interconnected.

- **Transparency**. Many have said that transparency is an enabler for everything else. With transparency comes a commitment to truth and not politics, a general common understanding of goals and status, and last but not least a sense of mutual respect.
- **Psychological Safety**. Many know of Amy Edmondson's work on Psychological safety and were convinced that achieving engagement hinges on the people's willingness to participate and speak up.
- **Respect and trust**. Engagement does not come without everybody showing and being shown respect. Every individual needs to be respected and appreciated for what they contribute. Once mutual respect is achieved, the next step of building trust can be taken. Develop trust in people and establish suitable guardrails that protect against abuse, but which are not experienced as oppressing control. This trust then allows the organization to cut down on monitoring and controlling overhead.
- **Common understanding**. There has to be a true common mental model of where the organization currently is, where it is heading, and

what we need to do to move in the right direction. This has to be communicated and discussed, not just declared from upstairs. It takes time and effort, but there is no way around it. This applies to specific areas as well such as hybrid work, people have to reach a common understanding of what works and what doesn't. There is also an important area in helping people to understand that complex work is a reality, what complexity is, how to work with it, and why traditional methods don't work. For some, it was a pronounced need to get their owners and board of directors educated in modern leadership principles so that they could have a meaningful dialog.

- **Improve career path.** Develop a better model for people's career moves, assigning status and value to other areas, rather than simply climbing the corporate ladder in the hierarchy.
- **Education.** It has to be a goal to educate people about what leadership is and what freedom is. It does not come just by announcing it. This also includes educating people currently in leadership positions on how they should act if they want a liberating and engaging organization.
- **Prioritize holistically.** Very often there is no formal way of ensuring that when choosing to apply resources to something, the whole system is taken into account. Silos prevent this.
- **Reduce the gaps between people.** This is perhaps a bit more complex objective, but it is relevant for people upstairs and downstairs, across cultures and across generations, where the older generations have to face up to the needs for freedom and fulfillment that the younger ones have, and the younger ones have to acknowledge that it cannot all be about them individually and their self-expression. There are other people in the organization that you need to work together with to find solutions, there is work that has to be accomplished now, although it doesn't feel like fun.

# Some Strategies

It became a bit harder to solicit concrete strategies from people, with strategies we meant practical things that could be done quickly to move toward the objectives. That is absolutely fair, as we only had 30 minutes, and the line of investigation was somewhat new to everybody. It takes time to get your thinking on a subject together. But there were some valuable spontaneous suggestions, they are presented here in no particular order.

- **Aligning values**. One interviewee told me that they were developing a sort of value matrix of company and personal values to try to align expectations when hiring new people. In that way, it would quickly become clear to both parties if there was a mismatch.
- **Honest answers to honest questions**. Implement a practice so that people can ask a question now and get an honest answer now. And if they need help, they will get it now, no whining or complaining.
- **Volunteering**. People have pretty much to be treated like volunteers, to be invited, if their commitment is wanted.
- **Bureaucracy weeding**. A visible, regular practice of identifying and weeding out bureaucratic practices whose value is questionable. Everybody will participate in this with great pleasure.
- **Change of compensation schemes.** Some interesting proposals were made, one was to link people's salary bracket to a commitment to actually showing up at the office and participating in the proactive building of relationships and culture.
- **Respect for competencies**. Develop a principle for giving private and public credit for people's achievements. Building competence takes time and practice, it is not enough to have watched a YouTube video on brain surgery to perform it.
- **Start with trust**. At the outset, unless there are previous bad examples of misuse, focus on trusting people and their commitments, however,

it is only fair to require a handshake around the fulfillment of commitments.

- **Time for reflection and learning**. Allow slack in the organization for people to learn, give and receive feedback, and allocate concrete time for this.
- **Onboarding of people**. This has to be very practical and concrete, it has to work, the clock is ticking, remember the new (often young) people represent the future.
- **Restart**. From time to time, force everybody to think about how we would do this if we started from scratch today. Often very valuable insights are discovered this way.

Some people provided us with quite personal recommendations, starting from the premise "What can I do today to improve conditions!", just one example:

> "*Some practical advice: Remind yourself that you are not always right, just because you have always done it this way!*"
>
> – *Michael Arp Christensen*

# List of Participants

90+ people participated in the interview sessions. The following people have approved that their names and email addresses are mentioned.

- **Agnete Djupvik** (agnete.djupvik@pwc.com)
- **Bård Kuvaas** (bard.kuvaas@bi.no)
- **Bjarte Bogsnæs** (bjarte@bogsnesadvisory.com)
- **Christoffer Motéus** (christoffer@yohrs.com)
- **Doug Kirkpatrick** (doug@dartagnanadvisors.com)
- **Espen Breivik** (espen.s.breivik@gmail.com)
- **Geir Garmannvik Pedersen** (geir.pedersen@gritera.com)
- **Gry Evita Sivertsen** (gry.evita.sivertsen@gritera.com)
- **Henrik Engmark Daae** (henrik@daae.dk)
- **Johanne Berg Bollingmo** (johanne@techpros.no)

- **John Coleman** (john@orderlydisruption.com)
- **Kristina Lausen** (kristina_lausen@hotmail.com)
- **Lesya Kolesnykova** (lesya.karpyn@gmail.com)
- **Lyubomyr Matsekh** (lyubomyr.m.u@gmail.com)
- **Marcus Albaeus** (marcus_henriksson2004@hotmail.com)
- **Michael Arp Christensen** (micharpc@gmail.com)
- **Michael Bagge** (mb@aheadcare.dk)
- **Per Wennersten** (per.wennersten@ramenvalves.com)
- **Rachel Bridges** (rachel.bridges@alfalaval.com)
- **René Figgé** (rfi@visuelprojektledelse.dk)
- **Rimantas Mažulis** (rimantas.mazulis@gmail.com)
- **Ståle Hansen** (stale.hansen@cloudway.com)
- **Tommy P. Storstein** (tommy@holmefjord.no)
- **Torben Grotkjær** (torben83@gmail.com)
- **Vincent Kruse** (vincentkruse@gmail.com)
- **Øystein Haaland** (ohaaland@lyse.net)

# Glossary

*One hundred specific Agile Lean Leadership terms*

**Acceptance Criteria**: Statements to highlight details of a Specification. Typically describing special situations, conditions, or outliers. For example, using the following template: *Given a-certain-context and some-more-context*. When *this-event* happens. Then *this-outcome another-outcome* must be the result.

**Acceptance Test**: Verifying the Specification and the Acceptance Criteria of a Deliverable or Backlog Item are fulfilled.

**Accomplishment**: A visible result that all stakeholders and/or Circle members can identify and relate to, typically during Review.

**Activity**: Often used interchangeably with the term Event.

**After Action Review**: Another term for a Retrospective.

**Agile Lean Leadership**: The framework presented in this book. It consists of values, principles, structures, and practices.

**Agile Lean Organization**: An Organization built using the Agile Lean Leadership framework.

**ALL**: Short for Agile Lean Leadership.

**Artifacts**: The tools used to visualize what to deliver, prioritization, tasks to do, impediments, and progress. The term normally refers to the Main Backlog or the Tactical Backlog, but can also refer to the Improvement Backlog, Product Burndown, and Sprint Burndown, if these are used.

**Backlog Item**: An item or entity of product or service with an identifiable result on a Backlog. In Scrum this is called a Product Backlog Item, sometimes also referred to as Stories, or for the larger ones Epics.

**Backlog Refinement**: A practice inherited from Scrum where the Team and the SO work on preparing Backlog Items for future iterations and tactical execution.

**Business Value**: The quantified value that the Strategy Owner (on behalf of the Customer) expects to reap from getting a particular Backlog Item done and delivered.

**Cadence**: An interval in time set up for planning and review purposes. The term is often used in Kanban; in Scrum the term is Sprint.

**Center Circle**: A circle in the Value Stream that serves other internal Circles and not normally real Customers out in the wild.

**Chair**: A term used for a person that assumes a special responsibility in Resolution, Secondary or Transient Circle. The Chair mediates the discussion and decision-making but also has the authority to switch to arbitrating if a deadlock exists.

**Circle**: An organizational unit with a certain mission and striking power, has defined roles, manifest, backlogs, and process guidelines.

**Commitments**: Definition of what the parties in a Relationship have promised each other. This communicates what the parties honestly believe can be accomplished and expresses that they will do their best to honor this.

**Constitution**: A set of overarching agreements governing collaboration in and among Circles, typically reflected in the Manifests of Circles and Organizations.

**Constitutional Organization**: A term used for an Agile Lean Organization, when stressing the special property of basing collaboration on mutual overarching agreements (A Constitution or a Covenant) and honoring commitments.

**Covenant**: Another term for Constitution.

**Cross-functional Team**: A team where the members together possess all the necessary skills and competencies to complete their Backlog Items.

**Customer**: The person who pays for the deliverables, the Backlog Items from a Frontline Circle. The Customer naturally wants maximum value and return on investment.

**Customer Circle**: A collection of Customers identified by the Organization with its manifest, typically such a Circle can be served by one Frontline Circle.

**Daily Coordination**: A gathering where a Team coordinates short-term plans and follows up on goals, progress, and impediments. This constitutes the shortest planning Cycle, it is also called *Tactical Meetup*. This event is called *Daily Scrum* in Scrum and in other Agile contexts *Daily Standup*.

**Daily Scrum**: A Scrum term for a Daily Coordination.

**Daily Standup**: Another term for a Daily Coordination.

**Definition of Done**: Specific criteria that a Team upholds to be as sure as possible that a Backlog Item is of acceptable quality so that they do not have to go back to it.

**Delegatee**: The Circle that accepts a request to deliver a Backlog Item to another.

**Delegation**: When one Circle asks another one to deliver one of its Backlog Items it is called Delegation.

**Delegator**: The Circle requesting a Backlog Item from another.

**Delivery-In**: A milestone on the Timeline specifies that at this time the plan is to receive certain deliveries into the circle, from other Circles or suppliers.

**Delivery-Out**: A milestone on the Timeline, specifying that at this time the plan is to deliver certain deliverables OUT of the project, for example to other Circles or to customers.

**Epic**: An Epic is a large Story (or generally a Backlog Item), typically one that later on will be broken down into appropriately sized Stories. Normally too big to execute in a Sprint or in Kanban.

**Escalation**: A form of delegation of an issue or an idea, that Teams cannot resolve alone or bilaterally, to a Resolution Circle, who will work on resolving it.

**ETA**: Estimated Time of Arrival. When is it expected that the Deliverable is handed back, completely done, to the one requesting it (the Delegator) from the one actually doing the work (Delegatee)?

**Event**: A meeting or an Activity conducted as part of the practices followed by a Circle or a Team.

**Executive Committee:** The forum of the three Chairs of the Resolution Circles. In times of crisis, this group may assume special responsibility and decide quickly.

**Expectations:** A definition of what the parties in a Relationship expect from each other. This communicates what the parties expect; there is normally some slack in how to accomplish this.

**Frontline Circle:** Aka Agile Customer Circle. A Circle in the Value Stream that has and serves customers out in the wild.

**Global Constraints:** Conditions for all the Circle's Backlog Items. Any solution that is delivered must be within the definition of this collection of constraints. This often includes performance, platforms, usability, documentation, etc.

**Idea:** Feedback from a customer or (delegator) about how products or services could be improved.

**Impediment:** Anything preventing a Team from performing at their very best. Impediments (sometimes called obstacles) are recorded on the Improvement Backlog and dealt with by the Operations Owner.

**Improvement Backlog:** An ordered list of the improvements and impediments currently being worked on, typically by the Operations Owner.

**Issue:** Feedback from a customer (or delegator) about problems with Backlog Items.

**Iteration:** A specific timebox in which the Team attempts to reach a committed goal and deliver a set of planned Backlog Items. In Scrum, this is called a Sprint.

**Iteration Planning:** An activity (one or two events) initiating an Iteration, it is a collaboration of the Strategy Owner and the Team, sometimes including Stakeholders as well. In Scrum, this is called *Sprint Planning*. The activity is often conducted as two events Planning 1, where the set of Iteration deliverables is agreed to, and Planning 2 where the Team determines *how* to deliver these.

**Kanban:** A way of managing work, by visualizing the workflow applying the definition of done criteria, and Work in Progress limits.

**Liberating Organization:** A term used for an Agile Lean Organization, when stressing the special property of setting the individual free to engage and take responsibility.

**Main Backlog:** An ordered list of everything a Circle has to work on and deliver. In Scrum, this is the Product Backlog.

**Manifest:** A short descriptive document, conveying what an Organization, a Circle, a Team, or a Relationship is and does.

**Milestone:** A general Milestone on the Timeline, typically specifying that certain conditions must be met by this time.

**OO:** Short for Operations Owner.

**Operations Owner (OO):** This role has the responsibility for the operational domain: the process guidelines, and how everybody works together. The OO owns the Improvement Backlog. This role is called the Scrum Master in Scrum.

**ORC:** Short for Operational Resolution Circle.

**PDSA**: Plan-Do-Study-Act, W. Edwards Deming's quality improvement process, constant learning.

**Phase**: Alternative word for Release, typically used in non-IT contexts.

**Practices**: A collection of recommended ways of doing things in Agile Lean Leadership.

**Primary Circles**: All the Circles participating in the Value Stream. They are also the home base of all members.

**Radical Transparency**: The requirement to represent the truth, the full truth, and nothing but the truth.

**Refactoring**: Changing the internals of a solution for long-term sustainability with easier maintenance, while keeping the external behavior the same.

**Relationship**: A defined connection between two Circles where delegations can be exchanged. A Manifest describes the nature and the properties of the relationship.

**Release**: A collection of Deliverables that together make up a portion of the total Product or Deliverable in some well-defined form and completeness that makes it usable to the User and the Customer.

**Release Milestone**: A Milestone on the Time-Line associated with a Release.

**Release Sprint**: The last Sprint before a Release, where certain different activities need to be performed (such as special deployment, tests, etc.).

**Representative decision-making**: The concept of granting a trusted representative the mandate to decide on behalf of a group, in this case, a Circle. This happens in Resolution and Secondary Circles.

**Resolution**: Resolved issues and ideas taken back to the Primary Circles after having been handled in one of the Resolution Circles.

**Resolution Circles**: Primary Circles have granted authority to these Circles to resolve Escalated issues and ideas. There are three resolution Circles that deal with Tactical, Strategic, and Operational matters that are escalated which Circles in the Value Stream cannot handle themselves.

**Retrospective**: An Event where the whole Circle discusses how the last Cadence of work went, what were they happy with? What could be improved? And what is going to be done? This is called *Sprint Retrospective* in Scrum.

**Return on investment**: A measure of the rate at which the Project generates value. Earlier value rather than later is of course preferable. This is a primary concern of the Strategy Owner.

**Review**: An Event where Stakeholders are invited to review Accomplishments by a Circle or Team, typically at the end of an Iteration or a Cadence. In Scrum, this is called Sprint Review.

**Roadmap**: The top-level view of time-based commitments in the Circle. Normally the Time-Line consists of 1) *Deadlines*, where certain achievements must be reached, 2) *Delivery In*, where something is delivered to the Circle, 3) *Delivery Out*, where the Team must deliver something to an outside party, 4) *Ordinary Milestones* defined internally for coordination purposes, and finally 5) *Release Milestones*, where the result of the Circle's work must exist in some well-defined form having reached a certain completeness that makes it usable to the User and Customer.

**Rules of Engagement**: Operating agreement between two Circles defining how requests for help or Backlog Items are handled. It includes form, response time, and mutual responsibilities. It always covers the handling of exceptions. This is documented in the Manifest.

**Scaled Down Circle**: A Circle with multiple streams of requests for deliverables or delegations coming in -- effectively multiple Main Backlogs, but still only one Team and one Tactical Backlog, the main issue is to prioritize effort in serving the multiple input streams.

**Scaled Up Circle**: A Circle that has multiple tactical Teams, each with their own Tactical Backlog. There is still only one Main Backlog and one SO, there may be more than one OO though.

**Secondary Circle**: The Secondary Circles are where people (who belong to primary Circles) spend some time from time to time on cross-cutting concerns (typically focused on skillsets) not directly moving value to customers in the Value Stream, hence Secondary.

**Self-managing**: People in a Circle and a Team do not have people from the outside telling them how to do things. Often used interchangeably with Self-organizing.

**Self-organizing**: People in a Circle and a Team organize in a way they find most appropriate for their work, their skill level, and their personality types. Often used interchangeably with Self-managing.

**Service Circle**: A Circle that primarily supports and services other Circles in the Value Stream, either by delivering things delegated to the Circles or having its Team members execute specific tasks as a sort of supplier to the requesting Circles.

**SO**: Short for Strategy Owner.

**Specification**: A description of a Backlog Item, that is precise enough (providing enough common understanding) so that somebody can take up the job of delivering the Backlog Item It often consists of a Sunshine Story (User Story) and a set of Acceptance Criteria.

**Sprint**: A Scrum term for an Iteration.

**SRC**: Short for Strategic Resolution Circle.

**Stakeholder**: A person with an interest in the Deliverables of a Circle, can be Users, Customers but also external Compliance people, and other internal people.

**Story**: A common term used as an alternative to a Backlog Item.

**Story Point**: A unitless measure of the size of a Backlog Item typically used in Scrum. It is used to estimate the relative size of Backlog Items compared to each other. It is customary to use the Fibonacci numbers for Stories (1, 2, 3, 5, 8, and 13), and for Epics (larger units of the project) it is customary to use 20, 40, and 100 as a scale.

**Strategy Owner (SO)**: This role is responsible for understanding and generating value and the best possible ROI. The SO owns the strategic domain in the form of the Main Backlog and prioritizes this. This role is called the Product Owner in Scrum.

**Sunshine Story**: The positive side of a Specification, including an explanation of the desired outcome -- why is this deliverable requested? It is often written as a User Story.

**Super Circle**: In a larger organization a Super Circle is a full organizational structure with Value Stream, Resolution Circles, etc. Multiple Super Circles collaborate in the whole organization, typically with an extra layer of Resolution Circles and Secondary Circles to decide and coordinate at the higher level.

**Supplier Circle**: An external organization that delivers components or services to a Circle in the Value Stream.

**Tactical Backlog**: The list of work a Team in a Circle is working on to deliver right now. In Scrum, this is Sprint Backlog. It can also be a Kanban Board or a combination of these.

**Task**: The smallest increment of work normally worked with. During Planning, Stories are normally decomposed into Tasks by team members.

**Team**: People in team roles are responsible for getting the actual work done, i.e. the *what* of the solutions. They have the responsibility for the tactical domain, they own the Tactical Backlog. They are currently called *Developers* in Scrum, which can be confusing in non-IT environments.

**Technical Debt**: Backlog Items delivered with known sub-standard implementation. The term is mostly used in Software development, but another example could be fixing a cooling pipe in a car with a bandaid while waiting for the real spare part.

**Timeboxing**: The concept of allocating a specific time to an activity. When the time has elapsed, the activity is over.

**Timeline**: Another term for a Roadmap.

**Transient Circle**: A Circle that is rapidly formed when a sudden drop into chaos is experienced in an Organization. It stabilizes the situation and then dissolves.

**Traveler**: A person in a Circle who has as a substantial part of his job to support other Circles. A traveler is typically called upon to give advice not to do the job. Sometimes a Traveller Circle is formed. Seen from the receiving Circle the Traveller is a special supplier.

**TRC**: Short for Tactical Resolution Circle.

**User**: A person who uses the deliverables, the Backlog Items, from a Circle. Users or their proxies are often involved in approving deliverables, e.g. performing acceptance tests.

**User Story**: A commonly used form of short specification using the following template: As *such-and-such a user*, I would like to have or do *this-and-that*, in order to get *yada-yada-yada*.

**Value Stream**: The collection of Primary Circles that deliver Backlog Items and hence value to the customers.

# Bibliography

Ackoff, Russel L.. *Differences That Make a Difference*. Triarchy Press, 2010.

Ackoff, Russel L.. *Systems Thinking for Curios Managers*. Triarchy Press, 2010.

Ackoff, Russel L.. *The Democratic Corporation*. Oxford University Press, 1994.

Ackoff, Russel L., and Addison, Herbert J.. *Management f-Laws*. Triarchy Press, 2007.

Ackoff, Russel L., and Addison, Herbert J.. *Ackoff's F/laws The Cure*. Triarchy Press, 2011.

Ackoff, Russel, and Magidsen, Jason, and Addison, Herbert. *Idealized Design*. Prentice Hall, Pearson, 2006.

Adzic, Gojko, and Evans, David. *Fifty Quick Ideas to Improve Your Userstories*. Neuri Consulting LLP, 2014.

Adzic, Gojko, and Evans, David, and Roden, Tom. *Fifty Quick Ideas to Improve Your Tests*. Neuri Consulting LLP, 2015.

Aguayo, Rafael. *Dr. Deming*. Simon & Schuster, 1990.

Allen, David. *Getting Things Done*. Piatkus, 2001.

Ambler, Scott W.. *Agile Modeling*. John Wiley and Sons, 2002.

Anderson, David J.. *Kanban*. Blue Hole Press, 2010.

Appelo, Jurgen. *Management 3.0*. Addison Wesley, 2010.

Beck, Kent. *Test-Driven Development*. Addison Wesley, 2002.

Beck, Kent, and Andres, Cynthia. *Extreme Programming Explained*. Addison Wesley, 2004.

Becker, Sebastian, and Bogsnes, Bjarte, and Larsson, Dag, and Morlidge, Steve, and Olesen, Anders, and Olsson, Rikard, and Röösli, Franz. *The Viable Map*. Beyond Books Press, 2023.

Bloch, Arthur. *Murphy's Law*. Price/Stern/Sloan Publishers Inc., 2000.

Bogsnes, Bjarte. *This is Beyond Budgeting*. Wiley, 2023.

Brougham, Greg. *The Cynefin Mini-Book*. C4 Media, 2015.

Brown, Tim. *Change by Design*. Harper Business, 2009.

Brown, Tim. *Change by Design*. Harper Business, 2009.

Buckingham, Marcus, and Coffman, Curt. *First, Break all the rules*. Simon & Schuster, 1998.

Cameron, Kim. *Positive Leadership*. Berrett-Koehler Publishers Inc., 2008.

Clark, Mike. *Pragmatic Project Automation*. Pragmatic Programmers, 2004.

Cloud, Henry. *Necessary Endings*. Morrow, 2010.

Cohn, Mike. *Succeeding with Agile*. Addison Wesley, 2009.

Cohn, Mike. *User Stories Applied*. Addison Wesley, 2004.

Cohn, Mike. *Agile Estimating and Planning*. Prentice Hall, 2005.

Collins, James C, and Porras, Jerry I.. *Built to Last*. HarperCollins Publishers, 1994.

Coplien, James, and Bjørnvig, Gertrud. *Lean Architecture*. John Wiley and Sons, 2010.

Coram, Robert. *Boyd, The fighter pilot who changed the art of war*. Back Bay Books, 2004.

Covey, Stephen R.. *The 7 Habits of Highly Effective People*. Simon & Schuster, 1989.

Crispin, Lisa, and Gregory, Janet. *Agile Testing*. Addison Wesley, 2008.

Davis, Christopher W.H.. *Agile Metrics in Action*. Manning Publication Co., 2015.

Delavigne, Kenneth, and Roberrtson, J.D.. *Demings Profound Changes*. PTR Prentice Hall, 1994.

Deming, W. Edwards. *Statistical Adjustment of Data*. John Wiley and Sons, 1984.

Deming, W. Edwards. *The Essentiel Deming*. McGraw-Hill, 2012.

Deming, W. Edwards. *Out of the Crisis*. MIT, 1982.

Deming, W. Edwards. *The New Economics*. MIT, 1991.

Denning, Stephen. *Radical Management*. Jossey-Bass, 2010.

Denning, Stephen. *The Leaders Guide to Storytelling*. Jossey-Bass, 2005.

Denning, Stephen. *The Secret Language of Leadership*. Jossey-Bass, 2007.

Derby Esther, and Larsen, Diana. *Agile Retrospectives*. Pragmatic Bookshelf, 2006.

Drucker, Peter F. *Management Challenges for the 21st Century*. Routledge, 2009.

Edmondson, Amy. *The Fearless Organization*. Wiley, 2018.

Edmondson, Amy C.. *Teaming*. Wiley, 2012.

Edmondson, Amy C.. *Teaming to Innovate*. Wiley, 2013.

Edmondson, Amy, and Harvey, Jean-Francios. *Extreme Teaming*. Emerald Publishing, 2017.

Epstein, Robert Ph.D. *The big book of creativity games*. McGraw-Hill, 2000.

Fenton, Traci. *Freedom at Work*. BenBella Books, 2022.

Freeman, Eric & Elisabeth. *Head First Design Patterns*. O'Reilly, 2004.

Gilb, Tom. *Principles of Software Engineering Management*. Addison Wesley, 1988.

Gilb, Tom. *Competitive Engineering*. Elsevier, Butterworth Heinemann, 2005.

Gillett, Jan. *Making your work work*. Infinite Ideas Ltd, 2014.

Gloger, Boris. *Scrum Checklists*. Sprint IT, 2011.

Gothelf, Jeff. *Lean vs Agile vs Design Thinking*. Gothelf Corp, 2017.

Gothelf, Jeff, and Seiden, Josh. *Lean UX*. O'Reilly, 2012.

Guinness, Os. *The Case for Civility*. HarperOne, 2008.

Guinness, Os. *The Magna Carta of Humanity*. InterVarsity Press, 2021.

Guinness, Os. *The Call*. Thomas Nelson, 1998.

Heath, Dan. *The Lean Startup*. Penguin Group, .

Heiman, Stephen, and Sanchez, Diane. *The New Strategic Selling*. Warner Books, 1985.

Hicks, Robert F., and Bone, Diane. *Self-Managing Teams*. Kogan Page, 1991.

Hohmann, Luke. *Innovation Games*. Addison Wesley, 2006.

Hopper, Kenneth, and Hopper, William. *The Puritan Gift*. I.B. Tauris, 2007.

Hunt, Andrew, and Thomas, David. *The Pragmatic Programmer*. Addison Wesley, 1999.

Hunter, James C. *The Servant*. Crown Business, 1998.

Jensen, Leise Astrid Passer, and Dahl, Brian John McCullen. *Damn Good Leadership: We are all Leaders. We are all Followers*. Jensen & Dahl, 2023.

Joiner, Brian L.. *Fourth Generation Management*. McGraw-Hill, 1994.

Kahneman, Daniel. *Thinking Fast and Slow*. Farrar, Straus and Giroux, 2011.

Kahneman, Daniel. *Workbook for Thinking Fast and Slow*. Book Tigers, 2023.

Kahneman, Daniel, and Sibony, Olivier, and Sunstein, Cass . *Noise*. Littlebrownspark, 2021.

Keller, Timothy. *Every Good Endeavour*. Hodder & Stoughton, 2012.

Kennedy, Michael N.. *Product Development for the Lean Enterprise*. The Oaklea Press, 2003.

Kim, W. Chan, and Mauborgne, Renée. *Blue Ocean Strategy*. Harvard Business Review Press, 2004.

Kirkpatrick, Doug. *The No-Limits Enterprise*. ForbesBooks, 2019.

Kniberg, Henrik. *Lean from the Trenches*. Pragmatic Bookshelf, 2011.

Kozak-Holland, Mark. *Titanic Lessons for IT Projects*. Multi-Media Publications, 2005.

Ladas Corey. *Scrumban*. Modus Cooperandi Press, 2008.

Laloux, Frederic. *Reinventing organizations*. Nelson Parker, 2014.

Larman, Craig, and Vodde, Bas. *Large-Scale Scrum*. Addison Wesley, 2016.

Larman, Craig, and Vodde, Bas. *Practices for Scaling Lean & Agile Development*. Addison Wesley, 2010.

Larman, Craig, and Vodde, Bas. *Scaling Lean & Agile Development*. Addison Wesley, 2008.

Liker, Jeffrey K.. *The Toyota Way* *. McGraw-Hill, 2005.

Liker, Jeffrey K., and Meier, David. *The Toyota Way Fieldbook*. McGraw-Hill, 2005.

Lipmanowicz, Henri, and McCandless, Keith. *The Surprising Power of Liberating Structures*. , 2014.

Marquet, Louis David. *Turn the Ship Around*. Portfolio Penguin, 2013.

Marquet, Louis David, and Worshek, Andy. *The Turn the Ship Around workbook*. Portfolio Penguin, 2018.

Maurya, Ash. *Running Lean*. O'Reilly, 2012.

McChrystal, General Stanley. *My share of the task*. Portfolio Penguin, 2013.

McChrystal, General Stanley. *Team of Teams*. Portfolio Penguin, 2015.

McChrystal, General Stanley, and Butrico, Anna. *Risk*. Penguin Random House, 2021.

Meadows, Donella H.. *Thinking in Systems*. Chelsea Green Publishing, 2008.

Moore, Geoffrey A. *Crossing the Chasm*. Capstone, 2006.

Moore, Geoffrey A. *Inside the Tornado*. HarperCollins Publishers, 1995.

Morrison, Edward, and Hutcheson, Scott, and Nilsen, Elizabeth, and Fadden, Janyce, and Franklin, Nancy. *Strategic Doing*. Wiley, 2019.

Murray, Andy. *Managing Successful Projects with Prince2*. TSO, 2009.

Neave, Henry R.. *The Deming Dimension*. SPC Press, 1990.

Nygard, Michael T.. *Release IT*. Pragmatic Bookshelf, 2007.

Olsen, Dan. *The Lean Product Playbook*. John Wiley and Sons, 2015.

Parkinson, C. Northcote. *Parkinsons Lov*. Fremad, 1958.

Patton, Jeff. *User Story Mapping*. O'Reilly Media Inc., 2012.

Pflaeging, Niels. *Organize for Complexity*. BetaCodex Publishing, 2014.

Pichler, Roman. *Agile Product Management with Scrum*. Addison Wesley, 2008.

Poppendieck, Mary, and Poppendieck, Tom. *Leading Lean Software Development*. Addison Wesley, 2009.

Poppendieck, Mary, and Poppendieck, Tom. *Implementing Lean Software Development*. Addison Wesley, 2006.

Powell, Colin. *It worked for me*. Harper Perennial, 2012.

Productivity Press Development Team. *Lean Culture*. Productivity Press, 2010.

Pugh, Ken. *Interface-Oriented Design*. Pragmatic Bookshelf, 2006.

Reinertsen, Donald G.. *Product Development Flow*. Celeritas Publishing, 2009.

Richardson, Jared, and Gwaltney, William Jr.. *Ship It*. Pragmatic Programmers, 2005.

Roden, Tom, and Williams, Ben. *Fifty Quick Ideas to Improve Your Retrospectives*. Neuri Consulting LLP, 2015.

Rubin, Kenneth S.. *Essential Scrum*. Addison Wesley, 2012.

Saul, John Ralston. *Voltaire's Bastards*. Simon & Schuster, 1992.

Scherkenbach, William W.. *The Deming route to Quality and Productivity*. Mercury Books, 1986.

Schneider, William N.. *The Reengineering Alternative*. McGraw-Hill, 1994.

Scholtes, Peter R.. *The Leaders Handbook*. McGraw-Hill, 1997.

Scholtes, Peter, and Joiner, Brian, and Streibel, B.. *The Team Handbook*. Oriel Stat A Matrix, 1988.

Schwaber, Ken. *Agile Project Management with Scrum*. Microsoft Press, 2004.

Schwaber, Ken. *The Enterprise and Scrum*. Microsoft Press, 2007.

Schwaber, Ken, and Beedle, Mike. *Agile Software Development with Scrum*. Pearson Education, 2001.

Schwaber, Ken, and Sutherland, Jeff. *Software in 30 days*. John Wiley and Sons, 2012.

Shewhart, Walter A.. *Statistical Method from the Wiewpoint of Quality Control*. Dover Publications Inc., 1987.

Shewhart, Walter A.. *Economic Control of Quality of Manufactured Product*. Martino Publishing, 2015.

Sinek, Simon. *Start with Why*. Penguin Group, 2009.

Skarin, Mattias. *Real-World Kanban*. Pragmatic Programmers, 2015.

Snowdon, Dave, and friends. *Cynefin*. Cognitive Edge, 2021.

Snyder, Timothy. *On Tyranny*. Random House LCC US, 2017.

Snyder, Timothy. *The Road to Unfreedom*. Random House LCC US, 2018.

Snyder, Timothy. *On Freedom*. Random House LCC US, 2024.

Spolsky, Joel. *Joel on Software*. Apress, 2004.

Stewart, Matthew. *The Management Myth, Debunking modern business Philosophy*. Norton, 2009.

Subramaniam Venkat, and Hunt, Andy. *Practices of an Agile Developer*. Pragmatic Bookshelf, 2006.

Sutherland, Jeff, and Coplien, James O.. *A Scrum Book: The Spirit of the Game *. Pragmatic Bookshelf, 2019.

Sutherland, Jeff, and Solingen,R, and Rustenburg, E. *The Power of Scrum*. Scruminc., 2011.

Tomasini, Andrea, and Kearns, Martin. *Agile Transition*. Agile42. 2012.

Verheyen, Gunther. *Scrum A Pocket Guide*. Van Haren Publishing, 2013.

Walton, Mary. *The Deming Management Method*. Dodd, Mead & Company Inc., 1986.

Webb, Nicholas J.. *The Digital Innovation Playbook*. Wiley, 2011.

Wheeler, Donald J.. *Understanding Variation*. SPC Press, 1993.

Wiefels, Paul. *The Chasm Companion*. Capstone, 2002.

Womack, James P, and Jones, Daniel T.. *Lean Thinking*. Simon & Schuster, 1996.

Womack, James P, and Jones, Daniel T/Roos, Daniel. *The Machine That Changed the World*. Harper Perennial, 1990.

341

# Alphabetical Index